5 STEPS TO A

5

500

AP English Literature Questions
to know by test day

5 STEPS TO A 5

500

AP English Literature Questions
to know by test day

Shveta Verma Miller

New York   Chicago   San Francisco   Lisbon   London   Madrid   Mexico City
Milan   New Delhi   San Juan   Seoul   Singapore   Sydney   Toronto

The McGraw-Hill Companies

SHVETA VERMA MILLER has taught English literature and English as a foreign language at the high school and college level in the United States, England, India, Japan, and China. Prior to that, she taught SAT preparation with both the Princeton Review and Kaplan. She has a bachelor's degree in English literature from the University of California, Berkeley, and a master's degree in modern literature from the University of London, England.

1 2 3 4 5 6 7 8 9 10 11 12 13 14 15   QFR/QFR   1 9 8 7 6 5 4 3 2 1 0

ISBN   978-0-07-175410-1
MHID   0-07-175410-5

Library of Congress Control Number 2010935999

Series interior design by Jane Tenenbaum

McGraw-Hill books are available at special quantity discounts to use as premiums and sales promotions or for use in corporate training programs. To contact a representative, please e-mail us at bulksales@mcgraw-hill.com.

This book is printed on acid-free paper.

CONTENTS

PREFACE

Even though students have been enrolling in AP English literature classes and taking the AP exam for decades, there is a noticeable shortage of multiple-choice practice and guides in the test prep world. This book is intended to *complement* a test-prep curriculum guidebook like McGraw-Hill's *5 Steps to a 5: AP English Literature*, which provides extensive instruction on the content covered in the exam, including terms, concepts, writing skills, and some multiple-choice practice. *5 Steps to a 5: 500 AP English Literature Questions to Know by Test Day*, however, is unique and essential in that it provides extensive practice for the multiple-choice section alone, which comprises 45 percent of the total AP exam score. The book provides 500 practice questions and detailed answer explanations. The questions are comparable to those found on the AP exam, covering similar content and genres.

This book is intended for students to use to prepare for the AP exam independently, in addition to the preparation they may be doing in an actual AP English literature classroom. The book is also useful for teachers to use in their AP and non-AP classrooms for extra practice and assessment. Students who do not intend to take the AP exam can still benefit from using this book because the passages, questions, and answer explanations will train any student of literature how to develop a subtle and insightful appreciation for and understanding of the technique, form, style, and purpose of complex literary texts, all skills necessary for the reading comprehension section of the SAT and other standardized exams in reading comprehension.

How to Use This Book

The book is divided into eight chapters that are categorized by geographic region and genre. The multiple-choice questions for the AP exam in English literature consist mostly of fiction and poetry. Of the fiction passages, most passages are taken from novels and short stories, while occasionally a passage from a play or even expository prose (excerpts from essays, prefaces, etc.) might be used.

Terms written in SMALL CAPITALS are terms and concepts that will reappear in multiple questions and should be reviewed for the AP exam. Many of these terms can be studied in McGraw-Hill's *5 Steps to a 5: AP English Literature*. In certain situations, words or letters that are *italicized* indicate this author's emphasis to make the answer explanations clearer.

The questions all ask you to **choose the best answer** from the available choices, so even though multiple answer choices may be "correct," the right answer is always the *best* answer because it may be more specific, detailed, or all-encompassing than the other choices.

For Students

- Identify a genre (American poetry, drama, expository prose, etc.) with which you are the least familiar and start with that chapter's passages. Which genre have you had the least experience or the most difficulty studying?
- Or, have you read and studied some of the texts or authors in the book? Try starting with those passages to test your ability on texts you already have some confidence with; then move on to unfamiliar texts, authors, and genres.

How to Study the Passages

- As you practice the questions, read the answer explanations of the questions you get wrong *and* the explanations of the questions you get right so you know *why* you got a question right and learn the logic of how right answers are reached on the exam.
- After completing a passage and questions, write your own explanations for your answers and then compare your explanations to the ones in the book. This exercise will force you to think carefully about why you are picking certain answers, and it may help you avoid picking certain answers on a whim if you know you will have to justify those choices later.
- Highlight the terms and concepts you are unfamiliar with that are written in SMALL CAPITALS in the answer explanations, even in the explanations of questions you get right. Once you have completed several passages, you will be able to notice which terms you consistently misunderstand in the questions. Review these terms by reading the answer explanations and looking up their definitions in *5 Steps to a 5: AP English Literature* or ask your teacher for a list of resources.

For Teachers

- When your students are beginning their practice, let them complete passages without a time limit so they can first adjust to the style, content, and expectations of the exam.
- While they are getting familiar with the test, you may also want to have them work in groups on one passage. They should discuss their rationale for choosing an answer and debate each other when there are disagreements. They will have to justify their own answers and explain their reasoning using references to the passages, which will train them to become more sensitive readers and to think carefully about *why* they are choosing an answer. While they are trying to convince their peers of their answer choice, they may realize they have misinterpreted something in the passage and they will come to appreciate the level of close reading and analysis the exam requires.
- When students are ready to practice on their own in a timed setting, have them practice a passage and check their answers but *not* read the answer explanations. Have them go back to the passage and write their own answer explanations for their chosen answers. Then they should test their explanations against the ones in the book to see exactly where and how their misinterpretation occurred.

AP Teachers: Assessments

- At the start of the year, create a full-length diagnostic exam from the passages in the book. Choose five to six passages totaling 50–60 questions. Select a balance of prose and poetry. The diagnostic exam will help you determine what types of passages (American poetry, drama, British fiction, etc.) and questions (vocabulary in context, main idea, inference, etc.) the students struggle with most, which can inform your teaching throughout the year.
- If you plan to teach one or more of the texts used in the book, you may want to use that text's passage and questions as a prereading assessment when beginning the unit on that text to see how well students are already reading that particular text on their own, before receiving instruction on it.
- If you plan to teach one or more of the texts used in the book, you may want to use that text's passage and questions as a quiz for your students.
- For practice and assessment throughout the year, create full-length practice exams that consist of five to six passages with a variety of prose (choose from novels, short stories, expository prose, and drama) and poetry.

All English Teachers

- Any teacher of English literature can make extensive use of the passages and questions provided in this book. Like AP teachers, non-AP teachers can use the passages as diagnostics and assessments if they are teaching units on any of the texts included in the book.
- Non-AP teachers can also use the book to prepare students who are on the AP track or to challenge the higher-performing students in their classes.

ACKNOWLEDGMENTS

I would first like to thank my AP English students of 2008–09 for their insightful contributions to our class discussions and written assignments on many of the texts used in this book.

Thank you to Dr. Sean Miller, Dr. Vikas Bhushan, and the editorial team at McGraw-Hill Professional for their editorial comments.

I would also like to acknowledge Mr. Robert Ayres and Mrs. Barbara Pfeiffer, two of my own high school English teachers who inspired me to pursue teaching English. Their teaching methods, styles, and lessons continue to inform my instruction.

INTRODUCTION

Congratulations! You've taken a big step toward AP success by purchasing *5 Steps to a 5: 500 AP English Literature Questions to Know by Test Day*. We are here to help you take the next step and score high on your AP exam so you can earn college credits and get into the college or university of your choice!

This book gives you 500 AP-style multiple-choice questions that cover all the most essential course material. Each question has a detailed answer explanation. These questions will give you valuable independent practice to supplement your regular textbook and the groundwork you are already doing in your AP classroom.

This and the other books in this series were written by expert AP teachers who know your exam inside out and can identify the crucial exam information as well as questions that are most likely to appear on the exam.

You might be the kind of student who takes several AP courses and needs to study extra questions a few weeks before the exam for a final review. Or you might be the kind of student who puts off preparing until the last weeks before the exam. No matter what your preparation style, you will surely benefit from reviewing these 500 questions, which closely parallel the content, format, and degree of difficulty of the questions on the actual AP exam. These questions and their answer explanations are the ideal last-minute study tool for those final few weeks before the test.

Remember the old saying "Practice makes perfect." If you practice with all the questions and answers in this book, we are certain you will build the skills and confidence needed to do great on the exam. Good luck!

Editors of McGraw-Hill Education

CHAPTER 1

British Poetry

Passage 1. Thomas Hardy, "Nobody Comes"

Tree-leaves labour up and down,
And through them the fainting light
Succumbs to the crawl of night.
Outside in the road the telegraph wire
To the town from the darkening land   5
Intones to travelers like a spectral lyre
Swept by a spectral hand.

A car comes up, with lamps full-glare,
That flash upon a tree:
It has nothing to do with me,   10
And whangs along in a world of its own,
Leaving a blacker air;
And mute by the gate I stand again alone,
And nobody pulls up there.

1. The first stanza contains all of the following devices *except*

   (A) consonance
   (B) personification
   (C) masculine rhyme
   (D) simile
   (E) enjambment

2. What is "Swept by a spectral hand" (7)?

   (A) the darkening land
   (B) travelers
   (C) an instrument
   (D) the speaker
   (E) the town

3. In context, the word "spectral" (6, 7) most likely means
    (A) mythical
    (B) invisible
    (C) shining
    (D) ghostly
    (E) loud

4. The purpose of the simile in line 6 is
    (A) to offer optimism in a dark situation
    (B) to emphasize the telegraph's power by humanizing it
    (C) to add a soothing tone to an otherwise ominous mood
    (D) to present modern technology as otherworldly
    (E) to highlight the irony of the telegraph wire

5. The rhyme scheme of the poem is
    (A) *abab cdcd efef gg*
    (B) *aabbccddeeffggh*
    (C) *ababcdc ababcdc*
    (D) *abbcdcd effgege*
    (E) *abbcdcdc efeefeg*

6. The first line of both stanzas
    I.   ends in a word that is never rhymed
    II. sets a scene
    III. contains a steady meter

    (A) I only
    (B) I and II only
    (C) II and III only
    (D) II only
    (E) I, II, and III

7. The alliteration in line 11
    (A) contrasts with the consonance in line 13
    (B) does not match the content of line 11
    (C) emphasizes the speaker's unity with the "world" (11)
    (D) coincides with the alliteration in the previous line
    (E) has no bigger purpose

8. We can interpret that the "air" becomes "blacker" (12) because of all of the following *except*

    (A) the speaker's isolation has become more palpable

    (B) it mimics the speaker's emotional state

    (C) the lights of the car have gone

    (D) it is later at night now

    (E) modern technology mars the natural environment

9. The overall tone of the poem is

    (A) self-pitying

    (B) eerie

    (C) nostalgic

    (D) irreverent

    (E) sardonic

10. The poem's theme can be interpreted as

    (A) the natural environment is lonely

    (B) the natural world is omnipotent

    (C) isolation is a common state

    (D) the benefits of modern technology are dubious

    (E) technology is bad

Passage 2. Robert Herrick, "To the Virgins, to Make Much of Time"

Gather ye rose-buds while ye may:
Old Time is still a-flying;
And this same flower that smiles to-day,
To-morrow will be dying.

The glorious lamp of heaven, the Sun,   5
The higher he's a-getting,
The sooner will his race be run,
And nearer he's to setting.

That age is best, which is the first,
When youth and blood are warmer;   10
But being spent, the worse, and worst
Times, still succeed the former.

—Then be not coy, but use your time,
And while ye may, go marry;
For having lost but once your prime,   15
You may for ever tarry.

11. The word "ye" in line 1 refers to
    (A) virgins
    (B) the speaker's friend
    (C) all women
    (D) the reader
    (E) a flower

12. The device used in line 2 is
    (A) anachronism
    (B) personification
    (C) allusion
    (D) sensory imagery
    (E) apostrophe

13. The rose-buds are
    (A) dying
    (B) an indication that the addressees are carefree
    (C) a symbol of young girls' leisure time
    (D) a metaphor for the ephemeral nature of youth and beauty
    (E) a symbol of women's beauty

14. In the second stanza, the sun is characterized as
    I. electric
    II. male
    III. a runner

    (A) I only
    (B) I and II only
    (C) I and III only
    (D) II and III only
    (E) I, II, and III

15. In line 12, "the former" refers to
    (A) the worse times
    (B) the worst times
    (C) the first age
    (D) the time of matrimony
    (E) the time of birth

16. The word "tarry" in line 16 most likely means

    (A) marry
    (B) regret
    (C) beautiful
    (D) delay
    (E) mourn

17. Alliteration is evident in which of the following lines?

    (A) line 2
    (B) line 3
    (C) line 4
    (D) line 5
    (E) line 8

18. In line 9, the words "best" and "first" create

    (A) masculine rhyme
    (B) internal rhyme
    (C) feminine rhyme
    (D) assonance
    (E) consonance

19. Where does enjambment occur in the poem?

    (A) line 4
    (B) line 11
    (C) line 13
    (D) line 14
    (E) line 15

20. A major theme of the poem can best be summarized as

    (A) everything is temporary, especially youth and beauty
    (B) time is a formidable foe
    (C) young women should indulge in sexual intercourse as soon as possible
    (D) everyone should wait to find the right person before marrying
    (E) "carpe diem"

21. The poem's rhyme scheme is

    (A) *ababcdcdefefghgh*
    (B) *aabbccddeeffgghh*
    (C) *abab cdcd efef ghgh*
    (D) *abab abab abab abab*
    (E) *aba cdc efe ghg*

22. The poem is a(n)

(A) ode
(B) ballad
(C) sonnet
(D) admonition
(E) lyric

23. In the poem, the speaker's tone can best be described as

(A) encouraging
(B) vehement
(C) desperate
(D) pushy
(E) maudlin

Passage 3. Gerard Manley Hopkins, "God's Grandeur"

The world is charged with the grandeur of God.
It will flame out, like shining from shook foil;
It gathers to a greatness, like the ooze of oil
Crushed. Why do men then now not reck his rod?
Generations have trod, have trod, have trod; 5
And all is seared with trade; bleared, smeared with toil;
And wears man's smudge and shares man's smell: the soil
Is bare now, nor can foot feel, being shod.
And for all this, nature is never spent;
There lives the dearest freshness deep down things; 10
And though the last lights off the black West went
Oh, morning, at the brown brink eastward, springs—
Because the Holy Ghost over the bent
World broods with warm breast and with ah! bright wings.

24. Lines 1–3 contain an abundance of

(A) alliteration
(B) asyndeton
(C) anaphora
(D) metaphor
(E) simile

25. The change in sound from the first three lines to line 4 is

    (A) a change from a mellifluous sound to a harsh sound
    (B) a change from a tranquil sound to a placid sound
    (C) a change from a confusing sound to a clear sound
    (D) a change from an inconsistent sound to a steady sound
    (E) a change from an indistinct sound to a distinct sound

26. The sound devices in line 4 serve to emphasize

    (A) the superiority of men to God
    (B) the unity between men and God
    (C) the fearless independence of men
    (D) man's obliviousness to God's grandeur
    (E) man's dislike of God's wrath

27. In context, the repetition in line 5 highlights

    (A) man's preference for the natural world
    (B) the inexorable nature of man's mistakes
    (C) the monotonous demands of an earthly life
    (D) man's temporary preference for industry and materiality over God
    (E) man's dissatisfaction with the material world

28. Line 6 contains all of the following devices *except*

    (A) internal rhyme
    (B) consonance
    (C) assonance
    (D) alliteration
    (E) enjambment

29. The change in tone from lines 1–3 to lines 4–8 is

    (A) a change from reverential to ambivalent
    (B) a change from perplexed to dismayed
    (C) a change from awe-inspired to dirgelike
    (D) a change from optimism to skepticism
    (E) a change from confident to pitiful

30. The structure and form of the poem indicates that it is

    (A) a pastoral
    (B) an elegy
    (C) a Petrarchan sonnet
    (D) an ode
    (E) a Shakespearean sonnet

31. The alliteration in the final six lines reinforces
    I. God's eminence
    II. the speaker's confidence
    III. God's harmony with the world

(A) I only
(B) I and II only
(C) III only
(D) II and III only
(E) I, II, and III

32. The last six lines differ from the first eight in that

(A) the sound changes but the tone stays the same
(B) God is portrayed as less powerful
(C) the focus is more on man than on God
(D) they reassure rather than question
(E) they contain skepticism instead of curiosity

33. The theme of the poem is best expressed by which one of its phrases?

(A) "It gathers to a greatness, like the ooze of oil" (3)
(B) "all is seared with trade; bleared, smeared with toil" (6)
(C) "Why do men then now not reck his rod" (4)
(D) "nature is never spent" (9)
(E) "Generations have trod, have trod, have trod" (5)

34. The rhyme scheme of the poem is

(A) *abbaabba cdccdc*
(B) *abcdefabcdefgg*
(C) *abab cdcd efef gg*
(D) *aba aba aba cdcdcd*
(E) *abbaabba cdcdcd*

35. The poem ends with

(A) bemusement
(B) unrestrained awe
(C) didacticism
(D) qualified hope
(E) constructive criticism

Passage 4. Andrew Marvell, "To His Coy Mistress"

Had we but world enough, and time,
This coyness, lady, were no crime.
We would sit down and think which way
To walk, and pass our long love's day;
Thou by the Indian Ganges' side   5
Shouldst rubies find; I by the tide
Of Humber would complain. I would
Love you ten years before the Flood;
And you should, if you please, refuse
Till the conversion of the Jews.   10
My vegetable love should grow
Vaster than empires, and more slow.
An hundred years should go to praise
Thine eyes, and on thy forehead gaze;
Two hundred to adore each breast,   15
But thirty thousand to the rest;
An age at least to every part,
And the last age should show your heart.
For, lady, you deserve this state,
Nor would I love at lower rate.   20

But at my back I always hear
Time's winged chariot hurrying near;
And yonder all before us lie
Deserts of vast eternity.
Thy beauty shall no more be found,   25
Nor, in thy marble vault, shall sound
My echoing song; then worms shall try
That long preserv'd virginity,
And your quaint honour turn to dust,
And into ashes all my lust.   30
The grave's a fine and private place,
But none I think do there embrace.

Now therefore, while the youthful hue
Sits on thy skin like morning dew,
And while thy willing soul transpires   35
At every pore with instant fires,
Now let us sport us while we may;
And now, like am'rous birds of prey,
Rather at once our time devour,
Than languish in his slow-chapp'd power.   40
Let us roll all our strength, and all

Our sweetness, up into one ball;
And tear our pleasures with rough strife
Thorough the iron gates of life.
Thus, though we cannot make our sun
Stand still, yet we will make him run.

45

36. The first stanza consists of all of the following *except*

(A) a steady meter
(B) metaphor
(C) end rhymes
(D) hyperbole
(E) anaphora

37. Which of the following lines contains internal rhyme?

(A) line 2
(B) line 16
(C) line 6
(D) line 4
(E) line 9

38. The word "coyness" in line 2 most likely means

(A) sedentary lifestyle
(B) hurried state
(C) procrastination
(D) seduction
(E) modesty

39. The references to the "Indian Ganges" (5), the "Humber" (7), the "Flood" (8), and the "Jews" (10) serve to

(A) flatter and impress
(B) confound and shock
(C) startle and mystify
(D) persuade and elude
(E) degrade and vilify

40. The phrase "vegetable love" (11) is

(A) an example of synesthesia
(B) an oxymoron
(C) intended to emphasize the speaker's immediate desire
(D) a symbol of the seductive powers of the natural environment
(E) a metaphor for the speaker's long-lasting love

41. The second stanza differs from the first in that
    I. the imagery changes from libidinous to morbid
   II. the tone changes from arrogant to desperate
  III. the sound changes from alluring to chilling

  (A) I and II only
  (B) I and III only
  (C) II only
  (D) II and III only
  (E) I, II, and III

42. "Time's winged chariot hurrying near" (22) can best be paraphrased as

  (A) we must catch up with time
  (B) time is our rescuer
  (C) time flies
  (D) time is all-powerful like God
  (E) death is near

43. The words at the ends of lines 23 and 24 and at the ends of lines 27 and 28 are examples of

  (A) slant rhyme
  (B) masculine rhyme
  (C) iambic pentameter
  (D) internal rhyme
  (E) enjambment

44. The simile in line 34 serves to

  (A) impress the addressee
  (B) underscore the addressee's ephemeral youth
  (C) distract the addressee
  (D) point out the addressee's natural beauty
  (E) question the addressee's beauty

45. In line 40, "his" refers to

  (A) the speaker
  (B) the addressee
  (C) "birds of prey"
  (D) "instant fires"
  (E) time

46. Which of the following devices enhances the speaker's point in the last two lines of the passage?

(A) assonance
(B) alliteration
(C) figures of speech
(D) pun
(E) simile

47. The speaker's strategy in the passage as a whole consists of

(A) an introduction to a problem, deductive reasoning, criticism, and solution
(B) soothing sounds, cogent examples, and personal anecdotes
(C) seduction, accurate data, and historical examples
(D) a major premise, minor premise, and conclusion
(E) agreement and contradiction

48. The poem is most similar in style and content to

(A) a lyric
(B) a panegyric
(C) an ode
(D) a sonnet
(E) a limerick

Passage 5. William Wordsworth, "The world is too much with us"

The world is too much with us; late and soon,
Getting and spending, we lay waste our powers:
Little we see in nature that is ours;
We have given our hearts away, a sordid boon!
This Sea that bares her bosom to the moon;   5
The Winds that will be howling at all hours

And are up-gathered now like sleeping flowers;
For this, for every thing, we are out of tune;
It moves us not—Great God! I'd rather be
A Pagan suckled in a creed outworn;   10
So might I, standing on this pleasant lea,
Have glimpses that would make me less forlorn;
Have sight of Proteus coming from the sea;
Or hear old Triton blow his wreathed horn.

49. The first two lines contain an abundance of

(A) couplets
(B) internal rhyme
(C) hyperbole
(D) consonance
(E) alliteration

50. The rhyme scheme of the poem is

(A) *aba aba aba aba*
(B) *abbaabba cdcdcd*
(C) *abab cdcd efef gg*
(D) *abaabaabacdcdcd*
(E) *abba abba abba cd*

51. The phrase "sordid boon" (4) is

(A) a call for an end to industry
(B) a sarcastic expletive that mocks our "hearts"
(C) a paradox that deplores human nature
(D) an oxymoron that points out the irony of society's advancement
(E) a celebration of nature's benefits

52. In context of the poem as a whole, we can infer that the word "world" means

(A) society
(B) England
(C) the man-made world
(D) nature
(E) people

53. The change in tone beginning in line 9 is best explained as

(A) a change from being wistful to willful
(B) a change from regretful to remorseful
(C) a change from scolding to lamenting
(D) a change from being forlorn to bitter
(E) a change from desperation to optimism

54. The metaphor in line 10 compares

(A) a religion to a mother's breast
(B) Paganism to an outdated belief system
(C) beliefs to mothers
(D) religion to breast milk
(E) Pagans to mothers

55. The poem's structure, style, and content are most like those of
    (A) a lampoon
    (B) a lyric
    (C) a Spenserian sonnet
    (D) a Petrarchan sonnet
    (E) an Elizabethan sonnet

56. The allusions in lines 13–14 illustrate
    (A) the speaker's sanguinity
    (B) the speaker's predicament
    (C) the speaker's fantasy
    (D) the speaker's knowledge
    (E) the speaker's solution

57. Personification is evident in which of the following lines?
    (A) line 14
    (B) line 5
    (C) line 6
    (D) line 8
    (E) line 13

58. The theme of the poem as a whole can best be stated as
    (A) nature is better than technology
    (B) the natural world has more to offer than people
    (C) the natural world is a panacea for our troubles
    (D) we should be reproached for having immersed ourselves in industry and lost touch with the natural world
    (E) we can forget our sins by personifying nature as godlike

Passage 6. William Butler Yeats, "That the Night Come"

She lived in storm and strife.
Her soul had such desire
For what proud death may bring
That it could not endure
The common good of life,   5
But lived as 'twere a king
That packed his marriage day
With banneret and pennon,
Trumpet and kettledrum,
And the outrageous cannon,   10
To bundle Time away
That the night come.

59. When measured, the beat and meter of lines 1–5 is called
    (A) trochaic pentameter
    (B) iambic trimeter
    (C) trochaic tetrameter
    (D) iambic tetrameter
    (E) iambic pentameter

60. The variation in beat is most evident in which line?
    (A) line 12
    (B) line 10
    (C) line 7
    (D) line 8
    (E) line 6

61. Lines 1–4 contain which of the following devices?
    (A) slant and exact rhyme
    (B) assonance and consonance
    (C) alliteration and personification
    (D) polysyndeton and asyndeton
    (E) oxymoron and chiasmus

62. The word "it" in line 4 refers to
    (A) "death"
    (B) "Her"
    (C) "soul"
    (D) "desire"
    (E) "She"

63. The main difference emphasized in the poem between "Her" and the "king" is
    (A) their gender
    (B) their way of living
    (C) the object of their desire
    (D) their attitude
    (E) their class status

64. In context, the words "banneret and pennon" most likely mean
    (A) men and women
    (B) food and beverage
    (C) wedding decorations
    (D) ammunition
    (E) types of fanfare

65. The use of multiple conjunctions in lines 8–10 is a device called

(A) asyndeton
(B) polysyndeton
(C) caesura
(D) epistrophe
(E) run-on sentence

66. The words "night come" (12) contain what type of beat?

(A) anapestic
(B) dactylic
(C) iambic
(D) trochaic
(E) spondaic

67. The simile in line 6 reveals

(A) the king's superiority to the woman
(B) the king's love for his wife
(C) the woman's anticipation of her wedding night
(D) the woman's regret that she did not marry
(E) the woman's excitement about death

68. The change in sound beginning in line 9 parallels

(A) the woman and the king's impatience
(B) the woman's dread
(C) the king's excitement
(D) the intense energy of a wedding celebration
(E) the first eight lines

69. The poem characterizes night as

  I. remote
 II. a panacea
III. interminable

(A) I only
(B) II only
(C) I and III only
(D) II and III only
(E) I, II, and III

70. The phrase "To bundle Time away" (11) means

(A) to pass time
(B) to protect time
(C) to waste time
(D) to save time
(E) to ignore time

CHAPTER 2

American Poetry

Passage 1. Anne Bradstreet, "The Author to Her Book"

Thou ill-form'd offspring of my feeble brain,
Who after birth did'st by my side remain,
Till snatcht from thence by friends, less wise than true,
Who thee abroad exposed to public view,
Made thee in rags, halting to th' press to trudge,   5
Where errors were not lessened (all may judge).
At thy return my blushing was not small,
My rambling brat (in print) should mother call.
I cast thee by as one unfit for light,
The visage was so irksome in my sight,   10
Yet being mine own, at length affection would
Thy blemishes amend, if so I could.
I washed thy face, but more defects I saw,
And rubbing off a spot, still made a flaw.
I stretcht thy joints to make thee even feet,   15
Yet still thou run'st more hobbling than is meet.
In better dress to trim thee was my mind,
But nought save home-spun cloth, i' th' house I find.
In this array, 'mongst vulgars may'st thou roam.
In critics' hands, beware thou dost not come,   20
And take thy way where yet thou are not known.
If for thy father askt, say, thou hadst none;
And for thy mother, she alas is poor,
Which caused her thus to send thee out of door.

71. The poem is developed mainly through
   (A) rhyme
   (B) iambic pentameter
   (C) simile
   (D) metaphor
   (E) conceit

72. The word "Thou" in line 1 indicates
    (A) the poem is a letter
    (B) the poem is an invocation
    (C) the speaker is employing apostrophe
    (D) the speaker uses arcane vocabulary to make a point
    (E) the poem is outdated

73. The poem contains all of the following devices *except*
    (A) enjambment
    (B) imagery
    (C) personification
    (D) explicit metaphor
    (E) exact rhyme

74. The words "trudge" (5) and "judge" (6) are examples of
    (A) internal rhyme
    (B) feminine rhyme
    (C) slant rhyme
    (D) masculine rhyme
    (E) iambs

75. The speaker implies her book is all of the following *except*
    (A) inchoate
    (B) disseminated prematurely
    (C) fallible
    (D) irreparable
    (E) polemical

76. Who is the subject of the verb "Made" (5)?
    (A) the press
    (B) friends
    (C) the speaker
    (D) the book
    (E) the offspring

77. The tone of the poem is
    (A) mournful
    (B) nurturing
    (C) self-deprecating
    (D) vengeful
    (E) acerbic

78. The poem's rhythm is composed of
    I. iambic pentameter
   II. terza rima
  III. heroic couplets

(A) I only
(B) I and II only
(C) II and III only
(D) I and III only
(E) I, II, and III

79. The relationship between the speaker and her addressee is most similar to the relationship between

(A) a teacher and a student
(B) a nurturing father and a child
(C) a boss and an employee
(D) a fastidious artist and her painting
(E) a director and an actor

80. The main topic of the poem is

(A) an artist's relationship with her work
(B) an artist's dislike for her work
(C) the need for editing before publication
(D) unreasonable critics
(E) the hardships of motherhood

Passage 2. Emily Dickinson, "Success is counted sweetest . . ."

Success is counted sweetest
By those who ne'er succeed.
To comprehend a nectar
Requires sorest need.

Not one of all the purple host   5
Who took the flag to-day
Can tell the definition,
So clear, of victory,

As he, defeated, dying,
On whose forbidden ear   10
The distant strains of triumph
Break, agonized and clear!

81. The alliteration in the first stanza serves to

(A) soothe the reader

(B) highlight the envious tone

(C) complement the assonance in the first stanza

(D) contrast the consonance in the second stanza

(E) emphasize the appeal of success by creating an appealing sound

82. The rhythm and beat of the poem as a whole can best be described as consisting of

(A) three to four feet of iambs

(B) iambic pentameter

(C) iambic trimeter

(D) three to four feet of trochees

(E) trochaic tetrameter

83. Line 5 is an example of what type of measured beat?

(A) iambic tetrameter

(B) iambic trimeter

(C) trochaic tetrameter

(D) iambic pentameter

(E) trochaic trimeter

84. The poem's language can be described as consisting of all of the following *except*

(A) aphorisms

(B) homilies

(C) epigrams

(D) axioms

(E) chiasmus

85. The poem's rhyme scheme is

(A) *abcb defe ghih*

(B) *abab abab abab*

(C) *abcb abcb abcb*

(D) *abcd efgh ijkl*

(E) *aabb ccdd eeff*

86. The word "comprehend" in line 3 most likely means

(A) to eat

(B) to figure out

(C) to determine

(D) to analyze

(E) to truly know

87. The words "day" (6) and "victory" (8) provide an example of
    (A) feminine rhyme
    (B) slant rhyme
    (C) double entendre
    (D) oxymoron
    (E) antithesis

88. The structure of the poem consists of
    (A) a hypothesis, reasoning, and a solution
    (B) a proposition and evidence
    (C) one axiomatic sentence and two sentences with images demonstrating the axiom
    (D) a theory and examples
    (E) a question answered by hypothetical situations

89. The overall tone of the poem is
    (A) pedantic
    (B) didactic
    (C) moralistic
    (D) adagelike
    (E) envious

90. The poem can be summarized by which of the following sentences?
    (A) Only those who have achieved success understand its sweetness.
    (B) Success comes only to those who risk and persevere.
    (C) Success is best won through hard work.
    (D) Only those who have not achieved success understand its sweetness.
    (E) The victor is always better off.

Passage 3. T. S. Eliot, "Morning at the Window"

They are rattling breakfast plates in basement kitchens,
And along the trampled edges of the street
I am aware of the damp souls of housemaids
Sprouting despondently at area gates.
The brown waves of fog toss up to me   5
Twisted faces from the bottom of the street,
And tear from a passer-by with muddy skirts
An aimless smile that hovers in the air
And vanishes along the level of the roofs.

91. In line 5, the "waves" are

    (A) so big they reach the speaker's window

    (B) a metaphor for the fog that carries the images of faces down below up to the speaker at his window

    (C) part of the poem's bigger conceit that compares the scene below to an ocean

    (D) part of a hypothetical situation thought up by the speaker

    (E) a hallucination that characterizes the speaker as depressed and delusional

92. The subject to which the word "tear" (7) refers is

    (A) a passer-by

    (B) the speaker

    (C) the brown waves

    (D) an aimless smile

    (E) damp souls

93. The words "fog . . . faces from" (5–6) are an example of

    (A) consonance

    (B) repetition

    (C) anaphora

    (D) assonance

    (E) alliteration

94. The poem's assonance

    (A) is found in the words "muddy skirts" (7) and emphasizes the ugliness of the scene being described

    (B) is found in the words "faces from" (6) and creates a soothing sound to ease the speaker's discomfort

    (C) is found in the words "fog toss" (5) and creates a feeling of upward movement to complement the movement of the waves

    (D) is found in the words "brown waves" (5) and emphasizes the disparity between ugliness and beauty

    (E) is found in the word "rattling" (1) and allows the reader to hear what the speaker hears

95. Regarding the scene he is describing, the speaker is

    (A) removed and observant

    (B) obsessed and upset

    (C) optimistic

    (D) fatalistic

    (E) apathetic

96. The people described in the poem are characterized mostly as

(A) ghostlike
(B) penurious
(C) starving
(D) pathetic
(E) grotesque

97. The speaker is differentiated from the people he describes by

I. his wealth
II. his location
III. his actions

(A) I only
(B) I and II only
(C) II only
(D) II and III only
(E) III only

98. The tone of the poem is developed through

I. diction
II. imagery
III. metaphor

(A) I only
(B) I and II only
(C) II and III only
(D) III only
(E) I, II, and III

Passage 4. Walt Whitman, "O Captain! My Captain!"

O Captain! my Captain! our fearful trip is done!
The ship has weathered every wrack, the prize we sought is won.
The port is near, the bells I hear, the people all exulting,
While follow eyes the steady keel, the vessel grim and daring.

But, O heart! heart! heart!   5
Leave you not the little spot
Where on the deck my Captain lies,
Fallen cold and dead.

O Captain! my Captain! rise up and hear the bells!
Rise up! for you the flag is flung, for you the bugle trills: 10
For you bouquets and ribboned wreaths; for you the shores a-crowding:
For you they call, the swaying mass, their eager faces turning.

O Captain! dear father!
This arm I push beneath you.
It is some dream that on the deck   15
You've fallen cold and dead!

My Captain does not answer, his lips are pale and still:
My father does not feel my arm, he has no pulse nor will.
But the ship, the ship is anchored safe, its voyage closed and done:
From fearful trip the victor ship comes in with object won!   20
Exult, O shores! and ring, O bells!
But I, with silent tread,
Walk the spot my Captain lies,
Fallen cold and dead.

99. Lines 5–8 can best be summarized as

(A) I should never forget the moment of my captain's death.
(B) I love my captain.
(C) My heart is breaking upon seeing my captain die.
(D) I will never leave this spot where my captain has died.
(E) I will never forget this moment.

100. The "bells," "flag," "bugle," "wreaths," and crowds in the second segment

(A) are meant to be ironic
(B) are part of the speaker's hallucination
(C) describe both a victory celebration and a funeral
(D) are metonymies for the captain
(E) are synecdoches for the captain

101. In lines 19–20, the ship is like the captain in all of the following ways *except*

(A) they have both ended their heroic journeys
(B) they have achieved their goals
(C) they are both metaphors
(D) they have both arrived home safely
(E) they are both celebrated

102. The rhyme of "bells" and "lies" differs from the rhyme of "tread" and "dead" (21–24) in that the former

(A) is a slant rhyme
(B) is a masculine rhyme
(C) is not a rhyme
(D) is an internal rhyme
(E) is an exact rhyme

103. The form of the poem's third segment differs from the form of the first two segments in that the former

(A) contains exact end rhymes
(B) contains a steady rhyme scheme
(C) lacks exclamations
(D) does not address the captain
(E) lacks metaphor

104. The references to the captain change

(A) from exclamations in the first and second segments to calm statements in the third segment
(B) to direct addresses in the third segment
(C) to internal thoughts in the third segment
(D) to dialogue in the second segment
(E) to exclamations in the third segment

105. The three segments of the poem are divided according to

(A) the speaker's shock, anger, and disbelief
(B) the speaker's discovery, denial, and acceptance
(C) death, funeral, and denial
(D) theory, research, and conclusion
(E) argument, counterargument, and solution

106. The repetition of the phrase "O Captain! my Captain" is called

(A) a refrain
(B) an echo
(C) anaphora
(D) epistrophe
(E) the chorus

107. The poem is developed mainly through

(A) a refrain
(B) an explicit metaphor
(C) a metaphor
(D) a simile
(E) an extended, implied metaphor

108. The captain in the poem is most likely

(A) a metaphor for a nation's leader
(B) an excellent seafarer who has suddenly died
(C) a metaphor for the speaker's father
(D) a symbol of the mighty naval industry
(E) the speaker himself

109. The poem's style and content are most similar to those of
- (A) a ballad
- (B) a sestina
- (C) a sonnet
- (D) an ode
- (E) an elegy

110. The poem ends with the speaker in a state of
- (A) optimism
- (B) disappointment
- (C) celebration
- (D) denial
- (E) mourning

Passage 5. William Carlos Williams, "Contemporania"

The corner of a great rain
Steamy with the country
Has fallen upon my garden.

I go back and forth now
And the little leaves follow me   5
Talking of the great rain,
Of branches broken,
And the farmer's curses!

But I go back and forth
In this corner of a garden   10
And the green shoots follow me
Praising the great rain.

We are not curst together,
The leaves and I,
Framing devices, flower devices   15
And other ways of peopling
The barren country.

Truly it was a very great rain
That makes the little leaves follow me.

111. The exclamation point in line 8 reveals

    (A) the speaker's dismay
    (B) the leaves' points of view
    (C) the farmer's hatred
    (D) the greatness of the rain
    (E) the evil of the rain's curse

112. When the speaker says, "The leaves and I,/ Framing devices, flower devices" (15), he means

    (A) the leaves frame and he flowers
    (B) they are not curst
    (C) plants frame the land and flower the land
    (D) both he and the plants are part of the life cycle
    (E) both leaves and people liven up the barren land by decorating it and by procreating

113. The speaker's attitude toward the rain is similar to

    (A) a stargazer's attitude toward the universe
    (B) an artist's attitude toward his muse
    (C) an acolyte's attitude toward his idol
    (D) a husband's attitude toward his wife
    (E) a child's attitude toward his favorite toy

114. The form and structure of the poem can best be described as

    (A) a sonnet
    (B) a villanelle
    (C) a sestina
    (D) free verse
    (E) closed form

115. The poem contains all of the following devices *except*

    (A) repetition
    (B) consonance
    (C) personification
    (D) assonance
    (E) alliteration

116. The title suits the poem in that

    (A) the poetic techniques are novel and groundbreaking
    (B) the speaker describes modernism
    (C) the poem includes details from contemporary life
    (D) the poem provides commentary on outdated modes of living
    (E) the poem is an artifact recording a moment in time

117. The poem's themes and style are most in line with

(A) neoclassicism
(B) postmodernism
(C) realism
(D) imagism
(E) naturalism

118. The rain reminds the speaker of

  I. his fertility
  II. the life cycle
  III. the similarities he shares with plants

(A) I only
(B) I and II only
(C) II and III only
(D) III only
(E) I, II, and III

119. The last two lines of the poem

(A) contain iambic pentameter
(B) make up the envoy
(C) communicate a theme
(D) make up a couplet
(E) make up a heroic couplet

120. A theme of the poem is

(A) the harshness of nature
(B) the speaker's realization that he is united with powerful nature
(C) the greatness of the rain
(D) the life cycle
(E) the positive and negative effects of nature

CHAPTER 3

World Poetry

Passage 1. Kahlil Gibran, "Defeat"

Defeat, my Defeat, my solitude and my aloofness;
You are dearer to me than a thousand triumphs,
And sweeter to my heart than all world-glory.

Defeat, my Defeat, my self-knowledge and my defiance,
Through you I know that I am yet young and swift of foot   5
And not to be trapped by withering laurels.
And in you I have found aloneness
And the joy of being shunned and scorned.

Defeat, my Defeat, my shining sword and shield,
In your eyes I have read   10
That to be enthroned is to be enslaved,
and to be understood is to be leveled down,
And to be grasped is but to reach one's fullness
and like a ripe fruit to fall and be consumed.

Defeat, my Defeat, my bold companion,   15
You shall hear my songs and my cries and my silences,
And none but you shall speak to me of the beating of wings,
And urging of seas,
And of mountains that burn in the night,
And you alone shall climb my steep and rocky soul.   20

Defeat, my Defeat, my deathless courage,
You and I shall laugh together with the storm,
And together we shall dig graves for all that die in us,
And we shall stand in the sun with a will,
And we shall be dangerous.   25

121. The poem as a whole is written as a(n)
    (A) allegory
    (B) anecdote
    (C) letter
    (D) speech
    (E) apostrophe

122. The repetitive use of the word "And" at the start of many lines in the poem is
    (A) grammatically incorrect
    (B) an example of hyperbole
    (C) a device known as asyndeton
    (D) repetitive
    (E) a device known as anaphora

123. In the second stanza, the speaker reveals that
    (A) "Defeat" is a characteristic of the young
    (B) "Defeat" is an actual person
    (C) he sees value in "Defeat" because it makes him incorrigible
    (D) he sees value in "Defeat" because it makes him self-aware
    (E) he has a sarcastic attitude toward "Defeat"

124. The metaphor of the "sword and shield" (9) is meant to
    (A) emphasize "Defeat's" emboldening powers
    (B) characterize the speaker as invincible
    (C) contradict the previous stanza's imagery
    (D) change the poem's tone from sarcastic to laudatory
    (E) emphasize "Defeat's" valiant nature

125. The third stanza reveals that the speaker thinks success is
    (A) hypocritical
    (B) unimaginable
    (C) overrated
    (D) easily obtained
    (E) better than "Defeat"

126. The speaker characterizes "Defeat" as all of the following *except*
    (A) second best to success
    (B) distinct
    (C) useful
    (D) brave
    (E) bold

127. The poem's refrain
    (A) is found in lines 1, 4, 9, 15, and 21 and characterizes "Defeat" as alone
    (B) is found in all lines beginning with "And" and highlights the theme
    (C) is found in all lines beginning with "And" and emphasizes the speaker's point
    (D) is found in lines 1, 4, 9, 15, and 21 and enhances the poem's odelike quality
    (E) is the entire last stanza and contains the theme

128. The speaker's address to "Defeat" as his "deathless courage" (21) shows
    (A) the poem's ironic tone
    (B) the speaker's appreciation of death
    (C) that courage and death are opposites
    (D) that with "Defeat" comes immortality
    (E) that with "Defeat" comes temerity

129. The speaker sees "Defeat" primarily as his
    (A) friend
    (B) mentor
    (C) adversary
    (D) obstacle
    (E) parent

130. The mood that is established by the end of the poem is one of
    (A) confidence
    (B) cynicism
    (C) desire
    (D) destruction
    (E) wistfulness

Passage 2. Jayadeva, Excerpt from *Gita Govinda*

Beautiful Radha, jasmine-bosomed Radha,
All in the Spring-time waited by the wood
For Krishna fair, Krishna the all-forgetful,—
Krishna with earthly love's false fire consuming—
And some one of her maidens sang this song:—   5

I know where Krishna tarries in these early days of Spring,
When every wind from warm Malay brings fragrance on its wing;
Brings fragrance stolen far away from thickets of the clove,
In jungles where the bees hum and the Koil flutes her love;

He dances with the dancers of a merry morrice one,   10
All in the budding Spring-time, for 'tis sad to be alone.

I know how Krishna passes these hours of blue and gold
When parted lovers sigh to meet and greet and closely hold
Hand fast in hand; and every branch upon the Vakul-tree
Droops downward with a hundred blooms, in every bloom a bee;   15
He is dancing with the dancers to a laughter-moving tone,
In the soft awakening Spring-time, when 'tis hard to live alone.

Where Kroona-flowers, that open at a lover's lightest tread,
Break, and, for shame at what they hear, from white blush modest red;
And all the spears on all the boughs of all the Ketuk-glades   20
Seem ready darts to pierce the hearts of wandering youths and maids;
Tis there thy Krishna dances till the merry drum is done,
All in the sunny Spring-time, when who can live alone?

Where the breaking forth of blossom on the yellow Keshra-sprays
Dazzles like Kama's sceptre, whom all the world obeys;   25
And Pâtal-buds fill drowsy bees from pink delicious bowls,
As Kama's nectared goblet steeps in languor human souls;
There he dances with the dancers, and of Radha thinketh none,
All in the warm new Spring-tide, when none will live alone.

Where the breath of waving Mâdhvi pours incense through the grove,   30
And silken Mogras lull the sense with essences of love,—
The silken-soft pale Mogra, whose perfume fine and faint
Can melt the coldness of a maid, the sternness of a saint—
There dances with those dancers thine other self, thine Own,
All in the languorous Spring-time, when none will live alone.   35

Where—as if warm lips touched sealed eyes and waked them—all the bloom
Opens upon the mangoes to feel the sunshine come;
And Atimuktas wind their arms of softest green about,
Clasping the stems, while calm and clear great Jumna spreadeth out;
There dances and there laughs thy Love, with damsels many a one,   40
In the rosy days of Spring-time, for he will not live alone.

131. The first verse serves as the poem's
    (A) overture
    (B) invocation
    (C) climax
    (D) denouement
    (E) coda

132. The appositives in the first verse provide
    (A) epithets for Radha and Krishna
    (B) examples
    (C) additional details about the setting
    (D) stereotypical descriptions
    (E) the problem that will be discussed in the poem

133. The overall mood of the poem can best be described as
    (A) jealous
    (B) exultant
    (C) reticent
    (D) admonishing
    (E) conciliatory

134. The sentence that makes up the third verse in lines 12–17 ("I know how Krishna passes these hours . . . hard to live alone") is the following kind of sentence:
      I. complex
     II. compound
    III. loose

    (A) I only
    (B) I and II only
    (C) II and III only
    (D) I and III only
    (E) I, II, and III

135. The beat and meter of each line in the second verse is measured as
    (A) five feet of iambs
    (B) six feet of iambs
    (C) seven feet of iambs
    (D) five feet of trochees
    (E) six feet of trochees

136. All of the following verses contain at least one end rhyme that is a slant rhyme *except*
    (A) verse 2
    (B) verse 3
    (C) verse 4
    (D) verse 5
    (E) verse 6

137. The simile in line 25 serves to
    (A) imply that nature can be destructive
    (B) emphasize Krishna's infidelity
    (C) compare the season to a war
    (D) compare flowers to people
    (E) highlight the commanding powers of spring

138. The phrase "pink delicious bowls" (26) is primarily
    (A) an example of personification
    (B) a metaphor for the nourishing flower petals
    (C) a description of a rare species of flower
    (D) an oxymoron
    (E) a symbol of the bees' hunger

139. In line 27, "Kama's nectared goblet steeps in languor human souls" most
    likely refers to
    (A) the drunken feeling of love
    (B) the smallness of human ambition
    (C) the awakening of desire
    (D) the wetness of springtime
    (E) the intoxicating effects of alcohol

140. Each of verses two through seven ends with the word "alone," which is an
    example of
    (A) chiasmus
    (B) anaphora
    (C) caesura
    (D) epistrophe
    (E) enjambment

141. The poem's refrain serves to
    (A) describe spring
    (B) reinforce the speaker's empathy for Krishna
    (C) make Radha feel lonelier
    (D) introduce new characters
    (E) question Krishna's intentions

142. Krishna's attitude toward Radha can best be described as
    (A) scornful
    (B) indifferent
    (C) ambivalent
    (D) coy
    (E) calculating

143. The sixth verse, which begins "Where the breath of waving Mâdhvi pours" (30), makes use of all of the following *except*

(A) alliteration
(B) em dashes
(C) asyndeton
(D) parallelism
(E) anastrophe

144. In line 34, "thine other self, thine Own" refers to

(A) Krishna
(B) Radha
(C) Mâdhvi
(D) Mogra
(E) Kama

145. The maidens' attitude toward Krishna can best be described as

(A) mercurial
(B) ambivalent
(C) sanctimonious
(D) incriminating
(E) apologetic

146. In context, the word "Love" (40) is a reference to

(A) Radha's possession
(B) Radha's desire
(C) spring
(D) Radha
(E) Krishna

147. We can infer from the poem's context that words like "Kroona," "Ketuk," "Keshra," "Pâtal," and "Mogras" are all

(A) allusions
(B) names of characters
(C) names of gods
(D) names of types of foliage
(E) names for spring

148. The implication from the maidens' song is that Krishna is all of the
following *except*
    (A) faithful
    (B) promiscuous
    (C) dexterous
    (D) charming
    (E) lonely

Passage 3. Rabindranath Tagore, "My Country Awake"

Where the mind is without fear and the head is held high;

Where knowledge is free;

Where the world has not been broken up into fragments by narrow
domestic walls;

Where words come out from the depth of truth;   5

Where tireless striving stretches its arms towards perfection;

Where the clear stream of reason has not lost its way into the
dreary desert sand of dead habit;

Where the mind is led forward by thee into ever-widening thought
and action—   10

Into that heaven of freedom, my Father, let my country awake.

149. The use of the word "Where" at the start of several clauses in the poem is a
device known as
    (A) analogy
    (B) apostrophe
    (C) parallelism
    (D) epistrophe
    (E) anaphora

150. The poem as a whole is made up of what type of sentence?
    (A) cumulative
    (B) compound-complex
    (C) periodic
    (D) compound
    (E) dependent

151. The words "head . . . held" (1) and "desert . . . dead" (8) contain

    (A) consonance and imagery
    (B) internal rhyme and assonance
    (C) oxymora and alliteration
    (D) assonance and consonance
    (E) alliteration and assonance

152. Lines 1, 3, 6, and 8 all contain which sound device?

    (A) enjambment
    (B) alliteration
    (C) consonance
    (D) assonance
    (E) rhyme

153. The "dreary desert sand of dead habit" (7–8)

    (A) is an implied metaphor stressing the hopelessness of chronic behavior
    (B) is an explicit metaphor emphasizing desperation
    (C) is a conceit that contains alliteration
    (D) contains a soothing sound to complement the speaker's dream of a desert country
    (E) is part of a bigger simile that uses the natural environment to describe what the speaker's country is and is not

154. In the grammatical structure of lines 9–10, "the mind" is

    (A) the dependent clause
    (B) the predicate
    (C) the subject
    (D) the object
    (E) the appositive

155. In the poem, the speaker addresses

    (A) his country
    (B) himself
    (C) a political leader
    (D) his parent
    (E) God

156. The speaker implies his country is all of the following *except*

    (A) fearful
    (B) limited
    (C) fettered
    (D) confined
    (E) irreparable

157. The poem as a whole is a

    I. supplication

   II. prayer

  III. speech

(A) I only

(B) I and II only

(C) II only

(D) II and III only

(E) I, II, and III

158. The tone of the poem can best be described as

(A) earnest

(B) plaintive

(C) pious

(D) optimistic

(E) fatalistic

Passage 4. Rabindranath Tagore, "The Home"

I paced alone on the road across the field while the sunset was
hiding its last gold like a miser.

The daylight sank deeper and deeper into the darkness, and the
widowed land, whose harvest had been reaped, lay silent.

Suddenly a boy's shrill voice rose into the sky. He traversed   5
the dark unseen, leaving the track of his song across the hush of
the evening.

His village home lay there at the end of the waste land, beyond
the sugar-cane field, hidden among the shadows of the banana and
the slender areca palm, the cocoa-nut and the dark green   10
jack-fruit trees.

I stopped for a moment in my lonely way under the starlight, and
saw spread before me the darkened earth surrounding with her arms
countless homes furnished with cradles and beds, mothers' hearts
and evening lamps, and young lives glad with a gladness that   15
knows nothing of its value for the world.

159. The simile in line 2

    (A) compares gold to a cheapskate to emphasize the town's poverty

    (B) compares the sun to a scrupulous saver to convey the disappearance of sunlight

    (C) contrasts the gold to a miser to show the town's poverty

    (D) contrasts the sun to a miser to show how dark it has become

    (E) symbolizes darkness

160. Line 3 contains an abundance of

    (A) anaphora

    (B) personification

    (C) hyperbole

    (D) assonance

    (E) alliteration

161. In context, the phrases "widowed land" (4) and "her arms" (13) are examples of

    (A) apostrophe

    (B) conceit

    (C) metaphor

    (D) personification

    (E) passive voice

162. The second sentence of the poem differs from the first in that

    (A) it is passive

    (B) it contains a simile

    (C) it contains only one independent clause

    (D) it contains a dependent clause

    (E) it contains an appositive

163. The third stanza contains a contrast between

    (A) night and day

    (B) boy and sky

    (C) boy and man

    (D) sound and silence

    (E) light and dark

164. The phrase "waste land" (8) implies that

(A) the setting is hellish
(B) the "home" is in the middle of nowhere
(C) a war has just taken place
(D) the people of this town are devastated
(E) the boy's home is isolated

165. The poem's final sentence can best be paraphrased as

(A) Happy families are unaware of how valuable their bliss is to the world.
(B) The dark, lonely earth is lit up by the people who inhabit it.
(C) I wish I were part of one of these families.
(D) Home is where the heart is.
(E) The natural world protects families and makes them glad.

166. The final stanza reveals the speaker's

(A) keen eye for detail
(B) love for his home
(C) love for his family
(D) loneliness
(E) appreciation for the natural world

167. The poem's form and style are characteristic of a(n)

(A) ballad
(B) ode
(C) elegy
(D) villanelle
(E) free-verse poem

168. The title of the poem

(A) contains the theme
(B) introduces the conceit
(C) begins the poem's metaphor
(D) is a symbol for heaven
(E) introduces the object of the speaker's desire

CHAPTER 4

British Fiction

Passage 1. Frances Burney, *Evelina*

We are to go this evening to a private ball, given by Mrs. Stanley, a very fashionable lady of Mrs. Mirvan's acquaintance.

We have been a-shopping as Mrs. Mirvan calls it, all this morning, to buy silks, caps, gauzes, and so forth.

The shops are really very entertaining, especially the mercers; there seem to be   5
six or seven men belonging to each shop; and every one took care by bowing and smirking, to be noticed. We were conducted from one to another, and carried from room to room with so much ceremony, that I was almost afraid to go on.

I thought I should never have chosen a silk: for they produced so many, I knew not which to fix upon; and they recommended them all so strongly, that I fancy   10
they thought I only wanted persuasion to buy every thing they showed me. And, indeed, they took so much trouble, that I was almost ashamed I could not.

At the milliners, the ladies we met were so much dressed, that I should rather have imagined they were making visits than purchases. But what most diverted me was, that we were more frequently served by men than by women; and such men!   15
so finical, so affected! they seemed to understand every part of a woman's dress better than we do ourselves; and they recommended caps and ribbands with an air of so much importance, that I wished to ask them how long they had left off wearing them.

The dispatch with which they work in these great shops is amazing, for they   20
have promised me a complete suit of linen against the evening.

I have just had my hair dressed. You can't think how oddly my head feels; full of powder and black pins, and a great cushion on the top of it. I believe you would hardly know me, for my face looks quite different to what it did before my hair was dressed. When I shall be able to make use of a comb for myself I cannot tell; for my   25
hair is so much entangled, frizzled they call it, that I fear it will be very difficult.

I am half afraid of this ball to-night; for, you know, I have never danced but at school: however, Miss Mirvan says there is nothing in it. Yet, I wish it was over.

Adieu, my dear Sir, pray excuse the wretched stuff I write; perhaps I may improve by being in this town, and then my letters will be less unworthy your read-   30
ing. Meantime, I am, Your dutiful and affectionate, though unpolished, EVELINA

169. The phrase "to be noticed" in line 7 implies that the mercers are

(A) solicitous
(B) officious
(C) cloying
(D) vigilant
(E) obsequious

170. The speaker's tone in the phrase "and such men!" (15) can best be described as

(A) perturbed
(B) frightened
(C) surprised and confused
(D) disappointed
(E) incredulous

171. In context, the word "affected" in line 16 most likely means

(A) unnatural
(B) superficial
(C) concerned
(D) moved
(E) stirred

172. The paragraph beginning "The dispatch with which they work" (20–21) suggests that the speaker is impressed by

(A) the dresses
(B) the shops' communication
(C) the milliners' and the mercers' haste
(D) the milliners' efficiency
(E) the ladies' demands

173. Regarding her "dressed" (22) hair, the speaker feels

(A) disillusioned
(B) relieved
(C) dissatisfied
(D) proud
(E) bemused

174. The speaker is "half afraid" (27) most likely because

(A) she fears the unpredictable
(B) her hair is odd but her clothes are beautiful
(C) she is perplexed and amazed by everything she has experienced
(D) she is insecure and apprehensive
(E) she does not know how to dance well

175. The final paragraph implies that the speaker is here

(A) to ingratiate herself
(B) to rise in social class
(C) to please her "dear Sir"
(D) to meet a husband
(E) to study

176. The closing lines (00–00) indicate that the passage is

(A) an interior monologue
(B) stream of consciousness
(C) nonfiction
(D) excerpted from a journal
(E) part of a missive

177. The qualification in the final line of the passage serves to

(A) characterize Evelina as obtuse
(B) underscore Evelina's self-awareness
(C) berate Evelina
(D) contrast Evelina with her addressee
(E) undermine Evelina's authority

178. The purpose of the passage as a whole is

(A) to criticize the values of a particular society
(B) to characterize the speaker as guileless and uncouth
(C) to detail the oddities of a culture from a stranger's perspective
(D) to reveal the speaker's perception of her experiences
(E) to characterize the speaker as tenacious and wise

Passage 2. Joseph Conrad, *Heart of Darkness*

The Nellie, a cruising yawl, swung to her anchor without a flutter of the sails, and was at rest. The flood had made, the wind was nearly calm, and being bound down the river, the only thing for it was to come to and wait for the turn of the tide.

The sea-reach of the Thames stretched before us like the beginning of an interminable waterway. In the offing the sea and the sky were welded together without a joint, and in the luminous space the tanned sails of the barges drifting up with the tide seemed to stand still in red clusters of canvas sharply peaked, with gleams of varnished sprits. A haze rested on the low shores that ran out to sea in vanishing flatness. The air was dark above Gravesend, and farther back still seemed condensed into a mournful gloom, brooding motionless over the biggest, and the greatest, town on earth.

The Director of Companies was our captain and our host. We four affectionately watched his back as he stood in the bows looking to seaward. On the whole river there was nothing that looked half so nautical. He resembled a pilot, which to

a seaman is trustworthiness personified. It was difficult to realize his work was not 5
out there in the luminous estuary, but behind him, within the brooding gloom.

Between us there was, as I have already said somewhere, the bond of the sea.
Besides holding our hearts together through long periods of separation, it had
the effect of making us tolerant of each other's yarns—and even convictions. The
Lawyer—the best of old fellows—had, because of his many years and many virtues, 10
the only cushion on deck, and was lying on the only rug. The Accountant had
brought out already a box of dominoes, and was toying architecturally with the
bones. Marlow sat cross-legged right aft, leaning against the mizzen-mast. He had
sunken cheeks, a yellow complexion, a straight back, an ascetic aspect, and, with
his arms dropped, the palms of hands outwards, resembled an idol. The director, 15
satisfied the anchor had good hold, made his way aft and sat down amongst us.
We exchanged a few words lazily. Afterwards there was silence on board the yacht.
For some reason or other we did not begin that game of dominoes. We felt meditative, and fit for nothing but placid staring. The day was ending in a serenity of
still and exquisite brilliance. The water shone pacifically; the sky, without a speck, 20
was a benign immensity of unstained light; the very mist on the Essex marsh was
like a gauzy and radiant fabric, hung from the wooded rises inland, and draping
the low shores in diaphanous folds. Only the gloom to the west, brooding over the
upper reaches, became more sombre every minute, as if angered by the approach
of the sun. 25

And at last, in its curved and imperceptible fall, the sun sank low, and from
glowing white changed to a dull red without rays and without heat, as if about
to go out suddenly, stricken to death by the touch of that gloom brooding over a
crowd of men.

179. The word "it" in line 3 refers to

    (A) a vessel
    (B) the water
    (C) the flood
    (D) the sun
    (E) the wind

180. In the first and second paragraphs, the setting is described using all of the
following devices *except*

    (A) sensory imagery
    (B) simile
    (C) metaphor
    (D) personification
    (E) oxymoron

181. The sentence in lines 9–11 ("The air was dark . . . earth") expresses what type of mood?

(A) wicked
(B) lugubrious
(C) irreverent
(D) diabolical
(E) placid

182. The Director of Companies is

(A) affectionate and authoritative
(B) demonstrative and trustworthy
(C) naval and venerable
(D) principled and brooding
(E) gregarious and esteemed

183. The word "yarns" in line 9 most likely means

(A) tales
(B) jokes
(C) clothing
(D) secrets
(E) convictions

184. How many people are with the narrator?

(A) three
(B) four
(C) five
(D) fewer than three
(E) more than five

185. The sentence in lines 20–23 ("The water shone . . .") is an example of

(A) a run-on sentence
(B) a periodic sentence
(C) a compound-complex sentence
(D) epanalepsis
(E) a cumulative sentence

186. The word "diaphanous" (23) describes

(A) the mist
(B) the landscape
(C) the water
(D) the light
(E) the shore

187. The narrator's tone in paragraphs 1–4 is

(A) dirgelike
(B) deferential
(C) inspired
(D) mordant
(E) saccharine

188. Lines 19–25, "The day was ending . . . approach of the sun," contrast

(A) the opening paragraph
(B) day and night
(C) the crew and their environs
(D) light and dark
(E) the west and the south

189. The passage's final sentence creates what type of mood?

(A) morbid
(B) ominous
(C) sanguine
(D) sorrowful
(E) regretful

190. The passage as a whole serves primarily to

    I. foreshadow later events
   II. establish a symbolic setting
  III. characterize the main character

(A) I only
(B) II only
(C) I and II only
(D) I and III only
(E) I, II, and III

191. The town described in the passage is

(A) Brussels
(B) London
(C) The Thames
(D) Gravesend
(E) England

Passage 3. Joseph Conrad, *Heart of Darkness*

"I left in a French steamer, and she called in every blamed port they have out there, for, as far as I could see, the sole purpose of landing soldiers and custom-house officers. I watched the coast. Watching a coast as it slips by the ship is like thinking about an enigma. There it is before you—smiling, frowning, inviting, grand, mean, insipid, or savage, and always mute with an air of whispering, 'Come and find out.' This one was almost featureless, as if still in the making, with an aspect of monotonous grimness. The edge of a colossal jungle, so dark-green as to be almost black, fringed with white surf, ran straight, like a ruled line, far, far away along a blue sea whose glitter was blurred by a creeping mist. The sun was fierce, the land seemed to glisten and drip with steam. Here and there greyish-whitish specks showed up clustered inside the white surf, with a flag flying above them perhaps. Settlements some centuries old, and still no bigger than pinheads on the untouched expanse of their background. We pounded along, stopped, landed soldiers; went on, landed custom-house clerks to levy toll in what looked like a God-forsaken wilderness, with a tin shed and a flag-pole lost in it; landed more soldiers—to take care of the custom-house clerks, presumably. Some, I heard, got drowned in the surf; but whether they did or not, nobody seemed particularly to care. They were just flung out there, and on we went. Every day the coast looked the same, as though we had not moved; but we passed various places—trading places—with names like Gran' Bassam, Little Popo; names that seemed to belong to some sordid farce acted in front of a sinister back-cloth. The idleness of a passenger, my isolation amongst all these men with whom I had no point of contact, the oily and languid sea, the uniform sombreness of the coast, seemed to keep me away from the truth of things, within the toil of a mournful and senseless delusion. The voice of the surf heard now and then was a positive pleasure, like the speech of a brother. It was something natural, that had its reason, that had a meaning. Now and then a boat from the shore gave one a momentary contact with reality. It was paddled by black fellows. You could see from afar the white of their eyeballs glistening. They shouted, sang; their bodies streamed with perspiration; they had faces like grotesque masks—these chaps; but they had bone, muscle, a wild vitality, an intense energy of movement, that was as natural and true as the surf along their coast. They wanted no excuse for being there. They were a great comfort to look at. For a time I would feel I belonged still to a world of straightforward facts; but the feeling would not last long. Something would turn up to scare it away. Once, I remember, we came upon a man-of-war anchored off the coast. There wasn't even a shed there, and she was shelling the bush. It appears the French had one of their wars going on thereabouts. Her ensign dropped limp like a rag; the muzzles of the long six-inch guns stuck out all over the low hull; the greasy, slimy swell swung her up lazily and let her down, swaying her thin masts. In the empty immensity of earth, sky, and water, there she was, incomprehensible, firing into a continent. Pop, would go one of the six-inch guns; a small flame would dart and vanish, a little white smoke would disappear, a tiny projectile would give a feeble screech—and nothing happened. Nothing could happen. There was a touch of insanity in the proceeding, a sense of lugubrious drollery in the sight; and it was not dissipated by somebody on board assuring me earnestly there was a camp of natives—he called them enemies!—hidden out of sight somewhere."

192. Lines 1–9 contain all of the following devices *except*

(A) simile
(B) personification
(C) sentence variety
(D) omniscient narration
(E) imagery

193. Lines 1–9, "'I left in a French steamer . . . a creeping mist,'" describe the sea as

   I. cryptic
   II. laconic
   III. obfuscated

(A) I only
(B) II only
(C) I and III only
(D) II and III only
(E) I, II, and III

194. Lines 13–18, "'We pounded along, . . . on we went,'" suggest that the speaker sees his job on the French steamer as

(A) perfunctory
(B) cumbersome
(C) onerous
(D) critical
(E) vexing

195. The tone of the sentence in lines 13–16 ("'We pounded along . . . presumably'") is enhanced by

(A) dependent clauses
(B) anaphora
(C) metaphor
(D) an em dash
(E) polysyndeton

196. All of the following keeps the speaker in a delusional state *except*

(A) idleness
(B) segregation
(C) the sea
(D) the uniformity of the coast
(E) a sordid farce

197. The speaker is relieved to see the '"black fellows"' (28) because

   (A) they provide him with comic relief
   (B) their grotesque faces are intriguing
   (C) they provide a sense of verity
   (D) they make the Europeans look better
   (E) they are an entertaining diversion

198. Lines 34–35 ('"but the feeling . . . away"') contain

   (A) regret
   (B) foreshadowing
   (C) antithesis
   (D) vacillation
   (E) paradox

199. The sentence in lines 37–39 ('"Her ensign . . . masts"') can be described as all of the following *except*

   (A) imagistic
   (B) compound-complex
   (C) figurative
   (D) periodic
   (E) alliterative

200. The word '"she"' in line 40 refers to

   (A) the hull
   (B) the sea
   (C) France
   (D) the man-of-war
   (E) the masts

201. Together, the two sentences in lines 41–43 ('"Pop . . . could happen"') demonstrate

   I. onomatopoeia and sentence variety
   II. asyndeton and personification
   III. parallel structure and metonymy

   (A) I only
   (B) II only
   (C) I and II only
   (D) II and III only
   (E) I, II, and III

202. In line 44, '"drollery"' most likely means

(A) boredom
(B) contention
(C) sadness
(D) dark absurdity
(E) insanity

203. The speaker's tone in the phrase '"he called them enemies!"' (46) communicates

(A) surprise and relief
(B) shock and incredulity
(C) vitriol and distress
(D) remorse and vehemence
(E) disappointment and fondness

204. The passage as a whole

(A) expresses yearning for an unforgettable journey
(B) questions assumptions about racial inequality
(C) questions the value of imperial outposts
(D) describes past events objectively
(E) describes experiences myopically

Passage 4. Mary Shelley, *Frankenstein*

St. Petersburgh, Dec. 11th, 17—
To Mrs. Saville, England

You will rejoice to hear that no disaster has accompanied the commencement of an enterprise which you have regarded with such evil forebodings. I arrived here yesterday, and my first task is to assure my dear sister of my welfare and increasing confidence in the success of my undertaking. 5

I am already far north of London, and as I walk in the streets of Petersburgh, I feel a cold northern breeze play upon my cheeks, which braces my nerves and fills me with delight. Do you understand this feeling? This breeze, which has travelled from the regions towards which I am advancing, gives me a foretaste of those icy 10 climes. Inspirited by this wind of promise, my daydreams become more fervent and vivid. I try in vain to be persuaded that the pole is the seat of frost and desolation; it ever presents itself to my imagination as the region of beauty and delight. There, Margaret, the sun is forever visible, its broad disk just skirting the horizon and diffusing a perpetual splendour. There—for with your leave, my sister, I will 15 put some trust in preceding navigators—there snow and frost are banished; and, sailing over a calm sea, we may be wafted to a land surpassing in wonders and in beauty every region hitherto discovered on the habitable globe. Its productions and features may be without example, as the phenomena of the heavenly bodies

undoubtedly are in those undiscovered solitudes. What may not be expected in a 20
country of eternal light? I may there discover the wondrous power which attracts
the needle and may regulate a thousand celestial observations that require only this
voyage to render their seeming eccentricities consistent forever. I shall satiate my
ardent curiosity with the sight of a part of the world never before visited, and may
tread a land never before imprinted by the foot of man. These are my enticements, 25
and they are sufficient to conquer all fear of danger or death and to induce me to
commence this laborious voyage with the joy a child feels when he embarks in a
little boat, with his holiday mates, on an expedition of discovery up his native river.
But supposing all these conjectures to be false, you cannot contest the inestimable
benefit which I shall confer on all mankind, to the last generation, by discovering a 30
passage near the pole to those countries, to reach which at present so many months
are requisite; or by ascertaining the secret of the magnet, which, if at all possible,
can only be effected by an undertaking such as mine.

205. The tone of the first sentence is best described as

    (A) acerbic

    (B) sincere

    (C) lethargic

    (D) sanctimonious

    (E) sagacious

206. The verb tense of lines 5–9 ("and my first task . . . this feeling?")

    (A) changes from past to present

    (B) changes from present continuous to present

    (C) changes from present to past

    (D) remains in present tense

    (E) changes from future to present

207. The sentence in lines 7–9 ("I am . . . delight") is

    (A) complex

    (B) compound

    (C) periodic

    (D) antithetical

    (E) balanced

208. The speaker indicates that he is traveling

    (A) from England to St. Petersburgh

    (B) from London to Russia

    (C) to a place that may or may not exist

    (D) to heaven

    (E) north

209. The speaker expects his destination to be

   (A) romantic
   (B) anticlimactic
   (C) unparalleled
   (D) dark
   (E) frosty

210. The simile in lines 19–20 ("as the phenomena . . . undiscovered solitudes")
compares

   (A) the speaker's destination's features to stars
   (B) undiscovered land to the solar system
   (C) the globe to heaven
   (D) snow to heaven
   (E) preceding navigators to phenomena

211. The repetition of the word "there" in lines 14–16 is an example of

   (A) redundancy
   (B) wordiness
   (C) epistrophe
   (D) anaphora
   (E) leitmotif

212. The speaker's "enticements" (25) include all of the following *except*

   (A) the promise of discovery
   (B) the hope of regulating
   (C) the chance of uncovering secrets
   (D) unlimited expectations
   (E) the hope of becoming notorious

213. The speaker's comparison in lines 27–28 ("with the joy . . . native river.")
emphasizes

   (A) the severity of the journey
   (B) the risks the speaker is willing to incur
   (C) the speaker's homesickness
   (D) the speaker's unfeigned enthusiasm
   (E) the speaker's apprehension

214. The first paragraph of the passage and lines 29–33 ("But supposing . . . such as mine.") emphasize the speaker's

(A) goals
(B) friendship with his sister
(C) need to convince
(D) doubts
(E) need for friendship

215. The word "inestimable" (29) most likely means

(A) praiseworthy
(B) immeasurable
(C) fathomable
(D) fallible
(E) factual

216. The style of the passage as a whole appears to be similar to that of

(A) a bildungsroman
(B) a myth
(C) an epistolary novel
(D) a legend
(E) an allegory

217. The passage includes which of the following devices?

I. sensory imagery
II. rhetorical questions
III. invocation

(A) I only
(B) I and II only
(C) II and III only
(D) I, II, and III
(E) III only

Passage 5. Mary Shelley, *Frankenstein*

There was a considerable difference between the ages of my parents, but this circumstance seemed to unite them only closer in bonds of devoted affection. There was a sense of justice in my father's upright mind which rendered it necessary that he should approve highly to love strongly. Perhaps during former years he had suffered from the late-discovered unworthiness of one beloved and so was disposed   5
to set a greater value on tried worth. There was a show of gratitude and worship in his attachment to my mother, differing wholly from the doting fondness of age, for it was inspired by reverence for her virtues and a desire to be the means of, in

some degree, recompensing her for the sorrows she had endured, but which gave inexpressible grace to his behaviour to her. Everything was made to yield to her 10 wishes and her convenience. He strove to shelter her, as a fair exotic is sheltered by the gardener, from every rougher wind and to surround her with all that could tend to excite pleasurable emotion in her soft and benevolent mind. Her health, and even the tranquillity of her hitherto constant spirit, had been shaken by what she had gone through. During the two years that had elapsed previous to their marriage 15 my father had gradually relinquished all his public functions; and immediately after their union they sought the pleasant climate of Italy, and the change of scene and interest attendant on a tour through that land of wonders, as a restorative for her weakened frame.

From Italy they visited Germany and France. I, their eldest child, was born at 20 Naples, and as an infant accompanied them in their rambles. I remained for several years their only child. Much as they were attached to each other, they seemed to draw inexhaustible stores of affection from a very mine of love to bestow them upon me. My mother's tender caresses and my father's smile of benevolent pleasure while regarding me are my first recollections. I was their plaything and their idol, 25 and something better—their child, the innocent and helpless creature bestowed on them by heaven, whom to bring up to good, and whose future lot it was in their hands to direct to happiness or misery, according as they fulfilled their duties towards me. With this deep consciousness of what they owed towards the being to which they had given life, added to the active spirit of tenderness that animated 30 both, it may be imagined that while during every hour of my infant life I received a lesson of patience, of charity, and of self-control, I was so guided by a silken cord that all seemed but one train of enjoyment to me. For a long time I was their only care. My mother had much desired to have a daughter, but I continued their single offspring. When I was about five years old, while making an excursion beyond the 35 frontiers of Italy, they passed a week on the shores of the Lake of Como. Their benevolent disposition often made them enter the cottages of the poor. This, to my mother, was more than a duty; it was a necessity, a passion—remembering what she had suffered, and how she had been relieved—for her to act in her turn the guardian angel to the afflicted. During one of their walks a poor cot in the foldings 40 of a vale attracted their notice as being singularly disconsolate, while the number of half-clothed children gathered about it spoke of penury in its worst shape. One day, when my father had gone by himself to Milan, my mother, accompanied by me, visited this abode. She found a peasant and his wife, hard working, bent down by care and labour, distributing a scanty meal to five hungry babes. Among these 45 there was one which attracted my mother far above all the rest. She appeared of a different stock. The four others were dark-eyed, hardy little vagrants; this child was thin and very fair. Her hair was the brightest living gold, and despite the poverty of her clothing, seemed to set a crown of distinction on her head. Her brow was clear and ample, her blue eyes cloudless, and her lips and the moulding of her face so 50 expressive of sensibility and sweetness that none could behold her without looking on her as of a distinct species, a being heaven-sent, and bearing a celestial stamp in all her features.

218. The opening phrases of the first, second, and fourth sentences create an example of

(A) anaphora
(B) doubts
(C) conjectures
(D) descriptions of the setting
(E) facts

219. In line 8, "it" refers to

(A) "doting"
(B) "his attachment"
(C) "a show of gratitude and worship"
(D) "fondness of age"
(E) "my mother"

220. The narrator's mother is presented as all of the following *except*

(A) virtuous
(B) munificent
(C) importunate
(D) convalescent
(E) enervated

221. The simile in line 11 characterizes

(A) the mother as distinct
(B) the mother as distinguished
(C) the father as nurturing
(D) the mother as a child
(E) the father as officious

222. What is the relationship between the first and second paragraphs?

(A) The first asks questions that the second answers.
(B) The first poses theories that the second explores.
(C) The second belies assumptions made in the first.
(D) The first provides background for comprehension of the second.
(E) The first sparks curiosity that the second satiates.

223. The metaphor in lines 21–23 emphasizes

(A) the parents' infinite capacity to love
(B) the parents' industriousness
(C) the parents' economic class
(D) the speaker's importance in the family
(E) the hierarchy within the family

224. The word "idol" in line 25 implies that

(A) the parents saw religious power in their child
(B) the child is like a prophet
(C) the parents admire their child
(D) the speaker is arrogant
(E) the parents worship their child

225. The sentence in lines 29–33 is

(A) simple
(B) periodic
(C) a run-on
(D) compound
(E) cumulative

226. The phrase "silken cord" (32) is an example of

(A) metonymy
(B) synecdoche
(C) metaphor
(D) synesthesia
(E) hyperbole

227. The word "penury" in line 42 most likely means

(A) destitution
(B) itinerancy
(C) sadness
(D) vagrancy
(E) selfishness

228. The girl described in lines 46–53 is characterized as

I. striking
II. inhuman and tow-headed
III. sartorially spartan

(A) I only
(B) I and II only
(C) II only
(D) II and III only
(E) I and III only

229. The description of the girl in lines 46–53 contains all of the following devices *except*

(A) allusion
(B) simile
(C) alliteration
(D) hyperbole
(E) polysyndeton

230. The tone of the passage can be described as

(A) grave
(B) factual
(C) mawkish
(D) resentful
(E) sardonic

231. The main purpose of the passage as a whole is

(A) to characterize the speaker's mother
(B) to characterize the speaker
(C) to characterize the father
(D) to describe the setting
(E) to characterize the speaker's family

Passage 6. Jonathan Swift, *Gulliver's Travels*

One morning, about a fortnight after I had obtained my liberty, Reldresal, principal secretary (as they style him) for private affairs, came to my house, attended only by one servant. He ordered his coach to wait at a distance, and desired I would give him an hour's audience; which I readily consented to, on account of his quality and personal merits, as well as of the many good offices he had done 5
me during my solicitations at court. I offered to lie down, that he might the more conveniently reach my ear; but he chose rather to let me hold him in my hand during our conversation.

He began with compliments on my liberty; said he might pretend to some merit in it. But however, added, that if it had not been for the present situation 10
of things at court, perhaps I might not have obtained it so soon. For, said he, as flourishing a condition as we may appear to be in to foreigners, we labor under two mighty evils: a violent faction at home, and the danger of an invasion, by a most potent enemy, from abroad. As to the first, you are to understand, that, for above seventy moons past, there have been two struggling parties in this empire, under 15
the names of *Tramecksan* and *Slamecksan*, from the high and low heels of their shoes, by which they distinguish themselves. It is alleged, indeed, that the high heels are most agreeable to our ancient constitution; but, however this may be, his majesty hath determined to make use only of low heels in the administration of

the government, and all offices in the gift of the crown, as you cannot but observe: 20
and particularly, that his majesty's imperial heels are lower, at least by a *drurr*, than
any of his court (*drurr* is a measure about the fourteenth part of an inch). The ani-
mosities between these two parties run so high, that they will neither eat nor drink
nor talk with each other. We compute the *Tramecksan*, or high heels, to exceed
us in number; but the power is wholly on our side. We apprehend his imperial 25
highness, the heir to the crown, to have some tendency towards the high heels; at
least, we can plainly discover that one of his heels is higher than the other, which
gives him a hobble in his gait. Now, in the midst of these intestine disquiets, we are
threatened with an invasion from the island of Blefuscu, which is the other great
empire of the universe, almost as large and powerful as this of his majesty. For, as 30
to what we have heard you affirm, that there are other kingdoms and states in the
world, inhabited by human creatures as large as yourself, our philosophers are in
much doubt, and would rather conjecture that you dropped from the moon or one
of the stars, because it is certain, that an hundred mortals of your bulk would, in
a short time, destroy all the fruits and cattle of his majesty's dominions. Besides, 35
our histories of six thousand moons make no mention of any other regions than
the two great empires of Lilliput and Blefuscu. Which two mighty powers have,
as I was going to tell you, been engaged in a most obstinate war for six-and-thirty
moons past. It began upon the following occasion: It is allowed on all hands, that
the primitive way of breaking eggs, before we eat them, was upon the larger end; 40
but his present majesty's grandfather, while he was a boy, going to eat an egg, and
breaking it according to the ancient practice, happened to cut one of his fingers.
Whereupon the emperor, his father, published an edict, commanding all his subjects, upon great penalties, to break the smaller end of their eggs. The people so
highly resented this law, that our histories tell us, there have been six rebellions 45
raised on that account, wherein one emperor lost his life, and another his crown.
These civil commotions were constantly fomented by the monarchs of Blefuscu;
and when they were quelled, the exiles always fled for refuge to that empire. It is
computed, that eleven thousand persons have, at several times, suffered death,
rather than submit to break their eggs at the smaller end. Many hundred large vol- 50
umes have been published upon this controversy, but the books of the Big-endians
have been long forbidden, and the whole party rendered incapable, by law, of holding employments. During the course of these troubles, the Emperors of Blefuscu
did frequently expostulate, by their ambassadors, accusing us of making a schism in
religion, by offending against a fundamental doctrine of our great prophet Lustrog, 55
in the fifty-fourth chapter of the *Blundecral* (which is their *Alcoran*). This, however,
is thought to be a mere strain upon the text; for the words are these: *That all true
believers break their eggs at the convenient end.* And which is the convenient end,
seems, in my humble opinion, to be left to every man's conscience, or, at least, in
the power of the chief magistrate to determine. Now, the Big-endian exiles have 60
found so much credit in the emperor of Blefuscu's court, and so much private
assistance and encouragement from their party here at home, that a bloody war
hath been carried on between the two empires for six-and-thirty moons, with various success; during which time we have lost forty capital ships, and a much greater

number of smaller vessels, together with thirty thousand of our best seamen and 65
soldiers; and the damage received by the enemy is reckoned to be somewhat greater
than ours. However, they have now equipped a numerous fleet, and are just preparing to make a descent upon us; and his imperial majesty, placing great confidence
in your valor and strength, hath commanded me to lay this account of his affairs
before you.   70

232. The opening sentence's syntactical style is distinct in its use of multiple

(A) aphorisms
(B) litotes
(C) proper nouns
(D) independent clauses
(E) appositives

233. The phrase "(as they style him)" (2) suggests

(A) Reldresal may not actually be suited for his title
(B) the speaker is envious of Reldresal's title
(C) Reldresal's title is a misnomer
(D) Reldresal's title is arbitrary
(E) Reldresal is addressed with the utmost reverence

234. The first paragraph implies that the speaker is all of the following *except*

(A) grateful
(B) recently emancipated
(C) obsequious
(D) gracious
(E) large

235. The phrase "pretend to some merit in it" (9–10) indicates that

(A) Reldresal's compliments are not genuine
(B) Reldresal is demonstrating guile
(C) the speaker's freedom was hard won
(D) the speaker's freedom was unwarranted
(E) Reldresal doubts whether the speaker earned his freedom

236. In line 11–12, the speaker of the passage changes

(A) from the speaker of the first paragraph to the principal secretary
(B) from gracious to severe
(C) from first person to second person
(D) from the speaker of the first paragraph to his majesty
(E) without warning

237. In lines 16–22, the speaker discusses the empire's problem of

(A) his majesty's shoes
(B) prejudice in their community
(C) the ancient constitution
(D) his majesty's partiality
(E) his majesty's impartiality

238. The speaker of lines 22–25 is a member of

I. the high heels
II. *Tramecksan*
III. *Slamecksan*

(A) I only
(B) II only
(C) III only
(D) I and III only
(E) I, II, and III

239. The heir's "hobble" (28) is worrying because

(A) he is in need of convalescence
(B) it suggests his defection
(C) it is unsightly
(D) it suggests he is partial to the *Slamecksan* party
(E) it suggests he and his father are estranged

240. In line 28, the phrase "intestine disquiets" most likely means

(A) physical illness
(B) municipal politics
(C) political intrigue
(D) domestic strife
(E) the speaker's inner turmoil

241. The speaker, in lines 30–35, cites all of the following as reasons that his addressee's claims are likely fallible *except*

(A) the empire's intact agriculture
(B) the empire's philosophers' conjectures
(C) the empire's annals
(D) the empire's ken
(E) Lilliput and Blefuscu's superiority in the world

242. In context, the word "fomented" in line 47 most likely means

(A) goaded
(B) quelled
(C) dispelled
(D) formed
(E) derided

243. The "*Alcoran*" (56) is

(A) the Blundecral
(B) the holy text of Big-endians
(C) the holy text of the *Slamecksan*
(D) the holy text of the *Tramecksan*
(E) the holy text of Lilliput

244. The argument between Blefuscu and Lilliput described in lines 53–60 is most similar to

(A) physical sparring
(B) moral disputes
(C) altercations about facts
(D) arguments about semantics
(E) ethical debates

245. The passage's style most closely resembles the style of

(A) a historical novel
(B) a Gothic novel
(C) a fable
(D) an epic
(E) a lampoon

246. In the passage, the words "*Slamecksan*," "*Tramecksan*," "*drurr*," "*Alcoran*," and "*Blundecral*" are all written in italics to indicate

(A) that they are the names of renowned people and places
(B) that they are important
(C) that they are words from a different language
(D) a lack of respect
(E) emphasis

247. The passage suggests that the imperial majesty expects the speaker of the first paragraph to assist him because
    I. he has recently been acquitted
   II. he is large
  III. he is doughty
(A) I only
(B) II only
(C) I and II only
(D) II and III only
(E) I, II, and III

248. The speaker of lines 11–70, as opposed to the passage as a whole, carries a tone of
(A) gravity
(B) irony
(C) absurdity
(D) amicability
(E) neutrality

Passage 7. Oscar Wilde, *The Picture of Dorian Gray*

The studio was filled with the rich odour of roses, and when the light summer wind stirred amidst the trees of the garden, there came through the open door the heavy scent of the lilac, or the more delicate perfume of the pink-flowering thorn.

From the corner of the divan of Persian saddle-bags on which he was lying, smoking, as was his custom, innumerable cigarettes, Lord Henry Wotton could 5 just catch the gleam of the honey-sweet and honey-coloured blossoms of a laburnum, whose tremulous branches seemed hardly able to bear the burden of a beauty so flamelike as theirs; and now and then the fantastic shadows of birds in flight flitted across the long tussore-silk curtains that were stretched in front of the huge window, producing a kind of momentary Japanese effect, and making him think 10 of those pallid, jade-faced painters of Tokyo who, through the medium of an art that is necessarily immobile, seek to convey the sense of swiftness and motion. The sullen murmur of the bees shouldering their way through the long unmown grass, or circling with monotonous insistence round the dusty gilt horns of the straggling woodbine, seemed to make the stillness more oppressive. The dim roar of London 15 was like the bourdon note of a distant organ. In the centre of the room, clamped to an upright easel, stood the full-length portrait of a young man of extraordinary personal beauty, and in front of it, some little distance away, was sitting the artist himself, Basil Hallward, whose sudden disappearance some years ago caused, at the time, such public excitement and gave rise to so many strange conjectures. 20

As the painter looked at the gracious and comely form he had so skillfully mirrored in his art, a smile of pleasure passed across his face, and seemed about to linger there. But he suddenly started up, and closing his eyes, placed his fingers upon the lids, as though he sought to imprison within his brain some curious dream from which he feared he might awake. "It is your best work, Basil, the best thing you have ever done," said Lord Henry languidly. "You must certainly send it next year to the Grosvenor. The Academy is too large and too vulgar. Whenever I have gone there, there have been either so many people that I have not been able to see the pictures, which was dreadful, or so many pictures that I have not been able to see the people, which was worse. The Grosvenor is really the only place." "I don't think I shall send it anywhere," he answered, tossing his head back in that odd way that used to make his friends laugh at him at Oxford. "No, I won't send it anywhere." Lord Henry elevated his eyebrows and looked at him in amazement through the thin blue wreaths of smoke that curled up in such fanciful whorls from his heavy, opium-tainted cigarette. "Not send it anywhere? My dear fellow, why? Have you any reason? What odd chaps you painters are! You do anything in the world to gain a reputation. As soon as you have one, you seem to want to throw it away. It is silly of you, for there is only one thing in the world worse than being talked about, and that is not being talked about. A portrait like this would set you far above all the young men in England, and make the old men quite jealous, if old men are ever capable of any emotion."

249. Lines 1–16 contain
    I. at least one simile
    II. passive voice
    III. compound sentences

  (A) I only
  (B) II only
  (C) III only
  (D) I and III only
  (E) I, II, and III

250. The "momentary Japanese effect" in line 10 sets up

  (A) a parallel between London and Tokyo
  (B) a contrast between movement and stillness
  (C) Lord Henry Wotton's preference for European art over Asian art
  (D) an emphasis on the pleasure offered by the setting
  (E) an attack on Japanese painters

251. In line 8, "theirs" refers to

  (A) innumerable cigarettes
  (B) a laburnum's blossoms
  (C) a laburnum's branches
  (D) Persian saddle-bags
  (E) birds' shadows

252. From the description of the setting in the first and second paragraphs, we can infer all of the following *except* that

  (A) Lord Henry Wotton would rather be somewhere else
  (B) the characters are familiar with the art of foreign countries
  (C) the characters are bourgeois
  (D) the abundance in nature is symbolic of the abundance of riches in the room
  (E) the mood is one of lethargy

253. The simile in line 16 serves to emphasize

  (A) the pollution and noise of London
  (B) the distance of the beauty the city has to offer
  (C) Lord Henry Wotton's preference for London over his current setting
  (D) the calmness of the current setting
  (E) the proximity of the current setting to the city of London

254. Lord Henry's speech is developed mostly through
  I. epigrams
  II. cliché
  III. counsel

  (A) I only
  (B) III only
  (C) I and III only
  (D) I and II only
  (E) II and III only

255. From the passage we can infer all of the following about Basil Hallward *except* that

  (A) he is a notable painter
  (B) he is well educated
  (C) he is insecure about his work
  (D) he is used to excoriation
  (E) he likes his painting

256. The dialogue in the passage serves primarily to

  (A) contrast Lord Henry Wotton with his environment
  (B) demonstrate the characters' level of education
  (C) develop Lord Henry Wotton's viewpoint
  (D) draw a parallel between riches and intellect
  (E) criticize old men

257. The characters of Lord Henry Wotton and Basil Hallward are both developed through all of the following *except*

(A) simile
(B) speech
(C) their physical descriptions
(D) references to their past
(E) their impressions of the room

258. The passage as a whole serves primarily to

(A) present Basil Hallward as a talented artist
(B) show the friendship between Lord Henry Wotton and Basil Hallward
(C) critique London's high society
(D) introduce main characters and their relationships with art
(E) demonstrate highly ornate descriptions of a natural setting

CHAPTER 5

American Fiction

Passage 1. Kate Chopin, "The Kiss"

It was still quite light out of doors, but inside with the curtains drawn and the smouldering fire sending out a dim, uncertain glow, the room was full of deep shadows.

Brantain sat in one of these shadows; it had overtaken him and he did not mind. The obscurity lent him courage to keep his eyes fastened as ardently as he liked upon the girl who sat in the firelight. 5

She was very handsome, with a certain fine, rich coloring that belongs to the healthy brune type. She was quite composed, as she idly stroked the satiny coat of the cat that lay curled in her lap, and she occasionally sent a slow glance into the shadow where her companion sat. They were talking low, of indifferent things 10 which plainly were not the things that occupied their thoughts. She knew that he loved her—a frank, blustering fellow without guile enough to conceal his feelings, and no desire to do so. For two weeks past he had sought her society eagerly and persistently. She was confidently waiting for him to declare himself and she meant to accept him. The rather insignificant and unattractive Brantain was enormously 15 rich; and she liked and required the entourage which wealth could give her.

During one of the pauses between their talk of the last tea and the next reception the door opened and a young man entered whom Brantain knew quite well. The girl turned her face toward him. A stride or two brought him to her side, and bending over her chair—before she could suspect his intention, for she did not 20 realize that he had not seen her visitor—he pressed an ardent, lingering kiss upon her lips.

Brantain slowly arose; so did the girl arise, but quickly, and the newcomer stood between them, a little amusement and some defiance struggling with the confusion in his face. 25

"I believe," stammered Brantain, "I see that I have stayed too long. I—I had no idea—that is, I must wish you good-by." He was clutching his hat with both hands, and probably did not perceive that she was extending her hand to him, her presence of mind had not completely deserted her; but she could not have trusted herself to speak. 30

"Hang me if I saw him sitting there, Nattie! I know it's deuced awkward for you. But I hope you'll forgive me this once—this very first break. Why, what's the matter?"

"Don't touch me; don't come near me," she returned angrily. "What do you mean by entering the house without ringing?"   35

"I came in with your brother, as I often do," he answered coldly, in self-justification. "We came in the side way. He went upstairs and I came in here hoping to find you. The explanation is simple enough and ought to satisfy you that the misadventure was unavoidable. But do say that you forgive me, Nathalie," he entreated, softening.   40

"Forgive you! You don't know what you are talking about. Let me pass. It depends upon—a good deal whether I ever forgive you."

At that next reception which she and Brantain had been talking about she approached the young man with a delicious frankness of manner when she saw him there.   45

"Will you let me speak to you a moment or two, Mr. Brantain?" she asked with an engaging but perturbed smile. He seemed extremely unhappy; but when she took his arm and walked away with him, seeking a retired corner, a ray of hope mingled with the almost comical misery of his expression. She was apparently very outspoken.   50

"Perhaps I should not have sought this interview, Mr. Brantain; but—but, oh, I have been very uncomfortable, almost miserable since that little encounter the other afternoon. When I thought how you might have misinterpreted it, and believed things"—hope was plainly gaining the ascendancy over misery in Brantain's round, guileless face—"Of course, I know it is nothing to you, but for my   55
own sake I do want you to understand that Mr. Harvy is an intimate friend of long standing. Why, we have always been like cousins—like brother and sister, I may say. He is my brother's most intimate associate and often fancies that he is entitled to the same privileges as the family. Oh, I know it is absurd, uncalled for, to tell you this; undignified even," she was almost weeping, "but it makes so much difference   60
to me what you think of—of me." Her voice had grown very low and agitated. The misery had all disappeared from Brantain's face.

"Then you do really care what I think, Miss Nathalie? May I call you Miss Nathalie?" They turned into a long, dim corridor that was lined on either side with tall, graceful plants. They walked slowly to the very end of it. When they turned to   65
retrace their steps Brantain's face was radiant and hers was triumphant.

Harvy was among the guests at the wedding; and he sought her out in a rare moment when she stood alone.

"Your husband," he said, smiling, "has sent me over to kiss you."

A quick blush suffused her face and round polished throat. "I suppose it's   70
natural for a man to feel and act generously on an occasion of this kind. He tells me he doesn't want his marriage to interrupt wholly that pleasant intimacy which has existed between you and me. I don't know what you've been telling him," with an insolent smile, "but he has sent me here to kiss you."

She felt like a chess player who, by the clever handling of his pieces, sees the   75
game taking the course intended. Her eyes were bright and tender with a smile as they glanced up into his; and her lips looked hungry for the kiss which they invited.

"But, you know," he went on quietly, "I didn't tell him so, it would have seemed ungrateful, but I can tell you. I've stopped kissing women; it's dangerous." Well, she had Brantain and his million left. A person can't have everything in this 80 world; and it was a little unreasonable of her to expect it.

259. The imagery in the opening paragraph ("uncertain glow," "deep shadows") creates what type of atmosphere?
    (A) lustful
    (B) romantic
    (C) morose
    (D) solemn
    (E) surreptitious

260. Brantain, as opposed to Mr. Harvy, is
    (A) a philanderer
    (B) penurious
    (C) libidinous
    (D) meek
    (E) astute

261. Lines 15–16 uncover Nathalie's
    (A) indifference
    (B) ardor
    (C) frankness
    (D) opportunism
    (E) venality

262. The phrase "'deuced awkward'" (31) is an example of
    (A) an oxymoron
    (B) a paradox
    (C) a colloquialism
    (D) a malapropism
    (E) slander

263. In context, Nathalie's "delicious frankness" of manner (44) implies
    (A) she is extremely frank
    (B) she is amorous for Brantain
    (C) she is ambivalent about Braintain
    (D) she is eager to mollify Brantain
    (E) she is more wily than frank

264. In context, the word "triumphant" (66) contributes most to

(A) imagery
(B) the characterization of Nathalie
(C) tone
(D) the characterization of Brantain
(E) mood

265. The phrase "Her eyes were bright and tender with a smile . . . " (76) suggests that Nathalie

(A) is still thinking about Brantain
(B) is torn between her love for Braintain and for Mr. Harvy
(C) is also interested primarily in Mr. Harvy's riches
(D) is guileful in her interactions with all men
(E) may have a genuinely romantic interest in Mr. Harvy

266. The simile in lines 75–76 coincides most with which other phrase?

(A) "Brantain's face was radiant and hers was triumphant" (66)
(B) "She was very handsome" (7)
(C) "'Don't touch me; don't come near me'" (34)
(D) "'but it makes so much difference to me what you think of—of me'" (60–61)
(E) "Her voice had grown very low and agitated" (61)

267. In the phrase "A person can't have everything in this world" (80–81), the word "everything" refers to

(A) unrequited affection
(B) having every man's attention
(C) kissing Mr. Harvy
(D) having her emotional and financial needs met
(E) "Brantain and his million"

268. Lines 80–81 are written in which narrative style?

(A) third person limited
(B) first person
(C) stream of consciousness
(D) third person rotating
(E) free indirect style

Passage 2. Nathaniel Hawthorne, *The Scarlet Letter*

A throng of bearded men, in sad-coloured garments and grey steeple-crowned hats, inter-mixed with women, some wearing hoods, and others bareheaded, was assembled in front of a wooden edifice, the door of which was heavily timbered with oak, and studded with iron spikes.

The founders of a new colony, whatever Utopia of human virtue and happiness they might originally project, have invariably recognised it among their earliest practical necessities to allot a portion of the virgin soil as a cemetery, and another portion as the site of a prison. In accordance with this rule it may safely be assumed that the forefathers of Boston had built the first prison-house somewhere in the Vicinity of Cornhill, almost as seasonably as they marked out the first burial-ground, on Isaac Johnson's lot, and round about his grave, which subsequently became the nucleus of all the congregated sepulchres in the old churchyard of King's Chapel. Certain it is that, some fifteen or twenty years after the settlement of the town, the wooden jail was already marked with weather-stains and other indications of age, which gave a yet darker aspect to its beetle-browed and gloomy front. The rust on the ponderous iron-work of its oaken door looked more antique than anything else in the New World. Like all that pertains to crime, it seemed never to have known a youthful era. Before this ugly edifice, and between it and the wheel-track of the street, was a grass-plot, much overgrown with burdock, pig-weed, apple-pern, and such unsightly vegetation, which evidently found something congenial in the soil that had so early borne the black flower of civilised society, a prison. But on one side of the portal, and rooted almost at the threshold, was a wild rose-bush, covered, in this month of June, with its delicate gems, which might be imagined to offer their fragrance and fragile beauty to the prisoner as he went in, and to the condemned criminal as he came forth to his doom, in token that the deep heart of Nature could pity and be kind to him.

This rose-bush, by a strange chance, has been kept alive in history; but whether it had merely survived out of the stern old wilderness, so long after the fall of the gigantic pines and oaks that originally overshadowed it, or whether, as there is fair authority for believing, it had sprung up under the footsteps of the sainted Ann Hutchinson[1] as she entered the prison-door, we shall not take upon us to determine. Finding it so directly on the threshold of our narrative, which is now about to issue from that inauspicious portal, we could hardly do otherwise than pluck one of its flowers, and present it to the reader. It may serve, let us hope, to symbolise some sweet moral blossom that may be found along the track, or relieve the darkening close of a tale of human frailty and sorrow.

269. The mood of the opening paragraph is best described as

    (A) somber and oppressive

    (B) claustrophobic and suffocating

    (C) peaceful and placid

    (D) misogynistic and domineering

    (E) religious and meditative

---

1. Ann Hutchinson (1591–1643) was a pioneer settler in Massachusetts, Rhode Island, and New Netherlands and the unauthorized minister of a dissident church discussion group. After a trial before a jury of officials and clergy, she was banished from the Massachusetts Bay Colony.

270. In line 6, "it" refers to

    (A) soil
    (B) cemetery
    (C) their first necessity
    (D) the new colony
    (E) Utopia

271. In context, "sepulchres" (12) means

    (A) the dead
    (B) prisoners
    (C) headstones
    (D) mourners
    (E) places of interment

272. The setting is described through all of the following devices *except*

    (A) metaphor
    (B) allusion
    (C) sentence variety
    (D) personification
    (E) anaphora

273. In line 33, "that inauspicious portal" refers to

    (A) the prison door
    (B) the sepulchres
    (C) the rose bush
    (D) the wilderness
    (E) the throng

274. The passage as a whole

    (A) presents a historical account of the settlement of the new colonies
    (B) introduces a tragic account
    (C) includes opprobrium of the penal system
    (D) serves as a panegyric of the human spirit
    (E) deplores human weakness

275. The narrator's attitude toward the society being described is

    (A) objective
    (B) critical
    (C) bewildered
    (D) reverential
    (E) frustrated

276. The purpose of the passage is to

    (A) lambaste the New World
    (B) create an eerie atmosphere
    (C) introduce the main characters of a story
    (D) establish motivation for a crime
    (E) set up the mood, setting, and symbols of a story

277. The narrator most likely mentions Ann Hutchinson to

    (A) deplore the colonies' disenfranchisement of its citizens
    (B) sympathize with Puritan leaders
    (C) suggest a theory
    (D) denigrate the symbol
    (E) introduce the main character of the story

278. The final paragraph does all of the following *except*

    (A) expounds a metaphor
    (B) speculates
    (C) anticipates
    (D) offers sanguinity
    (E) establishes a cynical tone

Passage 3. Nathaniel Hawthorne, *The Scarlet Letter*

It may seem marvellous that, with the world before her—kept by no restrictive clause of her condemnation within the limits of the Puritan settlement, so remote and so obscure—free to return to her birth-place, or to any other European land, and there hide her character and identity under a new exterior, as completely as if emerging into another state of being—and having also the passes of the dark, inscrutable forest open to her, where the wildness of her nature might assimilate itself with a people whose customs and life were alien from the law that had condemned her—it may seem marvellous that this woman should still call that place her home, where, and where only, she must needs be the type of shame. But there is a fatality, a feeling so irresistible and inevitable that it has the force of doom, which almost invariably compels human beings to linger around and haunt, ghost-like, the spot where some great and marked event has given the colour to their lifetime; and, still the more irresistibly, the darker the tinge that saddens it. Her sin, her ignominy, were the roots which she had struck into the soil. It was as if a new birth, with stronger assimilations than the first, had converted the forest-land, still so uncongenial to every other pilgrim and wanderer, into Hester Prynne's wild and dreary, but life-long home. All other scenes of earth—even that village of rural England, where happy infancy and stainless maidenhood seemed yet to be in her mother's keeping, like garments put off long ago—were foreign to her, in

comparison. The chain that bound her here was of iron links, and galling to her 20
inmost soul, but could never be broken.

It might be, too—doubtless it was so, although she hid the secret from herself,
and grew pale whenever it struggled out of her heart, like a serpent from its hole—
it might be that another feeling kept her within the scene and pathway that had
been so fatal. There dwelt, there trode, the feet of one with whom she deemed her- 25
self connected in a union that, unrecognised on earth, would bring them together
before the bar of final judgment, and make that their marriage-altar, for a joint
futurity of endless retribution. Over and over again, the tempter of souls had thrust
this idea upon Hester's contemplation, and laughed at the passionate and desperate
joy with which she seized, and then strove to cast it from her. She barely looked 30
the idea in the face, and hastened to bar it in its dungeon. What she compelled
herself to believe—what, finally, she reasoned upon as her motive for continuing
a resident of New England—was half a truth, and half a self-delusion. Here, she
said to herself had been the scene of her guilt, and here should be the scene of her
earthly punishment; and so, perchance, the torture of her daily shame would at 35
length purge her soul, and work out another purity than that which she had lost:
more saint-like, because the result of martyrdom.

279. In lines 1–19, all of the following devices are used *except*

    (A) periodic sentence
    (B) anaphora
    (C) simile
    (D) complex sentence
    (E) chiasmus

280. The passage as a whole is developed by which syntactical device(s)?
    I. parallelism
    II. loose sentences
    III. em dashes

    (A) I only
    (B) I and II only
    (C) III only
    (D) II and III only
    (E) I, II, and III

281. The afterthoughts expressed in lines 1–8 serve primarily to

    (A) distract the reader from the subject of the sentence
    (B) present a character as unstable
    (C) cast doubt upon the reliability of the narrator
    (D) elucidate the alternative possibilities to a problem
    (E) explain the reasons for a character's choice

282. For Hester, the "fatality" mentioned in line 10 is later suggested to be

(A) the sighting of a ghost
(B) her transgression
(C) the death of her child
(D) her choice to live in this place
(E) doom

283. The second paragraph focuses on Hester's

(A) secret
(B) sin
(C) ambivalence
(D) regret
(E) justification

284. In the phrase "the feet of one" in line 25, "one" refers to

(A) Hester's child
(B) Hester's mother
(C) the tempter of souls
(D) Hester's husband
(E) Hester's accomplice

285. The narrator's attitude towards Hester can best be described as

(A) condescending
(B) pejorative
(C) hagiographic
(D) intrigued
(E) aloof

286. The second paragraph suggests that Hester Prynne stays in New England because

(A) she has been exiled from her home
(B) she is ambivalent
(C) it is better than her birth-place
(D) she longs for eventual absolution
(E) it has been the most important place in her life

287. The content of the passage is most similar to that of

(A) a Gothic novel
(B) an expository essay
(C) a personal narrative
(D) an epistolary novel
(E) an Aristotelian tragedy

288. The narrator characterizes Hester Prynne as

    (A) pusillanimous
    (B) persevering
    (C) delusional
    (D) wild
    (E) ghost-like

Passage 4. Henry James, *The Turn of the Screw*

    I remember the whole beginning as a succession of flights and drops, a little seesaw of the right throbs and the wrong. After rising, in town, to meet his appeal, I had at all events a couple of very bad days—found myself doubtful again, felt indeed sure I had made a mistake. In this state of mind I spent the long hours of bumping, swinging coach that carried me to the stopping place at which I was to 5 be met by a vehicle from the house. This convenience, I was told, had been ordered, and I found, toward the close of the June afternoon, a commodious fly in waiting for me. Driving at that hour, on a lovely day, through a country to which the summer sweetness seemed to offer me a friendly welcome, my fortitude mounted afresh and, as we turned into the avenue, encountered a reprieve that was probably but a 10 proof of the point to which it had sunk. I suppose I had expected, or had dreaded, something so melancholy that what greeted me was a good surprise. I remember as a most pleasant impression the broad, clear front, its open windows and fresh curtains and the pair of maids looking out; I remember the lawn and the bright flowers and the crunch of my wheels on the gravel and the clustered treetops over 15 which the rooks circled and cawed in the golden sky. The scene had a greatness that made it a different affair from my own scant home, and there immediately appeared at the door, with a little girl in her hand, a civil person who dropped me as decent a curtsy as if I had been the mistress or a distinguished visitor. I had received in Harley Street a narrower notion of the place, and that, as I recalled it, 20 made me think the proprietor still more of a gentleman, suggested that what I was to enjoy might be something beyond his promise.

    I had no drop again till the next day, for I was carried triumphantly through the following hours by my introduction to the younger of my pupils. The little girl who accompanied Mrs. Grose appeared to me on the spot a creature so charming 25 as to make it a great fortune to have to do with her. She was the most beautiful child I had ever seen, and I afterward wondered that my employer had not told me more of her. I slept little that night—I was too much excited; and this astonished me, too, I recollect, remained with me, adding to my sense of the liberality with which I was treated. The large, impressive room, one of the best in the house, the 30 great state bed, as I almost felt it, the full, figured draperies, the long glasses in which, for the first time, I could see myself from head to foot, all struck me—like the extraordinary charm of my small charge—as so many things thrown in. It was thrown in as well, from the first moment, that I should get on with Mrs. Grose in a relation over which, on my way, in the coach, I fear I had rather brooded. The 35 only thing indeed that in this early outlook might have made me shrink again was the clear circumstance of her being so glad to see me. I perceived within half an hour that she was so glad—stout, simple, plain, clean, wholesome woman—as to be positively on her guard against showing it too much. I wondered even then a little why she should wish not to show it, and that, with reflection, with suspicion, might of course have made me uneasy. 40

289. Lines 1–4 describe the speaker's state of mind as

(A) tenacious
(B) penitent
(C) reserved
(D) impatient
(E) anxious

290. The "convenience" mentioned in line 6 refers to

(A) a spacious means of conveyance
(B) an insect
(C) "the bumping swinging coach"
(D) the stopping-place
(E) the nice June weather

291. The word "fortitude" in line 9 most likely means

(A) contentment
(B) amicability
(C) mental and emotional strength
(D) senses
(E) terror

292. Which of the following devices enhances the speaker's excitement in lines 12–16?

   I. polysyndeton and onomatopoeia
  II. imagery and hyperbole
 III. anaphora and idioms

(A) I only
(B) I and III only
(C) II only
(D) II and III only
(E) III only

293. From the first paragraph, we can infer that the speaker is

    (A) a precocious girl
    (B) not upper class
    (C) male
    (D) the overseer
    (E) the proprietor

294. The "drop" in line 23 refers to

    (A) the rain
    (B) a fall
    (C) doubts
    (D) sustenance
    (E) excitement

295. What "remained" with the speaker in line 29?

    (A) her employer's reticence
    (B) the beautiful child
    (C) the same thing that astonishes her
    (D) the generosity of her hosts
    (E) Mrs. Grose

296. The word "that" in line 40 refers to

    (A) "the only thing" (36)
    (B) Mrs. Grose's gregariousness
    (C) Mrs. Grose's snub
    (D) reflection
    (E) suspicion

297. Overall, the speaker feels she has been treated

    (A) gregariously
    (B) impecuniously
    (C) irreverently
    (D) munificently
    (E) suspiciously

298. The style of the passage is most similar to the style of a

    (A) panegyric
    (B) jeremiad
    (C) lampoon
    (D) historical novel
    (E) memoir

Passage 5. Sinclair Lewis, *Babbitt*

He was busy, from March to June. He kept himself from the bewilderment of thinking. His wife and the neighbors were generous. Every evening he played bridge or attended the movies, and the days were blank of face and silent.

In June, Mrs. Babbitt and Tinka went East, to stay with relatives, and Babbitt was free to do—he was not quite sure what.   5

All day long after their departure he thought of the emancipated house in which he could, if he desired, go mad and curse the gods without having to keep up a husbandly front. He considered, "I could have a reg'lar party to-night; stay out till two and not do any explaining afterwards. Cheers!" He telephoned to Vergil Gunch, to Eddie Swanson. Both of them were engaged for the evening, and sud- 10 denly he was bored by having to take so much trouble to be riotous.

He was silent at dinner, unusually kindly to Ted and Verona, hesitating but not disapproving when Verona stated her opinion of Kenneth Escott's opinion of Dr. John Jennison Drew's opinion of the opinions of the evolutionists. Ted was work- ing in a garage through the summer vacation, and he related his daily triumphs: 15 how he had found a cracked ball-race, what he had said to the Old Grouch, what he had said to the foreman about the future of wireless telephony.

Ted and Verona went to a dance after dinner. Even the maid was out. Rarely had Babbitt been alone in the house for an entire evening. He was restless. He vaguely wanted something more diverting than the newspaper comic strips to read. 20 He ambled up to Verona's room, sat on her maidenly blue and white bed, hum- ming and grunting in a solid-citizen manner as he examined her books: Conrad's "Rescue," a volume strangely named "Figures of Earth," poetry (quite irregular poetry, Babbitt thought) by Vachel Lindsay, and essays by H. L. Mencken— highly improper essays, making fun of the church and all the decencies. He liked 25 none of the books. In them he felt a spirit of rebellion against niceness and solid- citizenship. These authors—and he supposed they were famous ones, too—did not seem to care about telling a good story which would enable a fellow to forget his troubles. He sighed. He noted a book, "The Three Black Pennies," by Joseph Hergesheimer. Ah, that was something like it! It would be an adventure story, 30 maybe about counterfeiting—detectives sneaking up on the old house at night. He tucked the book under his arm, he clumped down-stairs and solemnly began to read, under the piano-lamp . . .

299. The first paragraph implies that Babbitt's life from March to June is

(A) intellectually stimulating
(B) perfunctory
(C) reclusive
(D) onerous
(E) pensive

300. In context, the phrase "blank of face and silent" (3) is an example of

(A) hyperbole
(B) simile
(C) personification
(D) synecdoche
(E) asyndeton

301. The structure of the second paragraph does which of the following?

(A) highlights a key characteristic of Babbitt that will be developed throughout the passage
(B) characterizes Babbitt's relationship with his wife
(C) stresses the importance of the new characters mentioned
(D) presents Babbitt as independent
(E) contrasts Babbitt with others

302. In context, the word "emancipated" (6) suggests that

(A) Mrs. Babbitt is unrelenting
(B) life from March to June is prescribed
(C) the house is forsaken
(D) Babbitt is lost without his routine
(E) Babbitt is suffering from ennui

303. From the passage, we can infer all of the following about Mrs. Babbitt *except*

(A) she is altruistic
(B) she is not a Bohemian
(C) she is the sole housekeeper
(D) she prefers Babbitt not stay out late
(E) she visits family

304. The tone of lines 12–14, "He was silent . . . evolutionists," is best described as

(A) vitriolic
(B) petulant
(C) sardonic
(D) splenetic
(E) sympathetic

305. The word "vaguely" in line 20 implies that Babbitt

(A) abhors comics
(B) is tenacious
(C) is frenetic
(D) is ambivalent
(E) is apathetic

306. Based on Babbitt's thoughts about the books, we can infer all of the following *except* that

(A) he is discomfited by their spirit
(B) he wants them to offer him an escape
(C) he is quick to judge them
(D) he dislikes their antisocial themes
(E) his interests are congruous with Verona's

307. The sentence "Ah, that was something like it!" (30) is an example of what narrative technique?

(A) omniscient
(B) third person rotating
(C) first person
(D) free indirect style
(E) first person plural

308. Lines 30–31, "It would be . . . night," coincide with which of the following statements?

   I. "He kept himself from the bewilderment of thinking." (1–2)
  II. "He vaguely wanted something more diverting than the newspaper comic strips to read." (19–20)
 III. "These authors . . . his troubles." (27–29)

(A) I only
(B) II only
(C) III only
(D) I, II, and III
(E) I and III only

Passage 6. Sinclair Lewis, *Babbitt*

The towers of Zenith aspired above the morning mist; austere towers of steel and cement and limestone, sturdy as cliffs and delicate as silver rods. They were neither citadels nor churches, but frankly and beautifully office-buildings.

The mist took pity on the fretted structures of earlier generations: the Post Office with its shingle-tortured mansard, the red brick minarets of hulking old 5 houses, factories with stingy and sooted windows, wooden tenements colored like mud. The city was full of such grotesqueries, but the clean towers were thrusting them from the business center, and on the farther hills were shining new houses, homes—they seemed—for laughter and tranquility.

Over a concrete bridge fled a limousine of long sleek hood and noiseless engine. These people in evening clothes were returning from an all-night rehearsal of a Little Theater play, an artistic adventure considerably illuminated by champagne. Below the bridge curved a railroad, a maze of green and crimson lights. The New York Flyer boomed past, and twenty lines of polished steel leaped into the glare.

In one of the skyscrapers the wires of the *Associated Press* were closing down. The telegraph operators wearily raised their celluloid eye-shades after a night of talking with Paris and Peking. Through the building crawled the scrubwomen, yawning, their old shoes slapping. The dawn mist spun away. Cues of men with lunch-boxes clumped toward the immensity of new factories, sheets of glass and hollow tile, glittering shops where five thousand men worked beneath one roof, pouring out the honest wares that would be sold up the Euphrates and across the veldt. The whistles rolled out in greeting a chorus cheerful as the April dawn; the song of labor in a city built—it seemed—for giants.

309. The first sentence of the first paragraph (1–2)
  I. is a loose sentence
  II. contains a simile
  III. contains polysyndeton
  (A) I and III
  (B) I and II
  (C) II and III
  (D) I, II, and III
  (E) II only

310. The tone of the first paragraph is
  (A) wry
  (B) reverential
  (C) deferential
  (D) objective
  (E) droll

311. In the second paragraph, the old is contrasted with the new to
  (A) show the Gothic elements of the town
  (B) contrast archaic architecture with modern design
  (C) hint at the possibly wrong assumption that contemporary society is superior to that of earlier generations
  (D) vilify earlier generations
  (E) laud the placid nature of the town

312. The thoughts set off by em dashes in lines 9 and 23 ("—they seemed—for laughter and tranquility" and "—it seemed—for giants") contribute most significantly to the passage's

   (A) symbolism
   (B) candor
   (C) allusions
   (D) tone
   (E) setting

313. In the passage, the name "Zenith" most likely signifies

   (A) the city's impression of itself
   (B) the apotheosis of modern architecture
   (C) the name of ascetic-type buildings
   (D) citadels and churches
   (E) the speaker's impression of the city being described

314. The passage is written primarily in which of the following narrative styles?

   (A) first person
   (B) second person
   (C) third person
   (D) stream of consciousness
   (E) third person rotating

315. The "twenty lines of polished steel" (14) refer to

   (A) the limousine
   (B) the train
   (C) the theater
   (D) the railroad tracks
   (E) a concrete bridge

316. All the people described in the passage have in common that they are

   (A) fatigued
   (B) employed
   (C) happy
   (D) of the same class
   (E) in clusters

317. The tone and the narrator's description of the setting

   (A) mock the values of the characters mentioned
   (B) show that modern industry has improved man's life
   (C) contrast the superiority of objects to inferior humans
   (D) question the superiority of objects and industry
   (E) deplore the loss of the natural environment

318. An appropriate title for the passage would be
  (A) Modern Grandeur
  (B) The Bemused Masses
  (C) The Beauty of Zenith
  (D) Progress?
  (E) Commercial Supremacy

Passage 7. Upton Sinclair, *The Jungle*

Jurgis had made some friends by this time, and he sought one of them and asked what this meant. The friend, who was named Tamoszius Kuszleika, was a sharp little man who folded hides on the killing beds, and he listened to what Jurgis had to say without seeming at all surprised. They were common enough, he said, such cases of petty graft. It was simply some boss who proposed to add a little 5
to his income. After Jurgis had been there awhile he would know that the plants were simply honeycombed with rottenness of that sort—the bosses grafted off the men, and they grafted off each other; and some day the superintendent would find out about the boss, and then he would graft off the boss. Warming to the subject, Tamoszius went on to explain the situation. Here was Durham's, for instance, 10
owned by a man who was trying to make as much money out of it as he could, and did not care in the least how he did it; and underneath him, ranged in ranks and grades like an army, were managers and superintendents and foremen, each one driving the man next below him and trying to squeeze out of him as much work as possible. And all the men of the same rank were pitted against each other; the 15
accounts of each were kept separately, and every man lived in terror of losing his job, if another made a better record than he. So from top to bottom the place was simply a seething caldron of jealousies and hatreds; there was no loyalty or decency anywhere about it, there was no place in it where a man counted for anything against a dollar. And worse than there being no decency, there was not even any 20
honesty. The reason for that? Who could say? It must have been old Durham in the beginning; it was a heritage which the self-made merchant had left to his son, along with his millions.

Jurgis would find out these things for himself, if he stayed there long enough; it was the men who had to do all the dirty jobs, and so there was no deceiving them; 25
and they caught the spirit of the place, and did like all the rest. Jurgis had come there, and thought he was going to make himself useful, and rise and become a skilled man; but he would soon find out his error—for nobody rose in Packingtown by doing good work. You could lay that down for a rule—if you met a man who was rising in Packingtown, you met a knave. That man who had been sent to 30
Jurgis' father by the boss, he would rise; the man who told tales and spied upon his fellows would rise; but the man who minded his own business and did his work—why, they would "speed him up" till they had worn him out, and then they would throw him into the gutter.

Jurgis went home with his head buzzing. Yet he could not bring himself to 35
believe such things—no, it could not be so. Tamoszius was simply another of
the grumblers. He was a man who spent all his time fiddling; and he would go to
parties at night and not get home till sunrise, and so of course he did not feel like
work. Then, too, he was a puny little chap; and so he had been left behind in the
race, and that was why he was sore. And yet so many strange things kept coming 40
to Jurgis' notice every day!

319. The word "this" in line 2 is later suggested to mean

(A) Jurgis's low wages
(B) the attaching of one thing to another
(C) an incident involving deception
(D) Tamoszius's job
(E) the superintendent's behavior

320. The word "simply" in line 5 implies

(A) the narrator's skepticism of Tamoszius's account
(B) Tamoszius's dismay at the corruption around him
(C) the obvious and overwhelming amount of graft in the company
(D) Jurgis's realization of the company's true nature
(E) the minor nature of the problems of the company

321. In the first paragraph from "They were common" through "with his
millions," which narrative device is used?

(A) first person
(B) interior monologue
(C) third person
(D) stream of consciousness
(E) free indirect style

322. Tamoszius's account of how the company works (first paragraph beginning
"It was") makes use of all of the following *except*

(A) metaphor and simile
(B) anaphora
(C) rhetorical questions
(D) examples
(E) speculation

323. In the second paragraph, the word "knave" most likely means

(A) a person who is law abiding

(B) a person who minds his own business

(C) a person who is industrious

(D) a skilled man

(E) a charlatan

324. The phrase *speed him up* (second paragraph) is in quotation marks because

   I. the speaker is mocking the bosses' euphemistic command

  II. the phrase is part of a dialogue

 III. the phrase is a figure of speech

(A) I only

(B) II only

(C) I and II only

(D) II and III only

(E) I, II, and III only

325. The change in the predominant narrative voice from the second paragraph to the third paragraph is signaled by which phrase?

(A) "no, it could not be so" (36)

(B) "and then they would throw him into the gutter" (33–34)

(C) "he was a puny little chap" (39)

(D) "Jurgis went home with his head buzzing." (35)

(E) "he could not bring himself to believe such things" (35–36)

326. Jurgis's response to Tamoszius's assessment of the company (third paragraph) is most like the response of

(A) someone who is firm in his or her beliefs

(B) someone who has successfully been disabused of his or her initial perceptions

(C) someone who is skeptical about new information

(D) someone corrupt

(E) someone extremely naive

327. The last sentence of the passage suggests that the next paragraph might

- (A) belie the three paragraphs in the passage
- (B) corroborate the details given in the first and second paragraphs
- (C) detail the hardships incurred by Jurgis
- (D) present Tamoszius as dubious
- (E) validate the company's behavior

328. According to the passage as a whole, the company being described seems to value workers who are

- (A) skilled, useful men
- (B) fast
- (C) fastidious
- (D) candid
- (E) unprincipled

CHAPTER 6

World Fiction

Passage 1. Miguel de Cervantes, *Don Quixote*

These preliminaries settled, he did not care to put off any longer the execution of his design, urged on to it by the thought of all the world was losing by his delay, seeing what wrongs he intended to right, grievances to redress, injustices to repair, abuses to remove, and duties to discharge. So, without giving notice of his intention to anyone, and without anybody seeing him, one morning before the dawning 5
of the day (which was one of the hottest of the month of July) he donned his suit of armour, mounted Rocinante with his patched-up helmet on, braced his buckler, took his lance, and by the back door of the yard sallied forth upon the plain in the highest contentment and satisfaction at seeing with what ease he had made a beginning with his grand purpose. But scarcely did he find himself upon the open plain, 10
when a terrible thought struck him, one all but enough to make him abandon the enterprise at the very outset. It occurred to him that he had not been dubbed a knight, and that according to the law of chivalry he neither could nor ought to bear arms against any knight; and that even if he had been, still he ought, as a novice knight, to wear white armour, without a device upon the shield until by his 15
prowess he had earned one. These reflections made him waver in his purpose, but his craze being stronger than any reasoning, he made up his mind to have himself dubbed a knight by the first one he came across, following the example of others in the same case, as he had read in the books that brought him to this pass. As for white armor, he resolved, on the first opportunity, to scour his until it was whiter 20
than an ermine; and so comforting himself he pursued his way, taking that which his horse chose, for in this he believed lay the essence of adventures.

Thus setting out, our new-fledged adventurer paced along, talking to himself and saying, "Who knows but that in time to come, when the veracious history of my famous deeds is made known, the sage who writes it, when he has to set forth 25
my first sally in the early morning, will do it after this fashion? 'Scarce had the rubicund Apollo spread o'er the face of the broad spacious earth the golden threads of his bright hair, scarce had the little birds of painted plumage attuned their notes to hail with dulcet and mellifluous harmony the coming of the rosy Dawn, that, deserting the soft couch of her jealous spouse, was appearing to mortals at the gates 30
and balconies of the Manchegan horizon, when the renowned knight Don Quixote of La Mancha, quitting the lazy down, mounted his celebrated steed Rocinante and

began to traverse the ancient and famous Campo de Montiel;'" which in fact he was actually traversing. "Happy the age, happy the time," he continued, "in which shall be made known my deeds of fame, worthy to be molded in brass, carved in 35 marble, limned in pictures, for a memorial for ever. And thou, O sage magician, whoever thou art, to whom it shall fall to be the chronicler of this wondrous history, forget not, I entreat thee, my good Rocinante, the constant companion of my ways and wanderings." Presently he broke out again, as if he were love-stricken in earnest, "O Princess Dulcinea, lady of this captive heart, a grievous wrong hast 40 thou done me to drive me forth with scorn, and with inexorable obduracy banish me from the presence of thy beauty. O lady, deign to hold in remembrance this heart, thy vassal, that thus in anguish pines for love of thee."

329. The narrator's attitude toward the protagonist can best be described as

(A) magnanimous

(B) sardonic

(C) acrimonious

(D) sympathetic

(E) dispassionate

330. The sentence in lines 26–33, "'Scarce had the rubicund Apollo . . . Campo de Montiel,'" uses all of the following *except*

(A) anaphora

(B) hyperbole

(C) alliteration

(D) euphony

(E) asyndeton

331. The tone of the sentence in lines 26–33, "'Scarce had the rubicund Apollo . . . Campo de Montiel,'" can best be described as

(A) ridiculous

(B) sarcastic

(C) sophisticated

(D) grandiloquent

(E) provincial

332. The "terrible thought" (11) that Don Quixote had refers to

(A) his leaving home without telling anyone

(B) his not knowing where he was going

(C) the wrongs that his lady had done him

(D) his status not being quite legitimate

(E) his ambitions being too great

333. According to the narrator, Don Quixote was able to overcome his initial hesitation because

    (A) he was unable to reason coherently

    (B) his fantasizing was resourceful

    (C) he had a tenuous grasp on reality

    (D) he had faith in his good fortune

    (E) he was unwilling to return home

334. The sentence in lines 36–39 ("And thou, O sage magician . . . and wanderings") is an example of all of the following *except*

    (A) self-reference

    (B) prosody

    (C) burlesque

    (D) lofty language

    (E) the use of appositives

335. In line 41, the word "obduracy" most likely means

    (A) cruelty

    (B) durability

    (C) unpredictability

    (D) stubbornness

    (E) loudness

336. The narrator's use of the expression "veracious history" in line 24 can best be described as

    (A) scrupulous

    (B) droll

    (C) ironic

    (D) disingenuous

    (E) emphatic

337. The genre of the narrative as a whole can best be described as

    (A) romance

    (B) epic

    (C) tragedy

    (D) comedy

    (E) farce

338. According to Don Quixote's chivalric code, a knight is not meant to do any of the following *except*

(A) travel directly and purposefully
(B) speak plainly and succinctly
(C) maintain a supercilious attitude about himself
(D) avoid romantic entanglement
(E) disregard unreasonable rules

Passage 2. Fyodor Dostoyevsky, *Crime and Punishment*

On an exceptionally hot evening early in July a young man came out of the garret in which he lodged in S. Place and walked slowly, as though in hesitation, towards K. bridge.

He had successfully avoided meeting his landlady on the staircase. His garret was under the roof of a high, five-storied house and was more like a cupboard than a room. The landlady who provided him with garret, dinners, and attendance, lived on the floor below, and every time he went out he was obliged to pass her kitchen, the door of which invariably stood open. And each time he passed, the young man had a sick, frightened feeling, which made him scowl and feel ashamed. He was hopelessly in debt to his landlady, and was afraid of meeting her. 10

This was not because he was cowardly and abject, quite the contrary; but for some time past he had been in an overstrained irritable condition, verging on hypochondria. He had become so completely absorbed in himself, and isolated from his fellows that he dreaded meeting, not only his landlady, but anyone at all. He was crushed by poverty, but the anxieties of his position had of late ceased to 15 weigh upon him. He had given up attending to matters of practical importance; he had lost all desire to do so. Nothing that any landlady could do had a real terror for him. But to be stopped on the stairs, to be forced to listen to her trivial, irrelevant gossip, to pestering demands for payment, threats and complaints, and to rack his brains for excuses, to prevaricate, to lie—no, rather than that, he would creep down 20 the stairs like a cat and slip out unseen.

This evening, however, on coming out into the street, he became acutely aware of his fears.

"I want to attempt a thing like that and am frightened by these trifles," he thought, with an odd smile. "Hm . . . yes, all is in a man's hands and he lets it all 25 slip from cowardice, that's an axiom. It would be interesting to know what it is men are most afraid of. Taking a new step, uttering a new word is what they fear most. . . . But I am talking too much. It's because I chatter that I do nothing. Or perhaps it is that I chatter because I do nothing. I've learned to chatter this last month, lying for days together in my den thinking . . . of Jack the Giant-killer. 30 Why am I going there now? Am I capable of that? Is that serious? It is not serious at all. It's simply a fantasy to amuse myself; a plaything! Yes, maybe it is a plaything."

The heat in the street was terrible: and the airlessness, the bustle and the plaster, scaffolding, bricks, and dust all about him, and that special Petersburg stench, so

familiar to all who are unable to get out of town in summer—all worked painfully 35
upon the young man's already overwrought nerves. The insufferable stench from
the pot-houses, which are particularly numerous in that part of the town, and the
drunken men whom he met continually, although it was a working day, completed the revolting misery of the picture. An expression of the profoundest disgust
gleamed for a moment in the young man's refined face. He was, by the way, excep- 40
tionally handsome, above the average in height, slim, well-built, with beautiful
dark eyes and dark brown hair. Soon he sank into deep thought, or more accurately
speaking into a complete blankness of mind; he walked along not observing what
was about him and not caring to observe it. From time to time, he would mutter
something, from the habit of talking to himself, to which he had just confessed. 45
At these moments he would become conscious that his ideas were sometimes in a
tangle and that he was very weak; for two days he had scarcely tasted food.

339. The passage is written from which narrative point of view?

    (A) third person limited
    (B) third person omniscient
    (C) first person singular
    (D) first person plural
    (E) third person rotating

340. The description of the setting serves to

    I. provide justification for the protagonist's feelings
    II. contrast with the protagonist
    III. critique the government of "Petersburg"

    (A) I only
    (B) I and II only
    (C) II and III only
    (D) I and III
    (E) III only

341. The last sentence of the second paragraph (9–10)

    (A) is redundant
    (B) is speculation
    (C) answers a question
    (D) provides clarification
    (E) characterizes the landlady

342. The third paragraph differs from the second in that

(A) the second paragraph does not contain dependent clauses

(B) the second paragraph does not contain simple sentences

(C) the third paragraph focuses on characterizing the protagonist's emotional state

(D) the third paragraph mentions a character that the second does not

(E) the tone is different

343. What is the "axiom" the protagonist refers to in line 26?

(A) that men who let things slip away are cowards

(B) that a man's timidity causes him to squander opportunities

(C) "'I want to attempt a thing like that and am frightened by these trifles'"

(D) his conjecture that doing nothing causes him to chatter

(E) his conjecture that chatter prevents him from doing things

344. The two sentences in lines 28–29 ("It's because I chatter that I do nothing. Or perhaps it is that I chatter because I do nothing") are

(A) chiastic

(B) axiomatic

(C) veracious

(D) hyperbolic

(E) delusional

345. The words "there," "that," and "It" in line 31 do all of the following *except*

(A) provoke curiosity

(B) characterize the protagonist's reluctance and fear

(C) elucidate the protagonist's desires

(D) create a sense of mystery

(E) hide the protagonist's actual fantasy from the reader

346. In the final paragraph, a contrast is established between

(A) beauty and ugliness

(B) rich and poor

(C) cleanliness and filth

(D) good and evil

(E) hunger and satiation

347. The protagonist is described as all of the following *except*

(A) emotionally detached
(B) proud
(C) petulant
(D) destitute
(E) intrepid

348. The narrator's tone can best be described as

(A) observant
(B) curious
(C) intrusive
(D) speculative
(E) sympathetic

Passage 3. Gustave Flaubert, *Madame Bovary*

We were in class when the head-master came in, followed by a "new fellow," not wearing the school uniform, and a school servant carrying a large desk. Those who had been asleep woke up, and every one rose as if just surprised at his work.

The head-master made a sign to us to sit down. Then, turning to the class-master, he said to him in a low voice: 5

"Monsieur Roger, here is a pupil whom I recommend to your care; he'll be in the second. If his work and conduct are satisfactory, he will go into one of the upper classes, as becomes his age."

The "new fellow," standing in the corner behind the door so that he could hardly be seen, was a country lad of about fifteen, and taller than any of us. His 10 hair was cut square on his forehead like a village chorister's; he looked reliable, but very ill at ease. Although he was not broad-shouldered, his short school jacket of green cloth with black buttons must have been tight about the armholes, and showed at the opening of the cuffs red wrists accustomed to being bare. His legs, in blue stockings, looked out from beneath yellow trousers, drawn tight by braces. 15 He wore stout, ill-cleaned, hobnailed boots.

We began repeating the lesson. He listened with all his ears, as attentive as if at a sermon, not daring even to cross his legs or lean on his elbow; and when at two o'clock the bell rang, the master was obliged to tell him to fall into line with the rest of us. 20

When we came back to work, we were in the habit of throwing our caps on the floor so as to have our hands more free; we used from the door to toss them under the form, so that they hit against the wall and made a lot of dust: it was "the thing."

But, whether he had not noticed the trick, or did not dare to attempt it, the "new fellow" was still holding his cap on his knees even after prayers were over. It 25 was one of those head-gears of composite order, in which we can find traces of the bearskin, shako, billycock hat, sealskin cap, and cotton nightcap; one of those poor

things, in fine, whose dumb ugliness has depths of expression, like an imbecile's face. Oval, stiffened with whalebone, it began with three round knobs; then came in succession lozenges of velvet and rabbit-skin separated by a red band; after that   30
a sort of bag that ended in a cardboard polygon covered with complicated braiding, from which hung, at the end of a long, thin cord, small twisted gold threads in the manner of a tassel. The cap was new; its peak shone.

349. The passage is written from which narrative point of view?

   (A)   third person omniscient
   (B)   second person
   (C)   first person plural
   (D)   third person
   (E)   first person singular

350. The fourth paragraph marks a change from the previous paragraphs in that it

   (A)   lacks objectivity
   (B)   includes speculation
   (C)   contains simile
   (D)   changes point of view
   (E)   contains dialogue

351. The speaker describes the "'new fellow'" sartorially (12–16) to emphasize

   (A)   that he does not want to be there
   (B)   how he does not fit in
   (C)   how varied the available school uniforms are
   (D)   how apprehensive the "new fellow" is
   (E)   that he is used to working, not going to school

352. The clause in lines 19–20 ("the master was obliged . . . rest of us") implies

   (A)   the new boy is misbehaving
   (B)   the new boy is recalcitrant
   (C)   the new boy is immersed in learning
   (D)   the new boy is an outcast
   (E)   the speaker is belittling the new boy

353. The phrase "'the thing'" (23) is in quotation marks because

   (A)   it is part of a dialogue
   (B)   it is a colloquial phrase used by the boys
   (C)   it is sarcastic
   (D)   it is ironic
   (E)   it is being mocked

354. The detailed description of the new boy's cap (25–33)

    (A) highlights similarities between the boy and others

    (B) serves as a symbol of the boy's nature

    (C) emphasizes the boy's piety

    (D) is intended to ridicule the boy

    (E) is a motif throughout the passage

355. The last two sentences of the passage can be described as

    (A) creating sentence variety

    (B) paradoxes

    (C) contradictions

    (D) redundant

    (E) run-ons

356. The overall tone of the passage is

    (A) attentive

    (B) critical

    (C) sentimental

    (D) detached

    (E) informal

357. The purpose of the passage as a whole is

    I. to introduce a story's setting

    II. to reveal one boy's reflections of his past

    III. to portray a character through others' observations

    (A) I and III only

    (B) II and III only

    (C) III only

    (D) I and II only

    (E) I, II, and III

358. The new boy differs from the speaker in all of the following ways *except*

    (A) his attire

    (B) his height

    (C) his deportment

    (D) his environs

    (E) his interests

Passage 4. Hermann Hesse, *Siddhartha*

In the shade of the house, in the sunshine of the riverbank near the boats, in the shade of the Sal-wood forest, in the shade of the fig tree is where Siddhartha grew up, the handsome son of the Brahman, the young falcon, together with his friend Govinda, son of a Brahman. The sun tanned his light shoulders by the banks of the river when bathing, performing the sacred ablutions, the sacred offerings. In the mango grove, shade poured into his black eyes, when playing as a boy, when his mother sang, when the sacred offerings were made, when his father, the scholar, taught him, when the wise men talked. For a long time, Siddhartha had been partaking in the discussions of the wise men, practicing debate with Govinda, practicing with Govinda the art of reflection, the service of meditation. He already knew how to speak the Om silently, the word of words, to speak it silently into himself while inhaling, to speak it silently out of himself while exhaling, with all the concentration of his soul, the forehead surrounded by the glow of the clear-thinking spirit. He already knew to feel Atman in the depths of his being, indestructible, one with the universe. 5 10 15

Joy leapt in his father's heart for his son who was quick to learn, thirsty for knowledge; he saw him growing up to become a great wise man and priest, a prince among the Brahmans.

Bliss leapt in his mother's breast when she saw him, when she saw him walking, when she saw him sit down and get up, Siddhartha, strong, handsome, he who was walking on slender legs, greeting her with perfect respect. 20

Love touched the hearts of the Brahmans' young daughters when Siddhartha walked through the lanes of the town with the luminous forehead, with the eye of a king, with his slim hips.

But more than all the others he was loved by Govinda, his friend, the son of a Brahman. He loved Siddhartha's eye and sweet voice, he loved his walk and the perfect decency of his movements, he loved everything Siddhartha did and said and what he loved most was his spirit, his transcendent, fiery thoughts, his ardent will, his high calling. Govinda knew: he would not become a common Brahman, not a lazy official in charge of offerings; not a greedy merchant with magic spells; not a vain, vacuous speaker; not a mean, deceitful priest; and also not a decent, stupid sheep in the herd of the many. No, and he, Govinda, as well did not want to become one of those, not one of those tens of thousands of Brahmans. He wanted to follow Siddhartha, the beloved, the splendid. And in days to come, when Siddhartha would become a god, when he would join the glorious, then Govinda wanted to follow him as his friend, his companion, his servant, his spear-carrier, his shadow. 25 30 35

Siddhartha was thus loved by everyone. He was a source of joy for everybody, he was a delight for them all.

359. The first sentence of the passage can be described as

      I. periodic
     II. containing repetition
    III. containing metaphor

  (A) II only
  (B) I and II only
  (C) II and III only
  (D) I and III only
  (E) I, II, and III

360. In context, the word "ablutions" (5) most likely means

  (A) forgiveness
  (B) prayers
  (C) rituals
  (D) religious cleansings
  (E) devotions

361. The dominant technique in the first paragraph is

  (A) anaphora
  (B) personification
  (C) asyndeton
  (D) allusion
  (E) metaphor

362. We can infer that "Om" is

  (A) a sedative
  (B) like an opiate
  (C) a prayer
  (D) a meditative recitation
  (E) a routine

363. Siddhartha's parents are impressed by all of the following *except*

  (A) his corpulence
  (B) his sagacity
  (C) his thirst for knowledge
  (D) his ecclesiastical talents
  (E) his litheness

364. In the passage as a whole, Siddhartha is described as all of the following *except*

(A) regal
(B) distinct
(C) luminous
(D) coveted
(E) proud

365. Govinda admires Siddhartha for all of the following *except* his

(A) nonconformity
(B) tenacity
(C) potential
(D) incantations
(E) amble

366. According to the passage, many Brahmans are
   I. supercilious
   II. venal
   III. banal

(A) I only
(B) II only
(C) III only
(D) I and III only
(E) I, II, and III

367. The tone of the passage as a whole is

(A) idyllic
(B) slanderous
(C) wistful
(D) nationalistic
(E) exalted

368. The passage's primary purpose is to

(A) portray a culture
(B) characterize Siddhartha through the perceptions of others
(C) introduce Siddhartha
(D) characterize Siddhartha through descriptions of his setting
(E) characterize Siddhartha through figurative language

Passage 5. James Joyce, "The Dead"

Lily, the caretaker's daughter, was literally run off her feet. Hardly had she brought one gentleman into the little pantry behind the office on the ground floor and helped him off with his overcoat than the wheezy hall-door bell clanged again and she had to scamper along the bare hallway to let in another guest. It was well for her she had not to attend to the ladies also. But Miss Kate and Miss Julia had 5 thought of that and had converted the bathroom upstairs into a ladies' dressing-room. Miss Kate and Miss Julia were there, gossiping and laughing and fussing, walking after each other to the head of the stairs, peering down over the banisters and calling down to Lily to ask her who had come.

It was always a great affair, the Misses Morkan's annual dance. Everybody 10 who knew them came to it, members of the family, old friends of the family, the members of Julia's choir, any of Kate's pupils that were grown up enough, and even some of Mary Jane's pupils too. Never once had it fallen flat. For years and years it had gone off in splendid style, as long as anyone could remember; ever since Kate and Julia, after the death of their brother Pat, had left the house in Stoney Batter 15 and taken Mary Jane, their only niece, to live with them in the dark, gaunt house on Usher's Island, the upper part of which they had rented from Mr. Fulham, the corn-factor on the ground floor. That was a good thirty years ago if it was a day. Mary Jane, who was then a little girl in short clothes, was now the main prop of the household, for she had the organ in Haddington Road. She had been through the 20 Academy and gave a pupils' concert every year in the upper room of the Ancient Concert Rooms. Many of her pupils belonged to the better-class families on the Kingstown and Dalkey line. Old as they were, her aunts also did their share. Julia, though she was quite grey, was still the leading soprano in Adam and Eve's, and Kate, being too feeble to go about much, gave music lessons to beginners on the 25 old square piano in the back room. Lily, the caretaker's daughter, did housemaid's work for them. Though their life was modest, they believed in eating well; the best of everything: diamond-bone sirloins, three-shilling tea and the best bottled stout. But Lily seldom made a mistake in the orders, so that she got on well with her three mistresses. They were fussy, that was all. But the only thing they would not stand 30 was back answers.

Of course, they had good reason to be fussy on such a night. And then it was long after ten o'clock and yet there was no sign of Gabriel and his wife. Besides they were dreadfully afraid that Freddy Malins might turn up screwed. They would not wish for worlds that any of Mary Jane's pupils should see him under the influ- 35 ence; and when he was like that it was sometimes very hard to manage him. Freddy Malins always came late, but they wondered what could be keeping Gabriel: and that was what brought them every two minutes to the banisters to ask Lily had Gabriel or Freddy come.

369. The phrase "literally run off her feet" (1) is an example of

(A) free indirect style
(B) a metaphor
(C) omniscient narration
(D) a malapropism
(E) the author's colloquial language

370. The characters in the passage are all introduced through all of the following *except*

(A) their points of view
(B) their vernacular
(C) their relationships to each other
(D) references to their past
(E) mention of their vocations

371. The structure of the second sentence of the passage

(A) is balanced
(B) is compound
(C) is simple
(D) emphasizes Lily's emotional state
(E) coincides with Miss Kate and Miss Julia's emotional states

372. The sentence in lines 10–13 ("Everybody who . . . pupils too") and the sentence in lines 13–18 ("For years . . . floor") are

(A) complex
(B) compound
(C) cumulative
(D) contradictory
(E) periodic

373. The mood in the house is predominantly

(A) pacific
(B) patient
(C) jovial
(D) nervous
(E) fearful

374. The phrase "if it was a day" (18) implies

(A) time has flown by for the two aunts
(B) time has flown by for Mary Jane
(C) time has flown by for the speaker
(D) the aunts are unsure of exactly when they moved to this house
(E) their history is foggy

375. The phrase "main prop" (19) reveals that

(A) the two aunts view Mary Jane as servile
(B) Mary Jane is the sole supporter of the household
(C) the two aunts use Mary Jane for their financial survival
(D) Mary Jane is the main provider in the family
(E) Mary Jane is objectified

376. From the passage as a whole, we can infer that the three women (Julia, Kate, and Mary Jane) are all of the following *except*

(A) epicures
(B) musically inclined
(C) not upper class
(D) abstemious
(E) finicky

377. The phrases "if it was a day" (18), "They were fussy . . . back answers" (30–31), "turn up screwed" (34), and "wish for worlds" (35) have what in common?

  I. They are examples of the characters' vernacular.
  II. They are examples of free indirect style.
  III. They are examples of third-person limited narration.

(A) I only
(B) I and II only
(C) I and III only
(D) II and III only
(E) I, II, and III

378. The second paragraph of the passage differs from the first in that

(A) the second contains Lily's perspective
(B) the first sets up a problem that the second solves
(C) the first sets the scene, and the second provides background
(D) the first contains simple sentences, and the second does not
(E) the first mentions characters that the second does not

Passage 6. Franz Kafka, "Metamorphosis"

One morning, when Gregor Samsa woke from troubled dreams, he found himself transformed in his bed into a horrible vermin.[2] He lay on his armor-like back, and if he lifted his head a little he could see his brown belly, slightly domed and divided by arches into stiff sections. The bedding was hardly able to cover it and seemed ready to slide off any moment. His many legs, pitifully thin compared with the size of the rest of him, waved about helplessly as he looked.

"What's happened to me?" he thought. It wasn't a dream. His room, a proper human room although a little too small, lay peacefully between its four familiar walls. A collection of textile samples lay spread out on the table—Samsa was a travelling salesman—and above it there hung a picture that he had recently cut out of an illustrated magazine and housed in a nice, gilded frame. It showed a lady fitted out with a fur hat and fur boa who sat upright, raising a heavy fur muff that covered the whole of her lower arm towards the viewer.

Gregor then turned to look out the window at the dull weather. Drops of rain could be heard hitting the pane, which made him feel quite sad. "How about if I sleep a little bit longer and forget all this nonsense," he thought, but that was something he was unable to do because he was used to sleeping on his right, and in his present state couldn't get into that position. However hard he threw himself onto his right, he always rolled back to where he was. He must have tried it a hundred times, shut his eyes so that he wouldn't have to look at the floundering legs, and only stopped when he began to feel a mild, dull pain there that he had never felt before.

"Oh, God," he thought, "what a strenuous career it is that I've chosen! Travelling day in and day out. Doing business like this takes much more effort than doing your own business at home, and on top of that there's the curse of travelling, worries about making train connections, bad and irregular food, contact with different people all the time so that you can never get to know anyone or become friendly with them. It can all go to Hell!" He felt a slight itch up on his belly; pushed himself slowly up on his back towards the headboard so that he could lift his head better; found where the itch was, and saw that it was covered with lots of little white spots which he didn't know what to make of; and when he tried to feel the place with one of his legs he drew it quickly back because as soon as he touched it he was overcome by a cold shudder.

He slid back into his former position. "Getting up early all the time," he thought, "it makes you stupid. You've got to get enough sleep. Other travelling salesmen live a life of luxury. For instance, whenever I go back to the guest house during the morning to copy out the contract, these gentlemen are always still

---

2. Modern translations indicate that the transformation is into a bug or insect, very likely a cockroach.

sitting there eating their breakfasts. I ought to just try that with my boss; I'd get kicked out on the spot. But who knows, maybe that would be the best thing for me. If I didn't have my parents to think about I'd have given in my notice a long 40 time ago, I'd have gone up to the boss and told him just what I think, tell him everything I would, let him know just what I feel. He'd fall right off his desk! And it's a funny sort of business to be sitting up there at your desk, talking down at your subordinates from up there, especially when you have to go right up close because the boss is hard of hearing. Well, there's still some hope; once I've got the 45 money together to pay off my parents' debt to him—another five or six years I suppose—that's definitely what I'll do. That's when I'll make the big change. First of all though, I've got to get up, my train leaves at five."

379. The structure of the sentences in the first paragraph

    (A) consists of dependent clauses
    (B) consists of simple sentences
    (C) consists of periodic sentences
    (D) consists of parallel clauses
    (E) is complex

380. The main purpose of the first paragraph is to

    (A) display figurative language
    (B) confound the reader
    (C) pique interest by setting up a problem
    (D) introduce the setting
    (E) characterize Gregor Samsa

381. The second paragraph differs from the first in that

    (A) it contains a metaphor
    (B) it characterizes Gregor through description of his personal items
    (C) it continues the description of the setting
    (D) it uses personification and simile
    (E) it contains a more facetious tone

382. The dominant technique used in the third paragraph is

    (A) repetition
    (B) polysyndeton
    (C) foreshadowing
    (D) imagery
    (E) dialogue

383. The inclusion of Gregor's thoughts in lines 23–28 serve to

(A) belittle Gregor's choice of career

(B) introduce a symbol

(C) reveal Gregor's primary preoccupation

(D) emphasize Gregor's frustration with his transformation into an insect

(E) divert our attention from his physical transformation

384. In context, the word "'stupid'" (35) most likely means

(A) disabled

(B) ignorant

(C) pointless

(D) stuporous

(E) without luxury

385. The purpose of almost all of the last paragraph is to

(A) display Gregor's vernacular

(B) elicit empathy for the main character

(C) critique the modern working world

(D) introduce the problems with Gregor's job

(E) elaborate on the metaphor introduced in the first paragraph

386. The narrative tone is

(A) clear and straightforward

(B) scientific

(C) arabesque

(D) cryptic

(E) passionate

387. In the last sentence of the passage the author seeks to interest us in the subject by

(A) confounding us with Gregor's indifference

(B) impressing us with Gregor's fastidiousness

(C) dumbfounding us with Gregor's obliviousness

(D) infuriating us with Gregor's tenacity

(E) distancing us from Gregor's situation

388. Gregor's tone contrasts with the narrator's in its

(A) frustration

(B) didacticism

(C) astonishment

(D) compassion

(E) sentimentality

CHAPTER 7

Drama

Passage 1. Euripides, *Medea*

MEDEA. From the house I have come forth, Corinthian ladies, for fear lest you be blaming me; for well I know that amongst men many by showing pride have gotten them an ill name and a reputation for indifference, both those who shun men's gaze and those who move amid the stranger crowd, and likewise they who choose a quiet walk in life. For there is no just discernment in the eyes of men, for they, or ever they have surely learnt their neighbour's heart, loathe him at first sight, though never wronged by him; and so a stranger most of all should adopt a city's views; nor do I commend that citizen, who, in the stubbornness of his heart, from churlishness resents the city's will.

But on me hath fallen this unforeseen disaster, and sapped my life; ruined I am, and long to resign the boon of existence, kind friends, and die. For he who was all the world to me, as well thou knowest, hath turned out the worst of men, my own husband. Of all things that have life and sense we women are the most hapless creatures; first must we buy a husband at a great price, and o'er ourselves a tyrant set which is an evil worse than the first; and herein lies the most important issue, whether our choice be good or bad. For divorce is not honourable to women, nor can we disown our lords. Next must the wife, coming as she does to ways and customs new, since she hath not learnt the lesson in her home, have a diviner's eye to see how best to treat the partner of her life. If haply we perform these tasks with thoroughness and tact, and the husband live with us, without resenting the yoke, our life is a happy one; if not, 'twere best to die. But when a man is vexed with what he finds indoors, he goeth forth and rids his soul of its disgust, betaking him to some friend or comrade of like age; whilst we must needs regard his single self.

5

10

15

20

25

And yet they say we live secure at home, while they are at the   30
wars, with their sorry reasoning, for I would gladly take my stand
in battle array three times o'er, than once give birth. But enough!
this language suits not thee as it does me; thou hast a city here, a
father's house, some joy in life, and friends to share thy thoughts,
but I am destitute, without a city, and therefore scorned by my   35
husband, a captive I from a foreign shore, with no mother,
brother, or kinsman in whom to find a new haven of refuge from
this calamity. Wherefore this one boon and only this I wish to win
from thee, thy silence, if haply I can some way or means devise
to avenge me on my husband for this cruel treatment, and on the   40
man who gave to him his daughter, and on her who is his wife.
For though woman be timorous enough in all else, and as regards
courage, a coward at the mere sight of steel, yet in the moment she
finds her honour wronged, no heart is filled with deadlier thoughts
than hers.   45

389. According to the first paragraph, Medea has come out of her house

- (A) because she is fearless
- (B) to criticize the lack of justice among men
- (C) to show her pride
- (D) to mitigate the people's judgment of her
- (E) because she fears the town's wrath

390. According to Medea, why is there "no just discernment in the eyes of men" (6)?

   I. because people hold grudges against those who have wronged them
  II. because people resent the city's will
 III. because people form immutable opinions of people they may not
     even know

- (A) I only
- (B) II only
- (C) III only
- (D) I and III only
- (E) I, II, and III

391. How does the second paragraph differ from the first?

- (A) The first is addressed to women and the second to men.
- (B) The first introduces the topic that the second develops.
- (C) The first poses a question that the second attempts to answer.
- (D) The first is general, and the second is specific.
- (E) The first excoriates, and the second justifies.

392. In context, the word "boon" (13) most likely means

(A) support
(B) dread
(C) life
(D) job
(E) pain

393. In context, the word "yoke" (25) most likely means

(A) egg
(B) husband
(C) life
(D) situation
(E) burden

394. Medea cites all of the following as examples of women being "hapless" (16) *except*

(A) their forced isolation from "some friend or comrade of like age"
(B) the fact that they have to "buy a husband"
(C) the fact that they have to bear offspring
(D) their submission to their husbands
(E) the fact that they cannot be unfettered

395. The phrase "But enough!" (32) can best be paraphrased as

(A) Pay attention!
(B) Do not disagree!
(C) Enough of this griping!
(D) But I digress!
(E) Stop distracting me!

396. Medea distinguishes herself from the other women by

(A) describing their families
(B) comparing their husbands
(C) cataloging all her misfortune
(D) assuming they have all that she lacks
(E) listing what she has that they lack

397. According to Medea, when a woman "finds her honour wronged" (44), she

(A) abandons her temerity
(B) is overcome with resilience
(C) fears the sight of steel
(D) becomes timorous
(E) gains temerity

398. Medea's tone is best described as

(A) resolute
(B) ruthless
(C) remorseful
(D) objective
(E) penitent

Passage 2. Euripides, *Medea*

MEDEA.   Ill hath it been done on every side. Who will gainsay it? but these
things are not in this way, do not yet think it. Still is there a contest for those lately married, and to those allied to them no small
affliction. For dost thou think I ever would have fawned upon this
man, if I were not to gain something, or form some plan? I would   5
not even have addressed him. I would not even have touched him
with my hands. But he hath arrived at such a height of folly, as
that, when it was in his power to have crushed my plans, by banishing me from this land, he hath granted me to stay this day in
which three of mine enemies will I put to death, the father, the   10
bride, and my husband. But having in my power many resources
of destruction against them, I know not, my friends, which I shall
first attempt. Whether shall I consume the bridal house with fire,
or force the sharpened sword through her heart having entered the
chamber by stealth where the couch is spread? But one thing is   15
against me; if I should be caught entering the house and prosecut-
ing my plans, by my death I shall afford laughter for my foes. Best
then is it to pursue the straight path, in which I am most skilled,
to take them off by poison. Let it be so. And suppose them dead:
what city will receive me? What hospitable stranger affording a   20
land of safety and a faithful home will protect my person? There
is none. Waiting then yet a little time, if any tower of safety shall
appear to us, I will proceed to this murder in treachery and silence.
But if ill fortune that leaves me without resource force me, I myself
having grasped the sword, although I should die, will kill them,   25
and will rush to the extreme height of daring. For never, I swear
by my mistress whom I revere most of all, and have chosen for my
assistant, Hecate, who dwells in the inmost recesses of my house,
shall any one of them wring my heart with grief with impunity.

Bitter and mournful to them will I make these nuptials, and bitter   30
this alliance, and my flight from this land. But come, spare none
of these sciences in which thou art skilled, Medea, deliberating and
plotting. Proceed to the deed of terror: now is the time of resolu-
tion: seest thou what thou art suffering? Ill doth it become thee to
incur ridicule from the race of Sisyphus, and from the nuptials of   35

Jason, who art sprung from a noble father, and from the sun. And thou art skilled. Besides also we women are, by nature, to good actions of the least capacity, but the most cunning inventors of every ill.

399. In the phrase "he hath granted me," "he" refers to

   (A) "the father" (10)
   (B) "those lately married" (3)
   (C) "thou" (4)
   (D) "this man" (4–5)
   (E) "mine enemies" (10)

400. The lines from "But having in my power . . ." to "rush to the extreme height of daring," (11–26) consist, in order, of

   (A) illogical reasoning and faulty conclusions
   (B) questioning, reasoning logically, drawing conclusions, and considering alternatives
   (C) hypotheses, theories, experiment, and conclusions
   (D) venting irrationally, reasoning rationally, and drawing conclusions
   (E) rhetorical questioning, weighing of consequences, and indecision

401. The phrase "any one of them" (29) refers to

   (A) Medea's victims
   (B) people in general
   (C) Hecate
   (D) hospitable strangers
   (E) men

402. In context, the word "impunity" (29) most likely means

   (A) intention
   (B) hate
   (C) care
   (D) license
   (E) audacity

403. From "But come," through "inventors of every ill" (31–39), Medea uses

   (A) first person plural
   (B) first person
   (C) third person
   (D) third person plural
   (E) first person singular

404. In those same lines from question 403, Medea

(A) doubts herself
(B) admonishes herself
(C) procrastinates
(D) motivates others
(E) motivates herself

405. Medea's tone is

I. proud
II. tenacious
III. rational

(A) I only
(B) I and II only
(C) II and III only
(D) III only
(E) I, II, and III

Passage 3. William Shakespeare, *Hamlet*

QUEEN.	Good Hamlet, cast thy nighted colour off,	
	And let thine eye look like a friend on Denmark.	
	Do not for ever with thy vailed lids	
	Seek for thy noble father in the dust:	
	Thou know'st 'tis common, —all that lives must die,	5
	Passing through nature to eternity.	
HAMLET.	Ay, madam, it is common.	
QUEEN.	If it be,	
	Why seems it so particular with thee?	
HAMLET.	Seems, madam! Nay, it is; I know not seems.	10
	'Tis not alone my inky cloak, good mother,	
	Nor customary suits of solemn black,	
	Nor windy suspiration of forc'd breath,	
	No, nor the fruitful river in the eye,	
	Nor the dejected 'havior of the visage,	15
	Together with all forms, moods, shows of grief,	
	That can denote me truly: these, indeed, seem;	
	For they are actions that a man might play;	
	But I have that within which passeth show;	
	These but the trappings and the suits of woe.	20
KING.	'Tis sweet and commendable in your nature, Hamlet,	
	To give these mourning duties to your father;	
	But, you must know, your father lost a father;	
	That father lost, lost his; and the survivor bound,	
	In filial obligation, for some term	25

To do obsequious sorrow: but to persevere
In obstinate condolement is a course
Of impious stubbornness; 'tis unmanly grief;
It shows a will most incorrect to heaven;
A heart unfortified, a mind impatient;   30
An understanding simple and unschool'd;
For what we know must be, and is as common
As any the most vulgar thing to sense,
Why should we, in our peevish opposition,
Take it to heart? Fie! 'tis a fault to heaven,   35
A fault against the dead, a fault to nature,
To reason most absurd; whose common theme
Is death of fathers, and who still hath cried,
From the first corse till he that died to-day,
'This must be so.' We pray you, throw to earth   40
This unprevailing woe; and think of us
As of a father: for let the world take note
You are the most immediate to our throne;
And with no less nobility of love
Than that which dearest father bears his son   45
Do I impart toward you. For your intent
In going back to school in Wittenberg,
It is most retrograde to our desire:
And we beseech you bend you to remain
Here in the cheer and comfort of our eye,   50
Our chiefest courtier, cousin, and our son.

406. The Queen's lines can best be summarized as
    I. You have mourned long enough, Hamlet.
   II. Put on a cheery disposition for your people, Hamlet.
  III. Your mourning is unwarranted, Hamlet.

(A) I only
(B) II only
(C) II and III only
(D) III only
(E) I, II, and III only

407. In the sentences "Seems, madam! Nay, it is; I know not seems" (10), Hamlet intends to express

(A) horror at the Queen's indifference
(B) confusion over the Queen's question
(C) shock and offense at the Queen's assumption
(D) his denial
(E) his accord with the Queen

408. The repetition four times of the word "nor" (12–15) is a device called

(A) redundancy
(B) affect
(C) litote
(D) asyndeton
(E) anaphora

409. The clause in lines 11–17 ("'Tis not alone . . . denote me truly") is

(A) periodic
(B) an example of asyndeton
(C) a run-on
(D) loose
(E) monotonous

410. The tone of lines 19–20 ("But I have . . . woe") is

(A) spiritual
(B) sanctimonious
(C) pitiful
(D) informative
(E) ironic

411. In line 20, "These" refers to

(A) fake mourners
(B) his tears
(C) his clothes
(D) "all forms, moods, shows of grief" (16)
(E) "that within which passeth show" (19)

412. Hamlet uses the word "suits" (20) as a double entendre because

(A) he intends to use two meanings of the word
(B) he wants to demonstrate his intellectual wit
(C) he intends to emphasize the word's sexual connotations
(D) he wants to use two meanings of the word for comic effect
(E) he wants to make a point by misusing the word

413. To make his point, the King condemns Hamlet for all of the following *except*

(A) lacking fortitude
(B) lacking masculinity
(C) being sinful
(D) being unintelligent
(E) being reasonable

414. The syntactical structure of the King's sentence in lines 40–46

    (A) is simple

    (B) is direct

    (C) is indirect

    (D) serves to emphasize his genuine love for Hamlet

    (E) allows for clarity

415. From the passage, we can infer that the King is Hamlet's

    I. new father

   II. confidant

 III. successor

    (A) I only

    (B) I and II only

    (C) II and III only

    (D) III only

    (E) I and III only

Passage 4. William Shakespeare, *Macbeth*

MACBETH.   Go bid thy mistress, when my drink is ready,
                 She strike upon the bell. Get thee to bed. *Exit Servant.*
                 Is this a dagger which I see before me,
                 The handle toward my hand? Come, let me clutch thee.
                 I have thee not, and yet I see thee still.   5
                 Art thou not, fatal vision, sensible
                 To feeling as to sight? Or art thou but
                 A dagger of the mind, a false creation,
                 Proceeding from the heat-oppressed brain?
                 I see thee yet, in form as palpable   10
                 As this which now I draw.
                 Thou marshal'st me the way that I was going,
                 And such an instrument I was to use.
                 Mine eyes are made the fools o' the other senses,
                 Or else worth all the rest. I see thee still,   15

                 And on thy blade and dudgeon gouts of blood,
                 Which was not so before. There's no such thing:
                 It is the bloody business which informs
                 Thus to mine eyes. Now o'er the one half-world
                 Nature seems dead, and wicked dreams abuse   20
                 The curtain'd sleep; witchcraft celebrates
                 Pale Hecate's offerings; and wither'd Murther,
                 Alarum'd by his sentinel, the wolf,
                 Whose howl's his watch, thus with his stealthy pace,
                 With Tarquin's ravishing strides, towards his design   25

> Moves like a ghost. Thou sure and firm-set earth,
> Hear not my steps, which way they walk, for fear
> Thy very stones prate of my whereabout,
> And take the present horror from the time,
> Which now suits with it. Whiles I threat, he lives;   30
> Words to the heat of deeds too cold breath gives.
> *A bell rings.*
> I go, and it is done; the bell invites me.
> Hear it not, Duncan, for it is a knell
> That summons thee to heaven, or to hell. *Exit.*   35

416. In the sentence in line 4 ("Come, let me clutch thee") and in lines 26–31 ("Thou sure and firm-set earth . . . breath gives"), the words "thee" and "thou" are examples of

(A) Old English
(B) dialogue
(C) apostrophe
(D) invocation
(E) hallucinations

417. The sentence in line 5 ("I have thee not, and yet I see thee still") is an example of

(A) dialogue
(B) metaphor
(C) allegory
(D) oxymoron
(E) antithesis

418. The syntactical arrangement of the phrase "Thou marshal'st me" (12)

(A) positions Macbeth as the subject
(B) positions Macbeth as the object
(C) positions Macbeth as the subject and the object
(D) characterizes Macbeth as purposeful
(E) is grammatically incorrect

419. The sentence in lines 14–15 ("Mine eyes . . . the rest") can best be paraphrased as

(A) My eyes better be the most reliable of all my senses.
(B) If my eyes are more foolish than my other senses, then I have no need for them.
(C) My eyes are useless in this situation.
(D) My senses deceive me.
(E) My sight is either less acute or sharper than my other senses.

420. The references to Hecate (22) and Tarquin (25) are examples of

(A) apostrophe
(B) anachronism
(C) hallucination
(D) illusion
(E) allusion

421. In the phrase "Moves like a ghost" (26), "moves" refers to

(A) Hecate
(B) a ghost
(C) Tarquin
(D) the wolf
(E) Murther

422. The reference to Tarquin serves to

  I. present a vivid image of the heinous act of murder
 II. emphasize Macbeth's cruelty
III. change the subject

(A) I only
(B) II only
(C) III only
(D) I and II only
(E) II and III only

423. The passage is written in which style?

(A) epic
(B) Gothic
(C) free verse
(D) ballad
(E) blank verse

424. The rhyme of "knell" and "hell" indicates that the last two lines of the passage

(A) are the least important
(B) make up a heroic couplet
(C) make up a couplet
(D) contain the spondee
(E) are the most important

425. We can infer from the passage that lines 3–35

(A) constitute a soliloquy
(B) constitute an aside
(C) are imagined
(D) are addressed to Macbeth's enemy
(E) are said in Macbeth's sleep

Passage 5. Sophocles, *Oedipus the King*

OEDIPUS. My children, fruit of Cadmus' ancient tree
New springing, wherefore thus with bended knee
Press ye upon us, laden all with wreaths
And suppliant branches? And the city breathes
Heavy with incense, heavy with dim prayer   5
And shrieks to affright the Slayer.—Children, care
For this so moves me, I have scorned withal
Message or writing: seeing 'tis I ye call,
'Tis I am come, world-honoured Oedipus.

Old Man, do thou declare—the rest have thus   10
Their champion—in what mood stand ye so still,
In dread or sure hope? Know ye not, my will
Is yours for aid 'gainst all? Stern were indeed
The heart that felt not for so dire a need.

PRIEST. O Oedipus, who holdest in thy hand   15
My city, thou canst see what ages stand
At these thine altars; some whose little wing
Scarce flieth yet, and some with long living
O'erburdened; priests, as I of Zeus am priest,
And chosen youths: and wailing hath not ceased   20
Of thousands in the market-place, and by
Athena's two-fold temples and the dry
Ash of Ismênus' portent-breathing shore.

For all our ship, thou see'st, is weak and sore
Shaken with storms, and no more lighteneth   25
Her head above the waves whose trough is death.
She wasteth in the fruitless buds of earth,
In parchèd herds and travail without birth
Of dying women: yea, and midst of it
A burning and a loathly god hath lit   30
Sudden, and sweeps our land, this Plague of power;
Till Cadmus' house grows empty, hour by hour,
And Hell's house rich with steam of tears and blood.

O King, not God indeed nor peer to God
We deem thee, that we kneel before thine hearth,   35
Children and old men, praying; but of earth
A thing consummate by thy star confessed
Thou walkest and by converse with the blest;
Who came to Thebes so swift, and swept away
The Sphinx's song, the tribute of dismay,   40
That all were bowed beneath, and made us free.
A stranger, thou, naught knowing more than we,
Nor taught of any man, but by God's breath
Filled, thou didst raise our life. So the world saith;
So we say.   45

Therefore now, O Lord and Chief,
We come to thee again; we lay our grief
On thy head, if thou find us not some aid.

426. The passage begins with

(A) a command
(B) a rhetorical question
(C) an invocation
(D) an inquiry
(E) an aside

427. In context, the word "us" (3) refers to

(A) Oedipus
(B) Cadmus
(C) the tree
(D) the land's people
(E) the rulers

428. In lines 4–6, personification is used to present the city as

(A) macabre
(B) diabolical
(C) desperate
(D) alive
(E) pious

429. The words "prayer" (5) and "care" (6) are examples of what type of rhyme?

(A) slant rhyme
(B) exact rhyme
(C) feminine rhyme
(D) masculine rhyme
(E) internal rhyme

430. In line 7, "this" refers to

(A) breathing, shrieks, and prayer
(B) care
(C) the Slayer
(D) the city
(E) children

431. The rhyme scheme of Oedipus's lines is

(A) *abacdcefeghg*
(B) *abc def ghi jkl*
(C) *aaba aaba aaba aaba*
(D) *aabbccddeeffgg*
(E) *ababcdcdefefgg*

432. According to the priest, the city has been harmed by

(A) a shipwreck
(B) a disease
(C) dying women
(D) deadly waves
(E) a ruthless scourge

433. The metaphor in lines 24–26

(A) compares a ship to the city and the sea to death
(B) emphasizes the futility of fighting back
(C) highlights the people's resilience
(D) contrasts life and death
(E) compares a ship to the priest; the sea to the gods

434. In lines 7–9 and lines 12–14, Oedipus characterizes himself as
  I. venerable
  II. concerned primarily for his citizens
  III. preoccupied

(A) I only
(B) II only
(C) I and II only
(D) I and III only
(E) I, II, and III

435. In context, "we" (35) refers to

(A) the priest and his friends
(B) all the citizens
(C) all men
(D) the young and senescent
(E) the clergy

436. In lines 34–45, the people view Oedipus as all of the following *except*

(A) a monarch
(B) a liberator
(C) God's peer
(D) their intellectual equal
(E) capable

437. The priest's tone differs from Oedipus's in that it is

(A) grave as opposed to compassionate
(B) bitter as opposed to reverent
(C) Gothic as opposed to patriotic
(D) elegiac as opposed to remorseful
(E) laudatory as opposed to naive

438. We can infer from the passage that Cadmus (1, 32) is

(A) the founder of Thebes
(B) the current king
(C) their God
(D) the city's name
(E) an ancient tree

CHAPTER 8

Expository Prose

Passage 1. Charles Darwin, *On the Origin of Species*

I have now recapitulated the chief facts and considerations which have thoroughly convinced me that species have been modified, during a long course of descent, by the preservation or the natural selection of many successive slight favourable variations. I cannot believe that a false theory would explain, as it seems to me that the theory of natural selection does explain, the several large classes of facts above specified. I see no good reason why the views given in this volume should shock the religious feelings of any one. A celebrated author and divine has written to me that "he has gradually learnt to see that it is just as noble a conception of the Deity to believe that He created a few original forms capable of self-development into other and needful forms, as to believe that He required a fresh act of creation to supply the voids caused by the action of His laws."

Why, it may be asked, have all the most eminent living naturalists and geologists rejected this view of the mutability of species? It cannot be asserted that organic beings in a state of nature are subject to no variation; it cannot be proved that the amount of variation in the course of long ages is a limited quantity; no clear distinction has been, or can be, drawn between species and well-marked varieties. It cannot be maintained that species when intercrossed are invariably sterile, and varieties invariably fertile; or that sterility is a special endowment and sign of creation. The belief that species were immutable productions was almost unavoidable as long as the history of the world was thought to be of short duration; and now that we have acquired some idea of the lapse of time, we are too apt to assume, without proof, that the geological record is so perfect that it would have afforded us plain evidence of the mutation of species, if they had undergone mutation.

But the chief cause of our natural unwillingness to admit that one species has given birth to other and distinct species, is that we are always slow in admitting any great change of which we do not see the intermediate steps. The difficulty is the same as that felt by so many geologists, when Lyell first insisted that long lines of inland cliffs had been formed, and great valleys excavated, by the slow action of the coast-waves. The mind cannot possibly grasp the full meaning of the term of a hundred million years; it cannot add up and perceive the full effects of many slight variations, accumulated during an almost infinite number of generations.

439. The first sentence in this passage does which of the following?

(A) summarize points made in previous paragraphs
(B) prove the writer's main point
(C) provide evidence of previous points
(D) emphasize the writer's authority
(E) provide a counterargument to opponents' points

440. The "false theory" (4) most likely refers to

(A) the immutability of species
(B) divine intervention
(C) spontaneous generation
(D) natural selection
(E) gaps in the geological record

441. It can be inferred from the question starting in line 12 that the writer

(A) discounts the opinion of geologists
(B) agrees with the opinion of geologists
(C) does not respect the opinion of geologists
(D) understands the opinion of geologists
(E) defers to the opinion of geologists

442. The word "mutability" (13) most nearly means

(A) variability
(B) silence
(C) persistence
(D) life
(E) death

443. The sentences in lines 13–19 contain

(A) epistrophe
(B) anastrophe
(C) chiasmus
(D) anaphora
(E) antithesis

444. The tone of the passage is

(A) polemical
(B) droll
(C) exasperated
(D) caustic
(E) expository

445. The sentence in lines 19–23 ("The belief that species . . . mutation.") refers to

(A) eschatology
(B) cosmogony
(C) teleology
(D) hermeneutics
(E) apostasy

446. According to the passage, natural selection is all of the following *except*

(A) theoretical
(B) falsifiable
(C) ephemeral
(D) religious
(E) coherent

447. In lines 29–30, the writer asserts that the "mind cannot possibly grasp the full meaning of the term of a hundred million years," in large part because
  I. few variations are slight
 II. changes accumulate over generations
III. human perception is limited

(A) I only
(B) III only
(C) I and III only
(D) I, II, and III
(E) II and III only

448. The writer assumes that the reader's attitude toward the theory of natural selection is one of

(A) incredulity
(B) accordance
(C) refraction
(D) skepticism
(E) intolerance

449. The ideas in this passage most closely resemble the ideas of

(A) theism
(B) atheism
(C) deism
(D) agnosticism
(E) animism

Passage 2. Nathaniel Hawthorne, "The Custom House" (Preface to *The Scarlet Letter*)

But the sentiment has likewise its moral quality. The figure of that first ancestor, invested by family tradition with a dim and dusky grandeur, was present to my
boyish imagination as far back as I can remember. It still haunts me, and induces a
sort of home-feeling with the past, which I scarcely claim in reference to the present
phase of the town. I seem to have a stronger claim to a residence here on account of 5
this grave, bearded, sable-cloaked, and steeple-crowned progenitor—who came so
early, with his Bible and his sword, and trode the unworn street with such a stately
port, and made so large a figure, as a man of war and peace—a stronger claim than
for myself, whose name is seldom heard and my face hardly known. He was a soldier, legislator, judge; he was a ruler in the Church; he had all the Puritanic traits, 10
both good and evil. He was likewise a bitter persecutor; as witness the Quakers,
who have remembered him in their histories, and relate an incident of his hard
severity towards a woman of their sect, which will last longer, it is to be feared, than
any record of his better deeds, although these were many. His son, too, inherited
the persecuting spirit, and made himself so conspicuous in the martyrdom of the 15
witches, that their blood may fairly be said to have left a stain upon him. So deep a
stain, indeed, that his dry old bones, in the Charter-street burial-ground, must still
retain it, if they have not crumbled utterly to dust! I know not whether these ancestors of mine bethought themselves to repent, and ask pardon of Heaven for their
cruelties; or whether they are now groaning under the heavy consequences of them 20
in another state of being. At all events, I, the present writer, as their representative,
hereby take shame upon myself for their sakes, and pray that any curse incurred
by them—as I have heard, and as the dreary and unprosperous condition of the
race, for many a long year back, would argue to exist—may be now and henceforth
removed. 25
Doubtless, however, either of these stern and black-browed Puritans would
have thought it quite a sufficient retribution for his sins that, after so long a lapse
of years, the old trunk of the family tree, with so much venerable moss upon it,
should have borne, as its topmost bough, an idler like myself. No aim that I have
ever cherished would they recognise as laudable; no success of mine—if my life, 30
beyond its domestic scope, had ever been brightened by success—would they deem
otherwise than worthless, if not positively disgraceful. "What is he?" murmurs one
grey shadow of my forefathers to the other. "A writer of story books! What kind
of business in life—what mode of glorifying God, or being serviceable to mankind
in his day and generation—may that be? Why, the degenerate fellow might as well 35
have been a fiddler!" Such are the compliments bandied between my great grand-
sires and myself, across the gulf of time! And yet, let them scorn me as they will,
strong traits of their nature have intertwined themselves with mine.

450. The phrase "a dim and dusky grandeur" in line 2

    (A) implies that the speaker does not revere his ancestor

    (B) implies that the speaker's ancestor was a man of enviable eminence

    (C) foreshadows the passage's dark mood

    (D) suggests that the nature of the ancestor's grandeur is murky

    (E) contains assonance

451. The speaker's ancestor is all of the following *except*

    (A) his family's progenitor and serious

    (B) formidable and a father

    (C) a philistine and religious leader

    (D) a Puritan and sinful

    (E) a fighter and remembered

452. In context, the word "port" in line 8 most likely means

    (A) head

    (B) costume

    (C) harbor

    (D) horse

    (E) demeanor

453. The sentence in lines 9–11 ("He was a . . . evil") contains an example of which device?

    (A) polysyndeton

    (B) asyndeton

    (C) onomatopoeia

    (D) antithesis

    (E) chiasmus

454. The two sentences from lines 11–16 ("He was likewise . . . upon him") are

    I. loose sentences

    II. simple sentences

    III. balanced sentences

    (A) I only

    (B) II only

    (C) I and II only

    (D) II and III only

    (E) I, II, and III

455. The relationship between the Quakers and the speaker's ancestor is characterized as similar to the relationship between

(A) two conspirators
(B) a husband and wife
(C) a disciplinarian and a student
(D) a president and a constituent
(E) a governess and her master

456. The phrase "either of these" (26) refers to

(A) the sins of the speaker's ancestors
(B) the progenitor and his offspring
(C) "their cruelties" (20)
(D) the speaker's repentance and shame
(E) the curses "incurred" (23) by the speaker's ancestors

457. The words "idler" (29) and "compliments" (36) are meant to be read

(A) gravely
(B) sarcastically
(C) jubilantly
(D) emphatically
(E) sympathetically

458. The dialogue in lines 32–36 serves primarily to

(A) exaggerate the perspective of those speaking
(B) validate the speaker
(C) distract the reader from the passage's theme
(D) liven up a dull paragraph
(E) create round instead of flat characters

459. The purpose of the passage as a whole is

(A) to lambaste Puritan ideals
(B) to explicate the nature of the speaker's origins
(C) to present the speaker as superior to his ancestors
(D) to lay the foundation for an autobiographical bildungsroman
(E) to portray the speaker as an innocent victim of a bad legacy

Passage 3. Thomas Hobbes, *Leviathan*

Whatsoever therefore is consequent to a time of Warre, where every man is Enemy to every man; the same is consequent to the time, wherein men live without other security, than what their own strength, and their own invention shall furnish them withall. In such condition, there is no place for Industry; because the fruit thereof is uncertain; and consequently no Culture of the Earth; no Navigation, nor use of the commodities that may be imported by Sea; no commodious Building; no Instruments of moving, and removing such things as require much force; no Knowledge of the face of the Earth; no account of Time; no Arts; no Letters; no Society; and which is worst of all, continuall feare, and danger of violent death; And the life of man, solitary, poore, nasty, brutish, and short.

It may seem strange to some man, that has not well weighed these things; that Nature should thus dissociate, and render men apt to invade, and destroy one another: and he may therefore, not trusting to this Inference, made from the Passions, desire perhaps to have the same confirmed by Experience. Let him therefore consider with himselfe, when taking a journey, he armes himselfe, and seeks to go well accompanied; when going to sleep, he locks his dores; when even in his house he locks his chests; and this when he knows there bee Lawes, and publike Officers, armed, to revenge all injuries shall bee done him; what opinion he has of his fellow subjects, when he rides armed; of his fellow Citizens, when he locks his dores; and of his children, and servants, when he locks his chests. Does he not there as much accuse mankind by his actions, as I do by my words? But neither of us accuse mans nature in it. The Desires, and other Passions of man, are in themselves no Sin. No more are the Actions, that proceed from those Passions, till they know a Law that forbids them; which till Lawes be made they cannot know: nor can any Law be made, till they have agreed upon the Person that shall make it.

It may peradventure be thought, there was never such a time, nor condition of warre as this; and I believe it was never generally so, over all the world: but there are many places, where they live so now. For the savage people in many places of America, except the government of small Families, the concord whereof dependeth on naturall lust, have no government at all; and live at this day in that brutish manner, as I said before. Howsoever, it may be perceived what manner of life there would be, where there were no common Power to feare; by the manner of life, which men that have formerly lived under a peacefull government, use to degenerate into, in a civill Warre.

But though there had never been any time, wherein particular men were in a condition of warre one against another; yet in all times, Kings, and persons of Soveraigne authority, because of their Independency, are in continuall jealousies, and in the state and posture of Gladiators; having their weapons pointing, and their eyes fixed on one another; that is, their Forts, Garrisons, and Guns upon the Frontiers of their Kingdomes; and continuall Spyes upon their neighbours; which is a posture of War. But because they uphold thereby, the Industry of their Subjects; there does not follow from it, that misery, which accompanies the Liberty of particular men.

460. The fourth sentence of the passage ("In such condition . . . and short") contains the following syntactical devices.

  I. ellipsis
  II. polysyndeton
  III. epanalepsis

(A) I only
(B) III only
(C) I and II only
(D) II and III only
(E) I, II, and III

461. The purpose of the first sentence of the second and third paragraphs is to

(A) anticipate counterarguments
(B) demonstrate the writer's skepticism
(C) undermine authoritative accounts
(D) cast doubt on the argument
(E) establish an ironic tone

462. The writer asserts in lines 22–23 that harmful "Desires" and "Actions" of man are "no Sin" under the following conditions *except*

(A) ignorance of the law
(B) a state of anarchy
(C) the installment of a legitimate sovereign
(D) the outbreak of civil war
(E) forgiveness from the church

463. The "some man" in line 11 refers to

(A) a known opponent
(B) the writer's alter ego
(C) the implied audience
(D) a hypothetical objector
(E) the writer's patron

464. The purpose of the passage as a whole is to

(A) elaborate on the natural state of man
(B) legitimize absolute monarchy
(C) cast aspersions on native savages
(D) question his readers' integrity
(E) argue against the value of liberty

465. According to the passage, "a time of Warre" (1) and "the Liberty of particular men" (42–43) share all of the following features *except*

(A) an atmosphere of fear
(B) a motivation for industry
(C) an absence of knowledge
(D) constraints on movement
(E) a general state of misery

466. In the last paragraph of the passage, the writer asserts that "Kings" are "in the state and posture of Gladiators," and their "Subjects" are not

(A) independent
(B) under scrutiny
(C) protected
(D) neighborly
(E) productive

467. In the third paragraph of the passage, the writer mentions Native Americans as an example of

(A) the effectiveness of small government
(B) people in an unnatural state
(C) the ideal of the noble savage
(D) people lacking an authority
(E) a society that values family

468. It can be inferred from the passage that the writer's attitude toward humanity is most likely one of

(A) aplomb
(B) cynicism
(C) contempt
(D) idealism
(E) realism

469. The argument that the writer makes in lines 11–17 is best described as

(A) apodictic
(B) empirical
(C) a priori
(D) deductive
(E) ad absurdum

Passage 4. Friedrich Nietzsche, *Beyond Good and Evil* (Translated by Helen Zimmern)

Inasmuch as in all ages, as long as mankind has existed, there have also been human herds (family alliances, communities, tribes, peoples, states, churches), and always a great number who obey in proportion to the small number who command—in view, therefore, of the fact that obedience has been most practiced and fostered among mankind hitherto, one may reasonably suppose that, generally   5
speaking, the need thereof is now innate in every one, as a kind of FORMAL CONSCIENCE which gives the command "Thou shalt unconditionally do something, unconditionally refrain from something," in short, "Thou shalt." This need tries to satisfy itself and to fill its form with a content, according to its strength, impatience, and eagerness, it at once seizes as an omnivorous appetite with little   10
selection, and accepts whatever is shouted into its ear by all sorts of commanders—parents, teachers, laws, class prejudices, or public opinion. The extraordinary limitation of human development, the hesitation, protractedness, frequent retrogression, and turning thereof, is attributable to the fact that the herd-instinct of obedience is transmitted best, and at the cost of the art of command. If one imag-   15
ine this instinct increasing to its greatest extent, commanders and independent individuals will finally be lacking altogether, or they will suffer inwardly from a bad conscience, and will have to impose a deception on themselves in the first place in order to be able to command just as if they also were only obeying. This condition of things actually exists in Europe at present—I call it the moral hypocrisy of the   20
commanding class. They know no other way of protecting themselves from their bad conscience than by playing the role of executors of older and higher orders (of predecessors, of the constitution, of justice, of the law, or of God himself), or they even justify themselves by maxims from the current opinions of the herd, as "first servants of their people," or "instruments of the public weal." On the other   25
hand, the gregarious European man nowadays assumes an air as if he were the only kind of man that is allowable, he glorifies his qualities, such as public spirit, kindness, deference, industry, temperance, modesty, indulgence, sympathy, by virtue of which he is gentle, endurable, and useful to the herd, as the peculiarly human virtues. In cases, however, where it is believed that the leader and bell-wether cannot   30
be dispensed with, attempt after attempt is made nowadays to replace commanders by the summing together of clever gregarious men. All representative constitutions, for example, are of this origin. In spite of all, what a blessing, what a deliverance from a weight becoming unendurable, is the appearance of an absolute ruler for these gregarious Europeans—of this fact the effect of the appearance of Napoleon   35
was the last great proof. The history of the influence of Napoleon is almost the history of the higher happiness to which the entire century has attained in its worthiest individuals and periods.

470. The purpose of the passage as a whole is to

    (A) justify the desire to disobey

    (B) expose the hypocrisy of leaders

    (C) celebrate the power of the collective

    (D) criticize group behavior

    (E) make a case against democracy

471. According to the passage, the most salient feature of "formal conscience" (6–7) is that

    (A) its ends justify its means

    (B) specific precepts are inconsequential

    (C) its appetite is easily sated

    (D) it contributes to sound rule

    (E) prohibitions are often unconditional

472. The simile in line 10 compares

    (A) a need to an appetite

    (B) a desire to satisfy to a desire to devour

    (C) a follower to an omnivore

    (D) content to an appetite

    (E) a need to a content

473. The expression "moral hypocrisy of the commanding class" (20–21) refers to

    (A) leaders calling leadership a form of service

    (B) the illegitimacy of the divine right of kings

    (C) rulers taking advantage of their position

    (D) the notion that might makes right

    (E) herds lacking the need for guidance

474. The tone of the passage is

    (A) ironic

    (B) apologetic

    (C) apodictic

    (D) polemical

    (E) expository

475. The writer mentions Napoleon (35) as an example of

    (A) herd instinct gone awry

    (B) command that requires no justification

    (C) the corrupting influence of power

    (D) a check on democratic institutions

    (E) the difficulty in serving the common good

476. The first sentence in this passage can be described as

    I. loose
   II. compound
  III. complex

(A) I only
(B) II only
(C) I and II only
(D) III only
(E) II and III only

477. According to the passage, human herds are all of the following *except*

(A) reprehensible
(B) obdurate
(C) autocratic
(D) self-perpetuating
(E) transitory

478. The writer's attitude toward democratic institutions can best be described as

(A) apathetic
(B) idealistic
(C) sanguine
(D) skeptical
(E) sarcastic

479. According to the writer, the inevitable consequence of the "herd-instinct of obedience" (14–15) is

(A) a dearth of strong leadership
(B) constitutional representation
(C) tyrants such as Napoleon
(D) persistent class conflict
(E) cohesive public opinion

480. According to the writer, European leaders "[protect] themselves from their bad conscience" (21–22) by all of the following *except*

(A) celebrating self-effacing virtues
(B) embracing public opinion
(C) vilifying rulers such as Napoleon
(D) encouraging collegiality
(E) respecting consensus

Passage 5. Oscar Wilde, Preface to *The Picture of Dorian Gray*

The artist is the creator of beautiful things. To reveal art and conceal the artist is art's aim. The critic is he who can translate into another manner or a new material his impression of beautiful things.

The highest as the lowest form of criticism is a mode of autobiography. Those who find ugly meanings in beautiful things are corrupt without being charming. This is a fault.

Those who find beautiful meanings in beautiful things are the cultivated. For these there is hope. They are the elect to whom beautiful things mean only beauty.

There is no such thing as a moral or an immoral book. Books are well written, or badly written. That is all.

The nineteenth century dislike of realism is the rage of Caliban[3] seeing his own face in a glass.

The nineteenth century dislike of romanticism is the rage of Caliban not seeing his own face in a glass. The moral life of man forms part of the subject-matter of the artist, but the morality of art consists in the perfect use of an imperfect medium. No artist desires to prove anything. Even things that are true can be proved. No artist has ethical sympathies. An ethical sympathy in an artist is an unpardonable mannerism of style. No artist is ever morbid. The artist can express everything. Thought and language are to the artist instruments of an art. Vice and virtue are to the artist materials for an art. From the point of view of form, the type of all the arts is the art of the musician. From the point of view of feeling, the actor's craft is the type. All art is at once surface and symbol. Those who go beneath the surface do so at their peril. Those who read the symbol do so at their peril. It is the spectator, and not life, that art really mirrors. Diversity of opinion about a work of art shows that the work is new, complex, and vital. When critics disagree, the artist is in accord with himself. We can forgive a man for making a useful thing as long as he does not admire it. The only excuse for making a useless thing is that one admires it intensely.

All art is quite useless.

481. The ideas expressed in the passage most closely resemble the ideas of

- (A) realism
- (B) naturalism
- (C) existentialism
- (D) aestheticism
- (E) romanticism

---

3. The ugly, beastlike slave of Prospero in Shakespeare's *The Tempest*

482. In lines 1–2, "To reveal art and conceal the artist is art's aim" means that

 (A) artists should hide from public view
 (B) art is about morality, not fame
 (C) artists who seek to advance their reputation are not true artists
 (D) the artist's purpose is irrelevant when we view art
 (E) the artist is a part of the art he creates

483. The "fault" the writer is referring to in line 6 is

 (A) artists reflecting their own lives in their art
 (B) people not appreciating the social value art has
 (C) people denigrating art altogether
 (D) people reading base meaning into art
 (E) people lacking charm

484. According to the passage, the difference between the corrupt and the cultivated is

 (A) optimism in the latter
 (B) cynicism in the latter
 (C) skepticism in the latter
 (D) sympathy in the former
 (E) banality in the former

485. The passage is developed through

 (A) epigrams and parallel structure
 (B) criticisms and blandishments
 (C) allegories and metaphors
 (D) questions and pontification
 (E) expostulations and hypotheses

486. The allusion to Caliban in lines 11–14 serves primarily to

 (A) describe nineteenth-century British citizens as slaves
 (B) explain that people of the nineteenth century have paradoxical expectations of art
 (C) express the author's distaste for romanticism
 (D) assert the moral rectitude of all art
 (E) question the legitimacy of romanticism

487. "The symbol" in line 23 refers to
    I. the didactic message underlying the art
    II. the morality imposed on the art by the artist
    III. the most important part of the art

    (A) I only
    (B) III only
    (C) II and III only
    (D) I, II, and III
    (E) I and II only

488. The tone of the passage is

    (A) vindictive
    (B) maudlin
    (C) sarcastic
    (D) vituperative
    (E) serious

489. According to the passage, art is none of the following *except*

    (A) theoretical
    (B) didactic
    (C) purposeful
    (D) ethical
    (E) reflective

490. The final sentence of the passage does which of the following?

    (A) employs varied syntax
    (B) states the passage's central theme
    (C) belies points made in previous paragraphs
    (D) indicates the author's frustration
    (E) offers a sarcastic conclusion

Passage 6. Zhuangzi

His cook was cutting up an ox for the ruler Wen Hui. Whenever he applied his hand, leaned forward with his shoulder, planted his foot, and employed the pressure of his knee, in the audible ripping off of the skin, and slicing operation of the knife, the sounds were all in regular cadence. Movements and sounds proceeded as in the dance of "the Mulberry Forest" and the blended notes of "the King Shou."   5

The ruler said, "Ah! Admirable! That your art should have become so perfect!"

(Having finished his operation), the cook laid down his knife, and replied to the remark, "What your servant loves is the method of the Dao, something in advance of any art. When I first began to cut up an ox, I saw nothing but the

(entire) carcass. After three years I ceased to see it as a whole. Now I deal with it 10
in a spirit-like manner, and do not look at it with my eyes. The use of my senses
is discarded, and my spirit acts as it wills. Observing the natural lines, (my knife)
slips through the great crevices and slides through the great cavities, taking advantage of the facilities thus presented. My art avoids the ligaments and tendons, and
much more the great bones. A good cook changes his knife every year; (it may have 15
been injured) in cutting—an ordinary cook changes his every month—(it may
have been) broken. Now my knife has been in use for nineteen years; it has cut up
several thousand oxen, and yet its edge is as sharp as if it had newly come from the
whetstone. There are the interstices of the joints, and the edge of the knife has no
(appreciable) thickness; when that which is so thin enters where the interstice is, 20
how easily it moves along! The blade has more than room enough. Nevertheless,
whenever I come to a complicated joint, and see that there will be some difficulty,
I proceed attentively and with caution, not allowing my eyes to wander from the
place, and moving my hand slowly. Then by a very slight movement of the knife,
the part is quickly separated, and drops like (a clod of) earth to the ground. Then 25
standing up with the knife in my hand, I look all round, and in a leisurely manner,
with an air of satisfaction, wipe it clean, and put it in its sheath."

The ruler Wen Hui said, "Excellent! I have heard the words of my cook, and
learned from them the nourishment of (our) life."

491. The second sentence in the first paragraph of this passage is
    I. compound
    II. periodic
    III. complex

(A) II only
(B) I and III only
(C) II and III only
(D) III only
(E) I, II, and III

492. The writer's attitude toward butchering meat is best described as one of

(A) caution
(B) indifference
(C) pragmatism
(D) avidity
(E) aversion

493. According to the cook, the "method of the Dao" is "in advance of any art" (8–9) because

(A) it is entirely mechanistic
(B) it transcends conscious effort
(C) it is in harmony with the ruler
(D) it requires only simple technology
(E) it makes work easier

494. The tone of the passage is

(A) insincere
(B) congenial
(C) ironic
(D) punctilious
(E) ecstatic

495. In line 17, the cook claims that he has had no need to replace his knife for nineteen years because

(A) the knife has magical properties
(B) he sharpens the knife regularly
(C) he leaves the carcasses intact
(D) his method prevents blunting
(E) he always proceeds slowly

496. Based on the ruler Wen Hui's responses to the cook (6), we can infer that Wen Hui is

(A) intrusive
(B) tolerant
(C) enlightened
(D) sarcastic
(E) permissive

497. According to the passage, the cook's method is none of the following *except*

(A) ambidextrous
(B) overwrought
(C) maladroit
(D) fractious
(E) meticulous

498. The cook's attitude toward the ox is best described as

(A) irreverent
(B) venerating
(C) religious
(D) animistic
(E) courteous

499. When the cook says that he deals with the ox carcass "in a spirit-like manner" (11), the reader can infer that

(A) he goes into a hypnotic trance
(B) his mastery is unconscious
(C) he is in a state of heightened sensitivity
(D) he defers to the ruler's wishes
(E) he relies entirely on instinct

500. The passage makes use of all of the following *except*

(A) allegory
(B) simile
(C) chiasmus
(D) hyperbole
(E) exclamation

ANSWERS

Chapter 1: British Poetry

Passage 1. Thomas Hardy, "Nobody Comes"

1. (A) The first stanza contains PERSONIFICATION (B) in lines 1 and 3 ("Tree-leaves labour" and "the crawl of night"). The words "land" and "hand" create a MASCULINE RHYME (C). The telegraph wire is compared to a spectral lyre in a SIMILE (6) (D). ENJAMBMENT (E) occurs at the ends of several lines (2, 4, 5, and 6). While there is an example of CONSONANCE in the *second* stanza ("m*u*te" and "g*a*te"), there are no examples of it in the first stanza.

2. (C) The telegraph wire is compared to a spectral lyre that is "Swept by a spectral hand." A lyre is a stringed musical instrument from ancient Greece.

3. (D) The word "spectral" refers to something that is ghostly, haunting, supernatural, etc. The first stanza introduces the setting of a dark, quiet town. No people are mentioned in this stanza, suggesting the town is desolate, emptied, at least at night. In this quiet emptiness, only the hum of the telegraph wire is heard, which sounds like a stringed instrument (a lyre) being played from afar. We can imagine that this lyre is ghostly (spectral) because it has an eerie, "intoning," beckoning sound from an unknown, unseen source, the only sound in a quiet town.

4. (E) A telegraph is a sign of industrialization and technological advancement. Its purpose was to increase communication among people across vast distances, to essentially make people feel more closely connected. The IRONY here in the poem, however, is that the telegraph "intones" to the town "from the darkening land," but there are no people in this stanza other than the isolated speaker, no other sounds, no light, and very little life. It is ironic that the technological symbol of human connectedness is calling to travelers that are not even there. It is compared to a spectral lyre because the sound is ghostly, shadowy, and out of place. The SIMILE does not offer optimism (A) because the lyre is "spectral" and ghost-like. The telegraph is not humanized (B) because the verb "intones" is something that an object (like a telegraph or a lyre) can do. The simile does not create a soothing TONE because the lyre is spectral and haunting, making the telegraph's "intoning" similarly haunting. If anything, the simile adds to the ominous mood (C). Perhaps technology (the telegraph) appears otherworldly (D) because of the comparison to something "spectral," but that does not seem to be the purpose of the simile when it is looked at in context.

5. (D) The RHYME SCHEME can be determined by observing the pattern of END RHYMES in each stanza. The first line (*a*) does not rhyme with any other line. The second line (*b*) rhymes with the third (*b*), and so on.

6. (C) Both lines set a scene by describing an object in the setting and its action ("Tree-leaves labour . . ." and "A car comes up . . .")—II. Both lines contain a steady METER that can be measured. Line 1 contains three and a half feet of TROCHEES, and line 4 contains four feet of IAMBS (IAMBIC TETRAMETER)—III. I is incorrect because even though the first line of the first stanza ends in a word that is never rhymed ("down"), the first line of the second stanza ends in a word that is rhymed ("glare" rhymes with "air" and "there").

7. (A) The ALLITERATION of "*wh*angs" and "*w*orld" cannot emphasize the speaker's unity with the "world" because the speaker is being characterized as alone ("I stand alone again") after the car "whangs along in a world of its own." The car and the speaker are a part of separate worlds, each alone (C). There is no ALLITERATION in the previous line (D). (E) is incorrect because there is always a purpose! The alliteration actually does match the content of line 11 because the car is in a world of its own and the similar "w" sound of "whangs" and "world" coincides with this cohesion and unity the car feels with its world (B). The alliteration does contrast with the CONSONANCE created by the words "m*u*te" and "g*a*te" in line 13. It makes sense that since the speaker and the car are both alone in their own separate worlds, each would have a contrasting sound device: the car has alliteration, and the speaker's line has consonance.

8. (D) Symbolically, the air is blacker because now that the car and its lights have left, the speaker finds himself "again alone" (13). His isolation is emphasized again in the final line, "And nobody pulls up there." The absence of the car's lights makes the air literally darker (C) while simultaneously the speaker feels darker and more alone (A, B). The air has become darker from the car's "whang[ing]" because cars are industrial, mechanized, and dirty. The gas and fumes from its engine have made the air "blacker" (E). There are no details to suggest that the air is darker because time has passed and it is later at night now (D).

9. (A) The title of the poem contributes to the self-pitying TONE. The poem focuses on the isolation the speaker feels. He mentions the light, the night, the telegraph wire, the spectral lyre, the car, the car's lights, and the black air all to emphasize how dark and isolated his setting is and how alone he feels. The JUXTAPOSITION of "I stand again alone" and "nobody pulls up there" conveys self-pity because he appears to remain focused on his loneliness. While parts of the poem sound eerie (B), the overall tone is one of self-pity.

10. (D) Of the options given, the only THEME that applies to the poem is (D) because the speaker feels alone in a town where technology is clearly widespread (the telegraph wire, the car, flashing lights), especially technology that is supposed to connect people (the telegraph wire). The isolation JUXTAPOSED with the technology supports the theme that the benefits of modern technology are dubious (in doubt). The speaker does not characterize his loneliness as a result of the natural environment (A); it is the car, for example, that "has nothing to do with [the speaker]" (10). (C) is not a complete or specific answer because a theme is expressed as a statement/message. (E) is supported by the poem but (D) is more specific than (E) and thus a better answer.

Passage 2. Robert Herrick, "To the Virgins, to Make Much of Time"

11. (A) The title already reveals that the speaker will be addressing virgins, so the address of "ye" in the opening line must refer to the title's virgins. (C) is a close answer, but the speaker is not referring to all women, only the ones who are virgins. Also, it is unclear whether he is talking only to female virgins; he could be addressing all virgins, both male and female.

12. (B) Time is PERSONIFIED as something that can fly. It is also capitalized, suggesting it has a name, like a person.

13. (D) The rose-buds can be a METAPHOR for numerous things—the female virgins who, like rose-buds, are not yet plucked, not yet matured, full of potential and promise. The rose-buds are a metaphor for the ephemeral (temporary) nature of the young women's beauty and youth (D), which, like the rose-buds, is full of beauty only for a short time before natural aging and decay. The speaker explains that though the flower "smiles to-day/ To-morrow will be dying" (3–4). (E) is true, but less specific than (D).

14. (E) The sun is the "lamp of heaven" (5), making it electric—I. It is referred to as "he" (6, 8) —II, and as a runner (7) because the speaker is indicating that the sun speeds through its task like a runner in a race, stressing the fleeting nature of time—III.

15. (A) The speaker first says that the "first" age is best (youth), but "being spent," meaning as time goes on, that first age is now "worse." He then says that "worst/ Times" will follow the former, the "worse" age that was just mentioned.

16. (D) The poem urges young virgins to take advantage of their youth and beauty and seize the day, to fall in love and marry, not to procrastinate until they are older and have lost their youthful beauty and energy. The speaker says that if they do not "use [their] time . . . [they] may for ever tarry," meaning they may forever delay.

17. (B) ALLITERATION occurs in line 3, with the words "*th*is . . . *th*at" and "*s*ame . . . *s*miles."

18. (E) The words "b*est*" and "fir*st*" create CONSONANCE because the ending consonants are the same but the vowels that precede them are different.

19. (B) ENJAMBMENT occurs only in line 11, which ends in the middle of a sentence or clause without any pause or punctuation. The phrase "worst/ Times" is broken abruptly by the end of the line. All the other lines end with a pause indicated by punctuation.

20. (E) A major THEME of the poem is for virgins to seize the day ("carpe diem" in Latin). The young virgins will be "rose-buds" for only a short time. The days will go by as fast as a runner runs a race. These virgins are encouraged to "use their time" and not "tarry." While (C) is a similar answer to (E), the speaker of the poem is not focusing only on sexual inter-course; rather, he is telling his addressees to "marry" while they are young. (A) and (B) do describe points made in the poem, but they are not themes of the poem because they do not encompass the poem's entire meaning.

21. (C) The words at the ends of each stanza's first and third lines rhyme, as do the words at the ends of each stanza's second and fourth lines. This RHYME SCHEME is written as *abab cdcd efef ghgh*.

22. (E) The poem is a LYRIC because it has a RHYME SCHEME (though a rhyme scheme is not absolutely necessary for a poem to be a lyric) and expresses the speaker's personal feelings. The poem is not an ELIZABETHAN SONNET (C) because it does not end in a COUPLET and it exceeds 14 lines. Though the speaker does encourage his addressees to seize the day, he does not admonish (severely warn) (D).

23. (A) The speaker exhorts (urges) the young virgins to seize the day and marry while they are still young and beautiful, but he is not desperate (C) to get them to follow his advice. He is also not vehement (heated, intense) (B) or pushy (D) about it; rather, he lightly encourages them in an almost jovial (lighthearted) TONE, far from maudlin (foolishly sentimental, tearfully and weakly emotional).

Passage 3. Gerard Manley Hopkins, "God's Grandeur"

24. (A) ALLITERATION is evident in the first three lines with the words "*g*randeur of *G*od," "*sh*ining from *sh*ook," "*g*athers to a *g*reatness," and "*o*oze *o*f *o*il." There are only two SIMILES (E): "*like* shining from shook foil," "*like* the ooze of oil." There is only one example of ANAPHORA (C) with the repetition of the word "It" at the start of lines 2–3. There is no *abundance* of ASYNDETON (B) or METAPHORS (D).

25. (A) The abundance of ALLITERATION (see question 24) in the first three lines creates a mellifluous (soothing) sound to mirror the praise the speaker feels for "God's grandeur." This sound changes, however, in the fourth line, where alliteration is mixed with ASSONANCE and different vowel sounds to create a cacophonous (harsh) and confusing sound, making the clause actually difficult to pronounce: "Why do men then now not reck his rod?" Alliteration is evident in "*n*ow *n*ot" and "*r*eck his *r*od." This otherwise soothing alliteration is then marred (spoiled) by the combination of ASSONANCE ("m*e*n th*e*n") and the similar but different sounds of "reck and rod."

26. (D) The words in line 4 are difficult to pronounce (see question 25) perhaps because they are describing behavior of men that the speaker finds hard to understand. After all, he *is* asking a question: How is it that men do not acknowledge God's magnificent power? He finds their obliviousness confusing and unwarranted considering how magnificent he thinks God is.

27. (B) The speaker repeats that "Generations have trod, have trod, have trod." The following clauses further clarify his point: "And all is seared with trade; bleared and smeared with toil;/ And wears man's smudge and shares man's smell: the soil/ Is bare now, nor can foot feel, being shod." The speaker is describing the numbing and tiring effects that modern industry, production, and technology have had on man. The "soil," which represents the natural world created by "God's grandeur," is "bare" because of man's folly. The repetition of "trod" emphasizes the repeated mistakes of man. Humanity persists habitually (inexorably) in its mistaken path rather than progressing. (E) does not work because the dissatisfaction is the speaker's and not necessarily man's. (D) does not work because the speaker's repetition indicates that man continues to prefer industry over God; this is not temporary. (A) and (E) are opposites of the answer.

28. (E) Line 6 contains INTERNAL RHYME (A) ("bleared" rhymes with "seared" *within* the same line), CONSONANCE (B) ("s*ea*red with tr*ade*"), ASSONANCE (C) ("bl*ea*red, sm*ea*red"), and ALLITERATION (D) ("*s*eared . . . *s*meared," "*t*rade . . . *t*oil"). There is no ENJAMBMENT at the end of the line because there is a punctuation mark indicating a pause.

29. (C) The ALLITERATION in the first three lines (see questions 24 and 25) helps emphasize the speaker's admiration for and wonder at "God's grandeur." He is in awe (C) of God's "shining," oozing, great, flaming grandeur. This TONE changes, however, in the next four lines, when the speaker focuses more on man's obliviousness to God's magnificence (see question 27). Man has toiled, "trod," worked in industry, and neglected God and the natural world. As a result, he is "seared with trade; bleared, smeared with toil." He smells and cannot feel his feet on the soil. The tone here is dirgelike (like a funeral song) because there is a steady rhythm to the descriptions of man's persistent and injurious mistakes. (E) is a close answer, but the tone of lines 4–8 is not as much pitiful as it is reproachful (disapproving, critical) and dirgelike.

30. (C) A sonnet always contains 14 lines, but a SHAKESPEAREAN SONNET will end in a COUPLET (the last two lines will have END RHYMES). This sonnet does not end in a couplet, so it must be a PETRARCHAN SONNET. Further evidence is that there is a clear change from the first eight lines to the last six lines (the separation of the OCTAVE from the SESTET).

31. (E) ALLITERATION is abundant in the opening three lines (see questions 24 and 25) and dominates again in the final six lines. In the opening lines, the alliteration coincides with the grand DICTION emphasizing God's brilliance, so when the alliteration returns in the final six lines, so does the description of God's grandeur, his eminence—I. The speaker also conveys confidence—II—in the resilience of nature: "for all this [man's desecration of the soil and earth], nature is never spent." The speaker is assured that God still loves and protects the world "with warm breast and with ah! bright wings." In these lines, the alliteration also coincides with the portrayal of God as in harmony with the world. God loves and protects the world, so "nature is never spent." The mellifluous (soothing) sounds of the alliteration in "with warm breast and with ah! bright wings" complement the harmonious partnership between God and the world—III.

32. (D) The first eight lines express dismay at why men do not acknowledge God's power when he, in fact, is so grand. The speaker actually asks the same question in line 4 after detailing how magnificent God is. The final six lines, however, provide some reassurance that even though men have spoiled and damaged the earth with their trodding and smearing and toil, God will still protect and care for the world. "[N]ature is never spent . . . Because the Holy Ghost over the bent/ World broods with warm breast and with ah! bright wings." In these last six lines God is not portrayed as any less powerful than in the opening lines (B); the focus is not on man; it is still on God (C); the speaker is not skeptical; he is in awe of God's generosity and love (E). The sound created by the ASSONANCE and ALLITERATION is similar to the sounds in the opening three lines (A) (see questions 24 and 25).

33. (D) The overall THEME of the poem can be expressed most closely by the phrase "nature is never spent" because this phrase encompasses the OCTAVE, in which the speaker explains that man has "spent" nature (he has toiled and emptied the soil, smeared and bleared with his modern industry and production), and the SESTET, which explains that even though man has done this, nature is never actually ruined because God protects the world. The other answer choices encompass only parts of the poem's message and not the entire theme.

34. (E) The RHYME SCHEME of the poem is *abbaabba cdcdcd* (the first line rhymes with the fourth, the second with the third, etc.). The first eight lines are the OCTAVE of the PETRARCHAN SONNET, and the last six lines comprise the SESTET.

35. (B) By the close of the poem, the speaker is very reassured that God will protect and nurture the world despite the damage man has done with his modern industry and production. The SESTET begins with "And for all this [damage caused by man] nature is never spent." We can still see "the dearest freshness" deep down inside things "[b]ecause the Holy Ghost [God] over the bent/ World broods with warm breast and with ah! bright wings." The exclamation point especially shows the speaker's unrestrained awe at God's munificence (generosity). There are no details to suggest that the hope expressed by the speaker is qualified or restrained (D). He is in wonder at God's power, but bemusement implies that he is perplexed by it (A). He is definitely not criticizing God (E).

Passage 4. Andrew Marvell, "To His Coy Mistress"

36. (E) The first stanza contains a steady METER of IAMBIC TETRAMETER (A). Line 11 contains a METAPHOR (B) comparing the pace of the speaker's love to the pace of vegetable growth. The last word of a line in the first stanza rhymes with the last word of the following line, creating END RHYMES (C). The speaker uses HYPERBOLE (D) when he uses numbers and descriptions that are clearly exaggerations and not realistic ("ten years before the Flood," "Vaster than empires," "hundred years," "thirty thousand"). There are no examples of ANAPHORA in this stanza (E) because we do not see a repeating sequence of words at the beginning of sequential clauses.

37. (C) Line 6 contains INTERNAL RHYME because two words within the same line rhyme with each other: "I" and "by."

38. (E) Throughout the first stanza, the speaker is making the point to his addressee that if there were plenty of time, it would be fine to delay their physical expressions of love. Since they do not, however, actually have a "hundred years" (13), he implies that the addressee's modesty ("coyness," hesitance, prudery, shyness) is a crime.

39. (A) The speaker flatters his addressee when he imagines her by the Indian Ganges finding rubies. He places her in (what is to them) an exotic locale with connotations of rare riches while he is back in England (the Humber). He intends to impress her with his intelligence by making biblical references to the Flood and the Jews. The point of this stanza is to compliment her and make her think she would be worth waiting an eternity for if they had an eternity.

40. (E) The speaker compares his love to vegetables, which grow slowly over time. He uses this METAPHOR to emphasize how strong and interminable (never ending) his love is for his addressee.

41. (B) The IMAGERY in the first stanza is libidinous (lustful, passionate) because the speaker wants his addressee to be convinced of his enduring passion for her—I. He conjures up images of endless infatuation and amorousness. He will adore her forehead, eyes, and breasts for hundreds and thousands of years. The second stanza, however, contains much more morbid, dark imagery—I—as the speaker now tries to emphasize the fact that they do not have thousands of years to wait; rather, they will soon face death ("marble vault") and faded beauty (25, 26). Their love will turn to "dust" (29) and "ashes" (30)—I. The sounds change from the first to the second stanza. In the first stanza, ALLITERATION abounds ("We would . . . which way," "long love's," "Thine thy," "thirty thousand," "should show," "love . . . lower"), creating an alluring, soothing sound—III—to match the speaker's intent—to flatter and cajole (convince). The alliteration is abandoned in the second stanza, however, to emphasize the chilling—III—sounds of the morbid descriptions. The TONE does change from the first to the second stanza, but it is not quite a change from arrogance to desperation—II—because the tone of the second stanza is not quite desperate—II; rather, the speaker here seems more chilling—III—sincere, and grave (serious, intense) than in the first stanza because the IMAGERY is of death and decay.

42. (C) The phrase essentially means "time flies." In fact, the speaker characterizes time as actually flying in his "winged" chariot. The phrase is also in the context of emphasizing how little time we have on earth, how we must "seize the day" and indulge in our desires. (E) is a valid answer, but (C) is a more specific paraphrase because it includes the detail of the "winged chariot."

43. (A) The words "lie" and "eternity" and "try" and "virginity" are meant to rhyme (as the rest of the poem contains END RHYMES that are exact), but they do not rhyme perfectly. They create SLANT RHYMES because they almost rhyme.

44. (B) By comparing his addressee's youth to "morning dew" on her skin, the speaker is emphasizing the ephemeral (short-lived) nature of her youth and beauty. Morning dew exists only in the morning; it does not even last more than a few hours. Dew also connotes freshness, virginity, and purity, which also describe the youthful and modest addressee. The speaker is trying to make the point that, as dew lasts only a short time, so will the addressee's youth.

45. (E) The speaker uses a SIMILE to compare himself and his addressee to "am'rous birds of prey" who, instead of being eaten by time's "slow-chapp'd power" (chaps are jaws—time slowly eats away at our youth), will devour time itself by seizing the day and indulging in their amorous desires.

46. (B) ALLITERATION permeates (fills) the last two lines: "*Th*us, *th*ough . . . *s*un/ *s*tand *s*till . . . *w*e *w*ill." The speaker uses alliteration in the first stanza, abandons it in the second, and returns to it with a flourish at the end, indicating that the alliteration helps communicate his passion and energy since the first and final stanzas focus on consummating desire.

47. (D) The speaker's argument follows the structure of a SYLLOGISM, which is a logical argument consisting of a major premise ("If . . . " in stanza one), minor premise ("But . . . " in stanza two) and conclusion ("Now therefore . . . " in stanza three). The speaker's argument does not culminate in a logical, airtight conclusion, but he mimics the syllogism's style, perhaps to create the appearance and sound of a foolproof argument.

48. (A) The poem is most similar to a lyric poem because a LYRIC poem always contains a speaker who is expressing personal feelings and emotions. ELEGIES, ODES, and SONNETS can all be described as lyric. Lyric poems often contain a RHYME SCHEME and measured beat, but they do not have to. The poem is not an ODE because it is not devoted solely to extolling (praising) one thing/person in particular (C). It does not follow the structure of any forms of the SONNET (D).

Passage 5. William Wordsworth, "The world is too much with us"

49. (E) ALLITERATION is evident in the words "*w*orld" and "*w*ith," "*s*oon" and "*s*pending," "*w*e" and "*w*aste." There are no examples of HYPERBOLE (C), CONSONANCE (D), COUPLETS, or INTERNAL RHYME (B).

50. (B) The RHYME SCHEME of the poem is *abbaabba cdcdcd* (the first line rhymes with the fourth, the second with the third, etc.). The first eight lines are the OCTAVE of the PETRARCHAN SONNET, and the last six lines comprise the SESTET.

51. (D) The phrase "sordid boon" is an OXYMORON because two opposite words are placed together for effect. "Sordid" describes something that is disgusting and distasteful, and a "boon" is a benefit, a gift, an advantage. The surrounding context explains that the speaker deplores (disapproves of) people's negligence of the natural world and preference for modern technological and industrial advancement. He claims, "we lay waste our powers:/ Little we see in nature that is ours" (2–3). He is saying that people do not bother to appreciate what they can see in nature because they prefer to look at their own man-made structures. They ignore the "Sea that bares her bosom to the moon;/ The Winds that will be howling at all hours" (5–6). We have lost the "tune" (8), the ability to harmonize with nature.

52. (C) The title and first line of the poem contain its THEME: "The world is too much with us." Here, "world" does not necessarily mean the environment of the earth and sky because we know that the speaker appreciates the "Sea" and the "Winds." He capitalizes them to emphasize their importance. So, if the "world" is "too much with us" in a negative way, then "world" must refer to the industrialized, modernized, technologically advanced world in which we are "Getting and spending . . . lay[ing] waste our powers" (2). The speaker characterizes this advancement as negative and destructive; it is a "sordid boon!" (4), a benefit/advantage that is dirty, grubby, foul.

53. (D) There is a clear change in TONE from the OCTAVE (first eight lines) to the SESTET (last six lines). The octave consists of the speaker's woeful complaints about how people have "given [their] hearts away" for "Getting and spending," and the sestet replaces the woeful complaints with a wish for an escape from the forlorn (sad) feelings expressed in the octave (D). Generally, in a PETRARCHAN SONNET, the octave sets up a problem that the sestet solves. This sestet does not necessarily solve the problem because the speaker merely wishes for a solution that he does not intend to execute: "I'd rather be/ A Pagan . . . so might I. . . ." His tone can be read in the sestet as a little bitter and sarcastic (D) because he realizes this wish is in vain, that he will not actually become a Pagan. When he says "I'd rather be/ A Pagan suckled in a creed outworn," he characterizes the Pagan in a negative way. The Pagan is "suckled" like a baby by an outdated belief system, and this is what the speaker prefers to following his peers' example. There is some anger in this "solution," this preference for something distasteful over something even more distasteful. In this regard, the tone is perhaps more cynical than it is optimistic (E).

54. (A) The METAPHOR compares the Pagan religion ("a creed outworn") to a mother's breast and a Pagan to a baby being "suckled" by that creed/breast. The comparison implies that the outworn creed of Paganism provides comfort and solace to a Pagan, the way a mother's breast offers the same consolation to a baby. Essentially, the speaker compares himself to a baby who is in dire need of such consolation. He would even go so far as to be a Pagan to get it.

55. (D) The poem has 14 lines, making it likely that it is a type of sonnet because a sonnet always contains 14 lines, but an ELIZABETHAN SONNET (also known as a Shakespearean or English sonnet) will end in a COUPLET, the last two lines having END RHYMES. This sonnet does not end in a couplet, so it cannot be an Elizabethan sonnet (E). This sonnet cannot be a SPENSERIAN SONNET (C) either because it does not contain a RHYME SCHEME of *abab bcbc cdcd ee*. The poem is a PETRARCHAN SONNET because it has 14 lines and there is a clear change from the OCTAVE to the SESTET (see question 53).

56. (C) When the speaker says he would "rather" be a Pagan so that he might glimpse Greek gods like Proteus and Triton, which would make him "less forlorn [sad]," he is expressing his fantasy. This is not an actual solution (E), even though it is found in the sonnet's SESTET, where a solution is generally expected to be. He says only that he would rather be a Pagan, not that he will actually convert to this "creed outworn" (10). While his references to the Greek gods do demonstrate his knowledge (D), that is not the primary intention of the ALLUSIONS. (B) is also a vague and incomplete answer. He does not express sanguinity (optimism) (A) through these allusions because he is not actually going to become a Pagan and escape his forlorn state.

57. (B) PERSONIFICATION is evident in line 5, when the "Sea" is personified as baring "her bosoms to the moon." Line 6 does not contain personification because the winds are merely described as "howling," which is what animals (the dog family in particular) are known to do, not people. This is not a human characteristic (C). In lines 13–14, the characterization of Proteus and Triton does not qualify as personification because these are Greek gods who would be expected to have human attributes like blowing a "wreathed horn."

58. (D) The THEME of the poem as a whole is best described by (D) because the speaker first reproaches (criticizes, scolds) people ("we") for allowing the "world" to be "too much with us," meaning we are consumed by "Getting and spending" and we "lay waste our powers. . . ." The "world" that is "too much with us" is the material world that we have created with our technological and industrial "powers," which the speaker describes as a "waste" because these powers only encourage "Getting and spending" and distract us from noticing Nature's "Sea" and "Winds." This is tragic because "we have given our hearts away." The "boon" (benefit) of progress is "sordid" (dirty, grimy) because we have paid a big price for such advancement. (A), while expressed in the poem, is an incomplete description of the overall theme. (B) is a slightly crude and extreme way to describe the theme. (C) and (E) are expressed in the SESTET (last six lines) but do not describe the poem as a whole.

Passage 6. William Butler Yeats, "That the Night Come"

59. (B) The stresses of the syllables in lines 1-5 follow the pattern of the IAMB, which is one unstressed syllable followed by a stressed syllable ("She *lived*" and "in *storm*"). One iamb is measured by the unit of a FOOT. There are three iambs in each of these lines, so the measurement of the line's meter is called TRIMETER (three FEET).

60. (A) The beat of line 12 is noticeably different from that of all the other lines in the poem. It consists of four stressed syllables made up of four one-syllable words: "*That the* *night come.*" This is unlike every other line in the poem in that all the other lines consist of varying stresses. Line 10 (B) is TROCHAIC and IAMBIC, lines 7 and 8—C, D—are iambic, and line 6 (E) is trochaic. Line 12, however, does not contain any combinations of unstressed and stressed syllables; it is SPONDAIC.

61. (C) Line 1 contains ALLITERATION with the words "storm" and "strife," and line 2 contains alliteration with the words "soul" and "such." The word "death" is PERSONIFIED as being "proud" in line 3. There are no examples of ASSONANCE or CONSONANCE (B), rhyme (A), ASYNDETON (D), or CHIASMUS (E).

62. (C) The subject to which "it" refers is the word "soul." When written as prose, the sentence reads, "Her soul had such desire for what proud death may bring that it could not endure the common good of life." The subject of the sentence is "soul," not "death" (A). It is the soul that cannot endure the common good of life, not the desire (D). "Her" and "She"—B, E—are not even in the sentence.

63. (C) The king is mentioned in a SIMILE that compares the woman's behavior to that of a king who cannot wait for his wedding night so he can consummate his marriage with his queen. The purpose of such a comparison is to further illustrate the emotional state of the woman, who is the main subject of the poem. The simile shows that the woman is anticipating her death as eagerly as the king anticipates his wedding night. While their emotion of eagerness is similar, the actual things they each desire are different: death and marriage. They are different in gender (A) and possibly class status since he is a king (E), but these differences are not emphasized in the poem. Their way of living (B) is the same (she lives like a king who . . .), as are their attitudes (D) toward life (they do not live for the moment but for the future).

64. (E) In anticipation of his wedding night, the king "packed his marriage day" with lots of energetic activity and fanfare to distract him from waiting for the day to pass. He "bundle[s] time away" by filling the day with "trumpet and kettledrum . . . the outrageous cannon" and "banneret and pennon." From the context, we can infer that "banneret and pennon" are, like the other items that "pack" the day, some kind of celebratory fanfare (flourish, display, elaboration) for distraction.

65. (B) Lines 8–10 contain the conjunction "and" three times to connect a list of items; this device is called POLYSYNDETON.

66. (E) A pair of syllables is called a *foot*. When a foot consists of two stressed syllables, the foot is described as SPONDAIC. The words "*night come*" consist of two stressed syllables and no unstressed syllables.

67. (E) The SIMILE compares the woman's anticipation for "what proud death may bring" (3) to a king who is so excited for his wedding night that he needs to fill his day with loud and exciting distractions to "bundle time away" (11). The comparison makes the woman's excitement for death more vivid by providing an image of an eager and impatient king.

68. (A) The poem's sound changes noticeably in line 9; the iambic feet change to a mixture of TROCHEES (a pattern of stressed/unstressed syllables), IAMBS (unstressed/stressed), and a SPONDEE (two stresses) in lines 9–12. These lines break the regular pattern of beats established in the first eight lines, paralleling the king's and the woman's frenetic (frantic) activity and impatience for their desired goals (marriage and death, respectively). The irregular beats mirror the king's and the woman's inability to endure the normal pace of time, the regular rhythmic beat of the first eight lines.

69. (A) Both the woman and the king are so impatient for something (death and the wedding night, respectively) to come that it seems remote and far away. Their impatience is emphasized by the SPONDAIC beat of the final line, "*That the night come*" (see question 66). The king longs for night because at night the king will be able to consummate his marriage, which is compared to the woman reaching "proud death" (3). Night, however, is not characterized as a panacea (a cure-all)—II—because night itself is not what will solve their problems; rather, night is only the setting in which the king (and the woman, through comparison) will obtain the cure to his impatience. Night is also not interminable (never ending)—III; it is only the day that is presented as interminable because the king (and woman, through comparison) must "bundle time away" (11) to pass time until night comes.

70. (A) The poem is about a woman who "had such desire/ For what proud death may bring" (3–4) that she lived like a king who filled his day with fanfare and distractions to pass time until his wedding night came. The woman's anticipation for "proud death" is equated with the king's impatience for his wedding night. Wasting time (C) implies that they indifferently idle away the hours, which is not what the king is doing when he packs his day with "[t]rumpet and kettledrum" (9). They definitely do not ignore time (E) because they see it is something that needs to be "bundle[d]" and spent; they see it as an obstacle in the way of attaining their desired goals.

Chapter 2: American Poetry

Passage 1. Anne Bradstreet, "The Author to Her Book"

71. (E) While the poem does contain RHYME (A), IAMBIC PENTAMETER (B), SIMILE (C), and METAPHOR (D), it is developed mainly through the device known as the CONCEIT (E). The entire poem hinges on the EXTENDED METAPHOR (a conceit) that compares the speaker's book to her child. The metaphor does not exist only in one line or one segment of the poem; rather, it continues throughout all 23 lines and drives the poem forward. All the other devices occur within the conceit.

72. (C) Throughout the entire poem, the speaker addresses her own book as "Thou," "thee," and "thy" in the EXTENDED METAPHOR that compares her book to her child. Since the book is not actually a person who can respond to her, this address to her book is an example of a device called APOSTROPHE.

73. (D) While the entire poem is developed mainly through an EXTENDED METAPHOR (see question 71), the metaphor is also an IMPLIED METAPHOR (not an EXPLICIT METAPHOR) because the speaker does not say, "My book *is* my offspring," which makes an explicit connection between one thing and another for purposes of comparison. In an implied metaphor, the comparison between two things is less explicit. The poem does not outwardly tell us that the book is a child; the connection is more subtle. The poem's metaphor hints at the book being a child by calling it an "ill-formed offspring of my feeble brain" (1). ENJAMBMENT (A) is evident at the end of line 11, where there is no punctuation to indicate a pause and the sentence is broken abruptly by the end of the line. The poem is full of IMAGERY (B) that allows us to see the book/child dressed raggedly (5) and being scrubbed by the mother/ writer (13–15). Since the book is being compared to a child in the extended, implied meta- phor, it is also being PERSONIFIED (C) and spoken to as if it were a person. EXACT RHYME (E) occurs at the end of most lines ("true" and "view," for example).

74. (D) The words "trudge" and "judge" are examples of MASCULINE RHYME because they consist only of one stressed syllable that is rhymed. FEMININE RHYME (B) consists of a stressed and unstressed pair of syllables that are rhymed. The poem does not contain any examples of feminine rhyme. SLANT RHYME (C) means the words almost rhyme, like "roam" and "come" (19–20). The poem does consist of IAMBS (E), but "trudge" and "judge" are not iambs.

75. (E) The speaker implies that her book is unfinished/unedited (inchoate) (A) when she describes it as "snatched" from her side when it was only dressed in "rags" (5). The book was disseminated prematurely (B) because it was "snatched . . . by friends, less wise than true,/ Who [the book] abroad exposed to public view" (3–4). She goes on to describe the numer- ous "errors" (6) in the book that make it fallible (C) and how she tried and tried to "amend" its "blemishes" by rubbing, washing, and stretching it. Regardless of all these attempts, though, "more defects [she] saw" (13), making the book irreparable (D). There are no details that imply the content of the book is polemical (controversially argumentative) (E).

76. (B) The "friends" are the ones who "snatched" the book and exposed [it] to public view." The next verb is "Made" in line 5, which refers to the same subject performing the previous actions of snatching and exposing: the friends.

77. (C) The speaker's TONE is self-deprecating (undervaluing oneself) because she has little confidence in her unedited and unrevised writing. She is mortified that her book would be "exposed to public view . . . in rags" (4–5). She is concerned that "all may judge" (6) her for a piece of writing she does not have confidence in. She admits that even with revi- sion (rubbing, washing, and stretching), the "more defects [she] saw" (13) and the revision itself "still made a flaw" (14). Even though she does compare the book to her offspring, her tone is not nurturing (B) because she speaks about the book/child with harsh diction like "rambling brat" (8), "unfit for light" (9), and "irksome" (10). She is also more concerned about what others will think of her because of her sloppy book/child; she is not as concerned for the actual book/child. The subject of the poem is the author and her relationship with and attitude toward her book, and she is not vengeful (D), acerbic (bitter) (E), or mourn- ful (A) toward it because she tries to improve it. Also, the poem is composed of HEROIC COUPLETS (see question 78), making the tone less severe and harsh, so while the speaker is disappointed in her work, she can make fun of herself (self-deprecate) and not get angry.

78. (D) The poem is composed of HEROIC COUPLETS, a series of two lines written in IAMBIC PENTAMETER—I— with END RHYME, III. Each line contains nearly five (*penta*meter) IAMBS (a pair of unstressed and stressed syllables), such as "Thou *ill*-formed *off*spring *of* my *fee*ble *brain*/ Who *after birth* did *by* my *side* re*main*" (1–2). Heroic couplets can lighten the tone of a poem because they create an almost childlike, songlike sound. The poem does not con- tain TERZA RIMA (stanzas made up of three lines with an interlocking rhyme scheme) —II.

79. (D) Like a fastidious (careful, picky) artist would view her painting with a critical eye (D), the speaker also views her book as not good enough to be published and read. She rubs, washes, and stretches (13–15) the book in an attempt to lessen the errors, but only creates more. She is embarrassed that her book has been "snatched" from her prematurely and "exposed to public view . . . in rags" (3–5). Though she does use the EXTENDED, IMPLIED METAPHOR (see question 73) of a child to talk about her relationship with her book, the relationship cannot be described as nurturing (B) because she speaks about the book/child with harsh diction like "rambling brat" (8), "unfit for light" (9), and "irksome" (10). Teachers (A), bosses (C), and directors (E) serve in supervisory roles, but the speaker implies, through the metaphor, that she is not merely disappointed in her pupil or subordinate; rather, she sees the flaws in her book as flaws in herself. She takes the criticism more personally than a teacher, boss, or director would. The book, like a child, is a part of her.

80. (A) Though she is disappointed in her unrevised writing, the poem conveys a lot more emotion than mere dislike (B). Through the METAPHOR, the speaker shows how a writer views her work as part of herself, that she has "affection" (11) for it and an innate drive to improve and take care of it, like a mother would a child. Though the poem does suggest a work can always undergo more and more revision and still not be perfect, this is not the overall purpose of the poem (C). The harsh critics are referred to, but they are not the focus of the poem (D). The hardships of motherhood (E) are implied only tangentially through the discussion of the poem's main topic, the artist's relationship with her work.

Passage 2. Emily Dickinson, "Success is counted sweetest"

81. (E) The ALLITERATION of "*s*uccess . . . *s*weetest . . . *s*ucceed . . . *s*orest" and "*n*ever . . . *n*ectar . . . *n*eed" in the first stanza creates a soothing, pleasing, appealing sound, which complements the appealing and pleasing feeling of success. While the alliteration may soothe the reader (A), (E) is a more specific answer. There is no ASSONANCE in the first stanza (C) or CONSONANCE in the second stanza (D). The TONE is not envious (B) (see question 89).

82. (A) The first line consists of three IAMBS and an extra unstressed syllable, "Su*cc*ess is *coun*ted *sweet*est." The fifth line, however, is written in IAMBIC TETRAMETER. "Not *one* of *all* the *pur*ple *host*."

83. (A) Line 5 consists of four even feet of iambs: "Not *one* of *all* the *pur*ple *host*," making it an example of IAMBIC TETRAMETER.

84. (E) Emily Dickinson's poetry is known for its HOMILETIC (inspirational sayings or clichés) style (B). Her poems often contain AXIOMATIC (D) (self-evident) truths that are expressed EPIGRAMMATICALLY (C) (short, terse, concise), like APHORISMS (A) (sayings, maxims). In this poem, the aphoristic axiom is that success is sweetest to those who have gone without it. This is a self-evident truth, a saying that is concise and wise. The axiom/homily/epigram/aphorism is not an example of CHIASMUS (E), a grammatical figure by which the order of words in one of two parallel clauses is inverted in the other.

85. (A) The poem consists of three four-line stanzas with the second and fourth lines rhyming. The RHYME SCHEME is written as *abcb defe ghih*. Though "to-day" (6) and "victory" (8) create a SLANT RHYME, they are still considered rhyming words even if they are not EXACT RHYMES. Many of Emily Dickinson's poems follow this rhyme scheme.

86. (E) The speaker says lines 3–4 ("To comprehend a nectar/ Requires sorest need") to provide an image that supports the AXIOM (self-evident truth) of the first sentence: "Success is counted sweetest/ By those who ne'er succeed" (1–2). In this context, "comprehend" means to truly know something. People who do not attain success *truly know* what success is, just as one must be in need of a nectar to truly know what it is. (B), (C), and (D) are all definitions of the word "comprehend," but in the context of the poem (E) makes the most sense.

87. (B) The words "day" and "victory" are meant to rhyme to fit the RHYME SCHEME of *abcb defe ghih*, in which the second and fourth lines of each stanza rhyme. However, these two words do not make an exact rhyme; they almost rhyme, which makes them an example of SLANT RHYME.

88. (C) The first sentence (1–2) of the poem is an example of an AXIOM, a self-evident truth, a proverb or wise saying. The other two sentences of the poem provide images (the nectar and the winning army) that demonstrate the truth of the axiom. The opening statement is not stated as a hypothesis (A) or a theory (D) that the speaker is proposing (B) for consideration or research; on the contrary, she is posing the statement as a known truth, which she elucidates with images.

89. (D) The speaker opens the poem with an AXIOM, (a wise saying, a self-evident truth), which can also be described as an adage (a wise saying, a proverb). The TONE of the poem is similar to the tone of an adage—it offers a piece of thought-provoking wisdom. (A), (B), and (C) assume that the speaker is lecturing to the reader when she is actually providing her own thought-provoking observation about life. She is not envious of those who have achieved success (E).

90. (D) The poem's main point is communicated in the first two lines, "Success is counted sweetest/ By those who ne'er succeed." The other two sentences offer more images to elucidate the same idea—the nectar is understood only by those who are in *need* of it and the sounds of triumph are clearest to the losing army.

Passage 3. T. S. Eliot, "Morning at the Window"

91. (B) In an IMPLIED METAPHOR, the speaker says, "The brown waves of fog toss up to me . . . " (5). The fog is presented as waves because it rises up from the street below to the speaker's window, from which he is observing the scene. The fog is also presented as a wave because it provides an image of how the fog carries the images of people's faces up to the speaker to see; it is as if the faces are riding the wave of fog.

92. (C) The sentence that contains the word "tear" reads "The brown waves of fog toss up to me/ Twisted faces from the bottom of the street,/ And tear from a passer-by with muddy skirts/ An aimless smile . . . " (5–8). The subject of the sentence is the waves, and they perform two actions: they toss and they tear. The waves tear an aimless smile from a passer-by and toss it up to where the speaker is.

93. (E) The words "*fog . . . faces from*" are an example of ALLITERATION because the same letter and sound is repeated at the start of multiple words in close succession.

94. (C) ASSONANCE occurs when the internal vowel sound of multiple words in close succession is the same, as in "fog" and "toss." In this example, our mouths open vertically to pronounce the sound of the "o," which complements the tall rise upward of the waves and fog being described. None of the other answer choices includes examples of assonance.

95. (A) The speaker is physically removed from the scene he is describing; he is up at his window, and the people are at "the bottom of the street" (6). He observes the people below from afar and describes his subjective impressions of their souls (3), clothes (7), and faces (6, 8). The speaker sees the scene as grubby and sad ("despondent"), which could indicate that he himself is upset (B) and depressed, but it is too extreme to say that he is obsessed (B) with the scene below his window. While there is a moment of optimism in the descriptions ("an aimless smile"), the rest of the descriptions are more gloomy and sad. Since there is that one moment of observing a smile, the speaker is not entirely fatalistic (D) either. He is definitely not apathetic (lazy, indifferent) (E); he vigilantly watches the people below and carefully describes what he observes in vivid detail.

96. (A) To describe the scene below his window, the speaker uses ghostly diction like "rattling" (1), "damp souls" (3), "waves of fog" (5), "twisted faces" (6), "muddy" (7), "aimless" (8), "hovers in the air" (8), and "vanishes" (9). Even though the people do appear to be penurious (poor) (B), the specific word choice clearly creates a ghostly image that communicates the people's poverty and their haunting, deadly, empty auras. Also, even though the people are poor, dirty, and working class, there are no details to suggest the speaker sees them as pathetic (D). Only the "twisted faces" characterize the people as grotesque (E).

97. (D) The speaker is, unlike the people he describes, up at the window—II. Also unlike the people he describes, he is merely observing the people who are "rattling breakfast plates" (1) and "[s]prouting despondently" (4) —III. While we can infer that the speaker is perhaps from a higher class than the working class he watches, there are no actual details to suggest he is wealthier—I.

98. (E) The TONE is developed through the speaker's ghostly DICTION ("rattling," "damp souls," "[s]prouting despondently," "fog," "twisted faces," "aimless smile," "hovers in the air," "vanishes"). The speaker also uses SENSORY IMAGES that allow us to hear the "rattling" of breakfast plates and see the "brown . . . fog" (5). The METAPHOR of the "waves of fog" (5) also communicates the speaker's attitude toward what he is describing—he sees the people below him as ghostlike; their faces rise up to him on the waves of fog and then vanish "along the level of the roofs" (9).

Passage 4. Walt Whitman, "O Captain! My Captain!"

99. (A) The speaker tells his heart to not leave "the little spot" where the Captain lies "cold and dead." In other words, he is telling himself (his heart) never to forget the moment and place of his captain's death. (E) is a close answer, but the command to his heart ("O heart! heart! heart!") indicates that he is telling himself not to forget.

100. (C) The "bells," "flag," "bugle," "wreaths," and crowds in the second segment serve dual purposes in that they describe the celebration the crowd planned to have upon the captain and the ship's victorious return and also happen to describe a funeral, which is appropriate since the victory parade must turn into a funeral upon receipt of the news that the captain has died.

101. (D) The captain has not arrived home safely; he has died on the ship. They both achieved their goals ("the victor ship") (B), ended their heroic journeys ("its voyage closed and done") (A), and are being celebrated (E). They are both METAPHORS; the captain is actually Abraham Lincoln, and the ship is the United States of America (see questions 107 and 108) (C).

102. (A) The third segment of the poem does have a more regulated RHYME SCHEME than the other two segments (see question 103), and since lines 22 and 24 have EXACT RHYMES ("tread" and "dread"), we can assume that lines 21 and 23 are also meant to rhyme. However, the words "bells" and "lies" do not rhyme exactly, making them SLANT RHYMES since they almost rhyme.

103. (B) When examining the rhyming patterns of each segment of the poem, it is clear that only the third stanza has a steady RHYME SCHEME (*aabbcdcd*). The first segment does contain some EXACT RHYMES (1-2 and 5-6), but they are not part of a clear pattern. The second segment contains no exact rhymes and only one or two examples of SLANT RHYME ("bells" and "trills").

104. (A) In the third segment, the speaker no longer refers to the captain in exclamatory sentences like "O Captain!" (1, 9, 13). Instead, his references are calm statements like "My Captain does not answer . . . " (17). While these calm statements may be called internal thoughts (C), this would not be considered a change because the references to the captain in the first two segments can also be considered internal thoughts.

105. (B) The first segment shows the speaker discovering his captain has just died (. . . on the deck my Captain lies,/ Fallen cold and dead"). The second segment shows the speaker is in a state of denial about the death ("It is some dream . . . "). The third segment shows the speaker accepting the reality of his captain's death (" . . . he has no pulse nor will").

106. (A) A REFRAIN is a phrase or group of lines that is repeated at significant moments within a poem, usually at the end of a stanza. Though the refrain of "O Captain! my Captain!" does not appear at the ends of stanzas, it is a significant phrase that is not only the title of the poem but also the opening phrase to two segments.

107. (E) In the poem, the captain and the ship are METAPHORS for a political leader and his citizens who have just achieved an important victory. The actual leader is Abraham Lincoln, the victory is the Civil War, and the country is the United States of America. Though this would be difficult to determine with just the poem at hand, the references to the captain and the ship are definitely metaphors for some kind of leader and group since the DICTION in the poem carries multiple levels of meaning. Since the comparison is not explicit (X is Y), it is an IMPLIED METAPHOR, and since the metaphor runs through the entire poem, it is an EXTENDED METAPHOR.

108. (A) See question 107.

109. (E) The poem commemorates the death of Abraham Lincoln (see question 107), making it an ELEGY, which is a mournful and melancholy poem that laments the dead.

110. (E) The speaker has moved from denial in the second segment ("It is some dream") to acceptance of the captain's death in the final segment. He acknowledges that the captain "does not answer" and "has no pulse or will" (17–18). Once he realizes this, he is in a mournful state as he decides to remain on "the spot [his] Captain dies" (23) while the shores and bells ring and "Exult" (21).

Passage 5. William Carlos Williams, "Contemporania"

111. (D) In the second stanza, the speaker says that he goes back and forth in the garden and the little leaves follow him, talking of the great rain. The "talk" is the subject of this question and they seem to be observing what the "great rain" has done: it has broken branches and upset the farmers because a great rain, perhaps a deluge, would ruin farmers' crops. The TONE indicated by the exclamation point, however, is not anger (C) or dismay (A) because they are merely observing how great (big, grand, powerful) (D) the rain is that it has done all of this.

112. (E) The sentence reads "We are not curst together,/ The leaves and I,/ Framing devices, flower devices/ And other ways of peopling/ The barren country" (13–17). The speaker is saying that the leaves and he are not curst because they "people" the barren land by "flowering" (creating life) and framing (filling, decorating) it. (D) is partially correct, but it does not include the detail of "framing" the barren land.

113. (A) The speaker is in awe of the "great rain" and appreciates it the way a stargazer stares in wonder at the universe. The speaker observes the "Steamy" (2) rain as it falls on his garden. He is very observant of the scene, personifying the leaves and shoots and appreciating how the rain makes the leaves "follow" him (19). An artist is inspired by his muse, but there is no indication that the speaker is inspired by the rain to do something (B). He is more appreciative of how it reminds him that he, the leaves, and the rain are part of the life cycle. While the speaker admires the rain, he is not like an acolyte who follows and worships his idol (C). The speaker is not necessarily in love with and committed to the rain like a husband is to his wife (D). A child enjoys playing with his favorite toy, also not similar to the speaker's attitude toward the rain (E).

114. (D) A poem written in FREE VERSE is a poem that does not adhere to an established poetic structure and format. Free-verse poems are not CLOSED-FORM poems (E); they are OPEN FORM because they are more "free" with their structure, rhythm, and rhyme scheme. This poem, though it contains its own logical structure, does not follow established patterns of rhythm, rhyme, meter, etc., so it is an example of free verse.

115. (B) In the poem, the phrase "I go back and forth" appears in lines 4 and 9, an example of REPETITION (A). The "little leaves" are PERSONIFIED (C) in being described as "talking" (6) and following (5). ASSONANCE (D) is evident in the phrase "great rain," which is also repeated several times. ALLITERATION is evident in the words "little leaves," which is also repeated several times, and "branches broken" (7). There are no instances of CONSONANCE (B).

116. (E) The word "Contemporania" can be understood to mean "the story of our times": "con-" and "temp-" mean "shared time," and with the suffix "-ania" the word means "a modern story/artifact, an artifact of modernity." William Carlos Williams was a leading figure in the poetic movement called IMAGISM (see question 117), which was revolutionary in its use of a few aptly chosen words and phrases to capture a moment in ordinary life. In essence, imagist poems are artifacts of moments in time. While (A) is true, it does not consider the poem's actual content/subject, so (E) is the better answer.

117. (D) William Carlos Williams was a leading figure in the poetic movement called IMAGISM, which was revolutionary in its use of a few aptly chosen words and phrases to capture a moment in ordinary life. Imagists took a snapshot of a seemingly commonplace occurrence in daily life and conveyed the image through poetic DICTION and sound. In essence, their poems are artifacts of moments in time.

118. (E) The "great rain" helps the speaker see how both he and the leaves "are not curst together," how they both "people" the "barren country" by "framing" and "flowering" (13–17). The word "barren" connotes infertility, so the rain reminds the speaker that both he and the plants—III— are fertile, I, and a part of the life cycle—II.

119. (C) Though the last two lines create their own stanza, they do not create a COUPLET because they are not rhymed (D). They definitely cannot be a HEROIC COUPLET (E) because they do not rhyme and they are not written in IAMBIC PENTAMETER (A). An ENVOY is a TERCET (three-line stanza) that ends a SESTINA and contains the THEME, so while the last two lines of this poem do contain a theme (see question 120) (C), they are only two lines and the poem itself is not a sestina.

120. (B) The speaker of the poem notices the "great rain" and observes how it makes the leaves "follow" him. In the fourth stanza, he realizes that both he and the leaves are united and similar in that they "are not curst together" and they "people" the barren country by "framing" and "flowering" it. Observing the rain makes the speaker realize how, like the plants in his garden, he contributes to the magnificent life cycle by procreating and filling/decorating the land. While (C) is definitely communicated in the poem, the purpose of the poem is not just to comment on how powerful the rain itself is, but to reflect on how man and plant are part of the life cycle. (D) does not say what the poem shows about the life cycle. While the farmers do curse the rain because it may ruin their crops, the poem as a whole is not about the harshness (A) or negative effects (E) of nature.

Chapter 3: World Poetry

Passage 1. Kahlil Gibran, "Defeat"

121. (E) The poem as a whole is written as an APOSTROPHE; the speaker addresses defeat as if it were a person who can answer back ("Defeat" is also capitalized as if it were the name of a person), even though it cannot.

122. (E) The repetitive use of the word "And" at the start of many lines in the poem is a device known as ANAPHORA.

123. (D) In the second stanza, the speaker refers to "Defeat" as "my self-knowledge" (4) because it is through "Defeat" that the speaker *knows* he is "young and swift of foot" (5). He has found joy in "being shunned and scorned" (8). "Defeat" is valuable in that it makes the speaker more self-aware.

124. (A) The METAPHOR of the "sword and shield" (9) is meant to emphasize "Defeat's" emboldening powers. The speaker calls defeat his sword and shield and then explains what he has learned from "Defeat"—namely, that success enslaves people and keeps them "leveled down" (12). The context does not indicate that "Defeat" is a sword and shield because it is brave or valiant (E), but rather that the knowledge "Defeat" has given the speaker has emboldened him the way a sword and shield would. It has made him feel strong, powerful, and protected.

125. (C) In the third stanza, the speaker describes different types of success ("enthroning," being "understood," and "grasped") and how they result not in happiness but in enslavement. In other words, success is overrated.

126. (A) The speaker characterizes "Defeat" as distinct (B) ("none but you"), useful (C) ("You are dearer to me than a thousand triumphs . . . ," "In your eyes I have read . . . "), brave (D) ("my deathless courage"), and bold ("my bold companion"). He does not, however, think "Defeat" is second best to success; rather, success is described as overrated in the second stanza (see question 125).

127. (D) The poem's REFRAIN is found in lines 1, 4, 9, 15, and 21 and enhances the poem's ode-like quality because, through the repetition of the same phrase, a lyrical, chorus-like sound is created, which coincides with the style of the ODE. The poem is also ode-like because the speaker addresses and praises "Defeat."

128. (E) The speaker's address to "Defeat" as his "deathless courage" (21) shows that with "Defeat" comes temerity (fearlessness). Even though "Defeat's" courage is "deathless," meaning it is without death, the speaker does not use the phrase to mean that "Defeat" is immortal (D) but rather that "Defeat" provides him with an almost invincible courage.

129. (B) The speaker sees "Defeat" primarily as his mentor in that "Defeat" teaches him ("Through you I know that I am . . . ") about himself and the world. Though "Defeat" is also his "companion" (15), their relationship is not primarily one of friendship (A), which implies an equal balance of give and take. The poem indicates that the speaker learns from and receives guidance from "Defeat" and does not necessarily offer the same in return.

130. (A) The MOOD that is established by the end of the poem is one of confidence: the speaker and "Defeat" will "laugh together" in a storm, "dig graves for all that die within" them, and "stand in the sun with a will" (22–24). These lines indicate that the speaker, with "Defeat" next to him, can face anything with confidence.

Passage 2. Jayadeva, Excerpt from *Gita Govinda*

131. (A) The first verse serves as the poem's OVERTURE, the introductory part or prologue. An introductory speaker (who is not the speaker for the remaining verses) sets up the scene by introducing Radha, her love-interest Krishna, and the maidens who will sing the remaining verses.

132. (A) The APPOSITIVES in the first verse provide EPITHETS for Radha and Krishna. An appositive is a noun or noun phrase that further describes a noun nearby. For example, the appositive after "Beautiful Radha" is "jasmine-bosomed Radha" (1), which is also an EPITHET, any word or phrase applied to a person or thing to describe an actual or attributed quality.

133. (B) The overall MOOD is exultant. As the first verse reveals, Radha waits with her maidens while her lover Krishna is elsewhere, cavorting with other women. Radha may very well be jealous (A), but it is some of her maidens who sing the song that follows. Rather than being admonishing (scolding) (D) , the maidens may be attempting to make excuses for Krishna's unfaithfulness through the song when they repeat at the end of each verse that it is "sad" or "hard" to be "alone" (11, 17). But this is hardly conciliatory (appeasing, soothing) for Radha (E). The maidens describe at great length the fertility and bounty of nature in springtime; the mood is celebratory, even ecstatic. Therefore, the best answer is (B), exultant.

134. (E) The entire verse is one sentence. There are two INDEPENDENT CLAUSES in the sentence: the one that begins "I know how Krishna passes the hours" (12) and the one that begins "He is dancing with the dancers" (16), making the sentence COMPOUND. The sentence also contains several DEPENDENT CLAUSES, making it COMPLEX. It is also LOOSE; the main clause comes at the beginning of the sentence, followed by a series of PARALLEL CONSTRUCTIONS.

135. (C) Each line of the second verse contains seven feet of IAMBS (iambic heptameter). There are seven sets of syllables that follow a pattern of unstressed and stressed, making them iambs.

136. (B) The second verse contains END RHYMES that are all EXACT RHYMES: "gold . . . hold," "tree . . . bee," and "tone . . . alone." The end rhymes of the other verses mentioned each contain an example of SLANT RHYME, two words that almost rhyme, like "one . . . alone" (10–11).

137. (E) The SIMILE in line 25 serves to highlight the commanding powers of spring when the speakers compare the dazzles from the blossoms to "Kama's sceptre, whom all the world obeys." Since everyone obeys Kama's sceptre, the simile makes us see how commanding spring's influence and bounty is, which almost justifies Krishna's infidelity—he has succumbed to spring's influence. The flowers are not compared to a person (D) but to a sceptre.

138. (B) The phrase "pink delicious bowls" (26) is primarily a METAPHOR for the nourishing flower petals that "fill drowsy bees." People eat from bowls, in the way the bees get their nourishment from the petals of a flower that look like and serve the purpose of bowls. While the bowls do evoke the bees' hunger, the phrase does not primarily symbolize their hunger (E); rather, it provides a new image of the flower petals.

139. (A) One can understand the meaning of the phrase based on both its vocabulary and the context. Throughout the poem, the maidens sing of the feelings of love that arise with the arrival of spring. A "goblet" is a drinking vessel; "nectar" means both the sweet secretions of flowers and, classically, the life-giving drink of the gods. This particular nectar "steeps" human souls in "languor" (27), languor being a feeling of laziness or tenderness. Therefore, the best answer is (A), the drunken feeling of love.

140. (D) The repetition of the same word or phrase at the end of lines, clauses, or sentences is called EPISTROPHE.

141. (B) The poem's REFRAIN serves to reinforce the speakers' empathy for Krishna by repeating the idea that "it is sad to be alone" (11) at the end of each verse (11, 17, 23, 29, 35, and 41), which serves as a type of justification for Krishna's flirting and cavorting with many women. The maidens who sing the song seem to have understanding and empathy for Krishna, given the difficulty of being alone during sensual springtime. While this refrain may make Radha feel lonelier (C) since she is, in fact, alone while Krishna is enjoying himself with other women, the refrain first and foremost shows the maidens' understanding of Krishna's actions, which they are describing throughout their song.

142. (B) The first verse is written in LIMITED THIRD PERSON, from the perspective of Radha. Although "fair," Krishna is "all-forgetful" and consumed with "earthly love's false fire" (3–4). This would suggest that Krishna's attitude toward Radha is best described as (B), indifferent (unconcerned, uninterested).

143. (C) The sixth verse does not contain any examples of ASYNDETON, which is the omission of conjunctions. Two examples of ALLITERATION (A) in the sixth verse are "*s*ilken-*s*oft" and "*f*ine and *f*aint" (32). The phrase that begins with "The silken-soft pale Mogra" is set off by EM DASHES (B), which indicate an interruption or afterthought to the main expression. "The coldness of a maid, the sternness of a saint" (33) is an example of PARALLELISM (D). ANASTROPHE (E) is the inversion of the normal word order in a sentence; in this verse it occurs here: "whose perfume fine and faint" (32), which normally would be "whose fine and faint perfume."

144. (A) In line 34, "thine other self, thine Own" refers to Krishna. The maidens sing this song to Radha. "Thine" is an archaic form of "your" and signifies familiarity. Therefore, the "you" here is Radha. Her "other self" then refers to her beloved Krishna, who dances with "those dancers" (34).

145. (E) While the maidens may be incriminating (D) Krishna by singing of his trysts with other women besides Radha, the best answer is (E), apologetic. In celebrating the fertility and bounty of springtime, they would seem to be justifying Krishna's behavior. He, too, is following the natural order of things. Furthermore, the repetition (REFRAIN) at the end of each verse that such an environment makes it impossible to be alone would seem to further excuse Krishna's transgressions (see question 141).

146. (E) In context, the word "Love" (40) is a reference to Krishna. The maidens sing this song to Radha, whose love is Krishna, and in this line they say to her, "There dances and there laughs thy Love, with damsels many and one." We also know "Love" is Krishna because he has already been described as dancing with other women and the word has a capital letter that suggests it is PERSONIFIED as Krishna.

147. (D) We can infer that all these names are the names of types of foliage. "Kroona" is paired with the word "flowers," indicating that it is a type of flower (18). "Ketuk" is paired with the word "glades," indicating that it is perhaps a type of grass or plant (20). "Keshra" is described as yellow and with blossoms (24), "Pâtal" is paired with the word "buds" and feeds sleepy bees (26), and "Mogras" are "silken" and exude a "perfume fine and faint" (31–32).

148. (A) The song does not imply that Krishna is at all faithful. He is certainly promiscuous (B); he flirts, dances, and cavorts with many others besides Radha. He must be dexterous (agile, skillful) in that he dances, presumably well, with the dancers in the jungle (C). He also must have some charm (D) to captivate these other lovers. And as the maidens point out repeatedly, part of what drives Krishna's unfaithfulness is the desire not to be alone (E).

Passage 3. Rabindranath Tagore, "My Country Awake"

149. (E) ANAPHORA is a device where a word/phrase is repeated at the start of several sentences/clauses, as the word "where" appears at the start of lines 1, 2, 3, 5, 6, 7, and 9.

150. (C) The poem consists of only one sentence, and it is PERIODIC in that the main clause is at the end of the sentence and is preceded by several introductory, descriptive clauses ("Where . . . where . . . where . . . Into that heaven of freedom, my Father, let my country awake"). While the sentence can be described as COMPLEX (B) because it contains one INDEPENDENT CLAUSE (the final clause) and several DEPENDENT CLAUSES (the "Where . . . " clauses), it is not COMPOUND—B, D—because it has only *one* independent clause and multiple dependent clauses.

151. (E) The words "head . . . held" (1) and "desert . . . dead" (8) contain ALLITERATION because "*h*ead" and "*h*eld" begin with the same letter, as do "*d*esert" and "*d*ead." Both pairs of words also contain ASSONANCE because their internal vowel sounds are also the same: "h*ea*d . . . h*e*ld" and "d*e*sert . . . d*ea*d."

152. (B) Lines 1, 3, 6, and 8 all contain ALLITERATION; each of these lines contains words that start with the same sound as another word in the same line. Line 1: "*W*here . . . *w*ithout . . . *h*ead *h*eld *h*igh." Line 3: "*W*here . . . *w*orld . . . *b*een *b*roken." Line 6: "*s*triving *s*tretches." Line 8: "*d*reary *d*esert . . . *d*ead." While ASSONANCE (D) does occur in some words (see question 151), it does not occur in all of the lines mentioned in this question.

153. (A) The "dreary desert sand of dead habit" (7–8) is an IMPLIED METAPHOR stressing the hopelessness of chronic behavior. The "dead habit" is being compared to the "dreary desert sand" to show how the country gets stuck in a routine way of doing things, so stuck it is as if they are in a dreary desert with no end. The metaphor is implied—no explicit (B) connection is made between habit and the desert (X is Y); rather, the connection is implied. While the phrase does contain ALLITERATION, the metaphor is not extended throughout the poem, so it is not a CONCEIT (C).

154. (D) In the grammatical structure of lines 9–10, "the mind" is the OBJECT. In the sentence, the mind "is led forward by" the SUBJECT of the sentence, "thee." The mind *receives* the action (led) from the subject, making it the object.

155. (E) In the poem, the speaker addresses God. Though the speaker refers to his addressee as "my Father" (D), he then asks him to lead his country into a "heaven of freedom," implying that this "Father," with a capital "F," is God and not his actual parent. He is clearly not addressing himself (B) since he says "thee" (9). He speaks about his country and not to his country (A). There are no details to suggest the speaker is addressing a political leader (C).

156. (E) The speaker does not imply his country is irreparable; if he thought his country was hopeless, he would not be requesting help. The whole poem is a plea to God for guidance, which implies the country does have some hope. The speaker hopes to be led to a place "without fear" (1), implying his country is fearful (A); to a place "where knowledge is free" (2), implying his country is limited (B) and fettered (C); to a place that "has not been broken up into fragments by narrow/ domestic walls," implying his country is confined (D).

157. (B) The poem as a whole is a supplication (plea, prayer)—I, II—to God requesting that he lead the speaker's country "Into that heaven of freedom" (11). While the poem may have later been incorporated into others' speeches, there are no details in the poem that imply it is actually a speech being delivered in front of an audience—III. Since the addressee is God (see question 155), the request is more likely a private prayer and supplication and not a public speech.

158. (A) The TONE of the poem can best be described as earnest because the speaker genuinely, seriously, and solemnly pleads to God for his country to be led out of its fearful and constricting environment and into "that heaven of freedom" (11). His tone is not plaintive; he is not exactly mourning something (B). Though he addresses God, the overall tone of the poem is not solely pious (C). Though the poem ends with a plea for help, which implies that the speaker sees some hope, the overall tone is not entirely optimistic (D) as much as it is earnest.

Passage 4. Rabindranath Tagore, "The Home"

159. (B) The SIMILE in line 2 compares the sun to a miser (scrupulous saver) to convey the disappearance of sunlight. The sun's light is compared to gold, and the sun holds on to its light (gold) as scrupulously as a miser (cheapskate) holds on to his money. (C) and (D) both say the simile contrasts two things when the purpose of a simile is to show similarities between two things, to compare them. While the simile does emphasize how dark it has become, similes do not symbolize things. (E) is not as specific as (B).

160. (E) Line 3 contains an abundance of ALLITERATION. Four words in this line start with the same letter/sound: "*d*aylight . . . *d*eeper . . . *d*eeper . . . *d*arkness."

161. (D) In context, the phrases "widowed land" (4) and "her arms" (13) are examples of PERSONIFICATION. The land is given the human characteristic of being a widow, and the "darkened earth" is given human characteristics with the phrase "surrounding with her arms."

162. (E) The second sentence of the poem differs from the first in that it contains an APPOSITIVE. The "widowed land" is further described in an appositive to be a land "whose harvest had been reaped." The first sentence, however, does not contain an appositive. Both sentences contain only one INDEPENDENT CLAUSE (C) and a DEPENDENT CLAUSE (D), so these are not differences between them. The first sentence has the SIMILE (see question 159), not the second sentence (B). Neither of the two sentences contains PASSIVE VOICE (A); the subject precedes the action in both sentences ("I paced . . . " and "daylight sank").

163. (D) The third stanza contains a contrast between sound and silence, describing the boy's voice as "shrill" and the "track of his song" is noticeable against the "hush of the evening." There are no references to light (E) or day (A), only the "dark" and the "evening." The boy's boyhood is not compared to manhood (C), and even though the boy and the sky are mentioned (B), it is the boy's noise that contrasts with the sky's hush.

164. (E) The fourth stanza describes the location of the boy's village home; it is "at the end of the waste land," implying that it is somewhat isolated, being at the end of a long stretch of unused land. It is also "beyond/ the sugar-cane field" and "hidden among the shadows. . . ."

165. (A) The speaker notices that the families are happy ("glad") and their happiness does not know its own "value for the world;" in other words, happy families are unaware of how valuable their bliss is to the world (A). The earth is described as "darkened" (13), but there are no clear details that suggest the families light it up (B). The final sentence can be interpreted to mean that the speaker wishes he were a part of these families (C), but this is an inference and the question asks for a paraphrase. The earth opens "her arms" around the glad families, but there are no details that suggest the earth makes the families happy (E).

166. (D) The final stanza reveals the speaker's loneliness. The speaker walks in his "lonely way" (12) and appreciates how "glad" the families in their homes are and how valuable their existence is to the world. He establishes a contrast between the happy families who are together and himself, who is outside their homes, observing alone.

167. (E) The poem's form and style are characteristic of a FREE-VERSE poem because the poem does not adhere to any regulated, standard patterns and styles of poems. There is no RHYME SCHEME or consistent BEAT, so it cannot be a BALLAD (A) or a VILLANELLE (D). It does not overtly praise something, so it is not an ODE (B), and it does not commemorate a death, so it is not an ELEGY (C).

168. (E) The title of the poem introduces the object of the speaker's desire, a home. The speaker walks in his "lonely way" (12), he "paced alone" (1), and he appreciates how "glad" the families in their homes are and how valuable their existence is to the world. He establishes a contrast between the happy families who are together and himself, who is outside their homes, observing alone. The title does not contain the THEME (A) because the theme is not just "the home"; a theme is phrased as a statement—what is the poem communicating about the home? There are no details to suggest the speaker is not actually speaking of a home but is using the home as a metaphor or symbol—B, C, D—for something else.

Chapter 4: British Fiction

Passage 1. Frances Burney, *Evelina*

169. (A) The mercers "took care . . . to be noticed" because they are eager to be noticed by the patrons, perhaps so that they may receive more business, making them solicitous (anxiously concerned, eager to please).

170. (C) The speaker is most "diverted" by the fact that the women are served by men who "seemed to understand every part of a woman's dress better than" they do themselves. She is surprised and confused as to how and why this can be the case, indicated also by the exclamation point. She cannot be incredulous (E) because she does not express doubt that they actually do know more than women; she is more surprised and confused that they do.

171. (A) In context, the word "affected" means assuming or pretending to possess that which is not natural. The speaker finds it abnormal that "such men!" exist, men who know women's clothes better than women. She finds this unnatural, affected.

172. (C) The speaker remarks, "The dispatch with which they work in these great shops is amazing, for they have promised me a complete suit of linen against the evening." While the previous paragraph describes the milliners, the speaker is impressed by "these great shops," and not solely the milliners' shop, suggesting that she is impressed by the dispatch (efficiency, haste) of the mercers and the milliners.

173. (E) The speaker is bemused; she finds her hair "odd" and wonders when she will be able to comb it. She is confused, perplexed, and a little bewildered by this strange new style.

174. (D) She is insecure about dancing well in front of different people, outside of her "school" (28). She is apprehensive (nervous, fearful) and wishes "it was over" despite reassurances from Miss Mirvan.

175. (B) It is stated that the speaker is here to "improve by being in this town." She claims that once she has improved, her letters will not contain this "wretched stuff" and "will be less unworthy." The wretched stuff likely refers to the subject matter of the letter we have been reading, which reflects her confusion and naiveté about her upper-class environment. Since she is here to improve, and she describes her experiences only with shopping and balls, we can infer that she is here to rise in social class.

176. (E) The closing of the passage is written as the closing of a letter. The passage is clearly an excerpt of a missive (a letter) from Evelina to her "dear Sir" (29).

177. (B) Evelina closes her letter, "Your dutiful and affectionate, though unpolished, Evelina," which emphasizes her balanced perception of herself. She acknowledges her strengths and what she perceives to be a temporary weakness, her unrefined nature, which she is currently devoting herself to improving.

178. (D) In the passage, the speaker describes what she has seen and experienced and how she felt about it. She reveals emotions such as "half afraid," "almost afraid," and "almost ashamed" to express her reactions to what she has experienced. While she does appear to be tenacious (determined) because she is dedicated to "improving" herself, she is not characterized as wise (E) because she is naive and new to the environment. She is merely recording all that is new and weird to her, not insightful analyses or criticism of her society (A). Also, while she does appear guileless (open, honest), she does not appear uncouth (bad-mannered, rude). This adjective is too extreme (B).

Passage 2. Joseph Conrad, *Heart of Darkness*

179. (A) The word "it" in line 3 refers to the "*Nellie*," a cruising yawl, which is a boat or a vessel.

180. (E) The first and second paragraphs contain SIMILE ("*like* the beginning of an interminable waterway"), METAPHOR ("red clusters of canvas"), PERSONIFICATION (the air broods, "the haze rested"), and SENSORY IMAGERY ("the air was dark"). However, there are no examples of OXYMORON, two words that have opposite meanings paired together.

181. (B) The MOOD of this sentence is lugubrious (gloomy, sorrowful), as indicated by the "mournful" gloom that "broods."

182. (C) The Director of Companies is described as "nautical" (naval) and venerable (deserving of respect) when the speaker claims that he and the other crew members "affectionately watched his back" and saw him as the equivalent of a pilot, who is "trustworthiness personified."

183. (A) Yarns are stories, which are woven together as yarn is woven into fabric. The context also suggests that their common interest in the sea held them together, creating a bond that allowed them to tolerate each other's "yarns."

184. (B) The narrator mentions four people who are on the boat with him: the accountant, the lawyer, Marlow, and the Director of Companies.

185. (C) The sentence is a COMPOUND-COMPLEX SENTENCE; it has two or more INDEPENDENT CLAUSES (there are three, separated by semicolons) and one or more DEPENDENT CLAUSES ("hung from the wooded rises inland . . .").

186. (A) The "mist" on the marsh is compared to a "gauzy and radiant fabric" that "drapes" in "diaphanous folds." The folds are part of the METAPHOR that compares the mist to gauze-like fabric. "Diaphanous" describes thin, gauzelike transparent fabric.

187. (C) The narrator's attitude toward the subject, his TONE, is best described as inspired (enthused and stimulated). In paragraphs 1–4, the speaker is in awe of his environment and describes it in great detail, suggesting he is stimulated by the subject he is describing.

188. (D) Lines 19–25 compare light and dark. The ending of the day creates "exquisite brilliance," shining water, "unstained light," and radiance. This light is contrasted with the "*gloom*" in the west, which can be interpreted as darkness because it is "angered by the approach of the sun [the light]," as if they are in battle.

189. (B) The final sentence creates an ominous (threatening) mood. The light, which is described as magnificent throughout the passage, is suddenly extinguished by the darkness—it has lost the battle and disappears as if "stricken to death by the touch of that gloom brooding over a crowd of men." This sentence is threatening in that something that *was* great and brilliant has suddenly been extinguished.

190. (C) The passage appears to use SYMBOLISM to FORESHADOW later events because the descriptions of the setting (the battles/conflicts between light and dark, the waterway/horizon and land, nature and man) are likely symbolic of future conflicts that are only hinted at by the descriptions of the setting. It is unclear who the main character—III—is from this passage. Several people are mentioned, but the narrator reveals more about the setting than himself and the actual main character of the novel (Marlow) is barely mentioned in this passage.

191. (B) The narrator and his crew members are on a boat on the Thames River, which runs through the city of London. This is evidenced in line 4.

Passage 3. Joseph Conrad, *Heart of Darkness*

192. (D) The entire passage is marked in quotation marks, indicating that the speaker of the passage is merely a character in the book who is speaking to other characters. We do not get the voice of the book's actual narrator in the passage (D). There is a SIMILE in lines 3–4 ("*like* thinking about an enigma") and line 7 ("*as* to be almost black"), PERSONIFICATION in line 4 ("there it is . . . smiling, frowning"), and IMAGERY is evident in line 7, which allows us to *see* the "dark-green" jungle. SENTENCE VARIETY is evident in lines 1–3, where a sentence consisting of one INDEPENDENT CLAUSE follows a sentence with one independent clause and multiple DEPENDENT CLAUSES.

193. (E) The sea's glitter is "blurred by a creeping mist" (9), making it obfuscated (concealed)—III. It is also "always mute with an air of whispering" (5), making it laconic (not talkative)—II. The sea is also compared to an enigma and described as "smiling, frowning, inviting, grand, mean, insipid, or savage . . ." (4–5) and as whispering, "'Come and find out'" (5), making it cryptic (mysterious)—I.

194. (A) The speaker describes his job as perfunctory (done in a routine way without much care or passion) when he implies that the crew on the boat just "pounded along" (13), doing the same thing every day, in a monotonous routine that "nobody seemed particularly to care" (17) about.

195. (B) The repetition of the word "landed" at the start of three clauses in the sentence is an example of ANAPHORA, which, in this context, helps establish the speaker's attitude, or TONE, of how repetitive and perfunctory he noticed the work to be.

196. (E) The speaker remains "within the toil of a mournful and senseless delusion" (24) because of "idleness" (A), "isolation" (B), "the oily and languid sea" (C), and the "uniform sombreness of the coast" (23) (D). He does not mention a sordid farce as a cause.

197. (C) When the speaker describes his fascination with the "black fellows," he explains that they were "as natural and true as the surf. . . . They wanted no excuse for being there" (31–32). This is why "They were a comfort to look at" and why he felt "for a time" he "belonged still to a world of straightforward facts" (32–34). They provide him with a sense of verity (truth).

198. (B) In these lines, the speaker FORESHADOWS what will happen later in his story—that, for him, the world of truth would not last long.

199. (D) The sentence is not PERIODIC because the main point does not appear at the end of several introductory phrases. The sentence can be described as COMPOUND-COMPLEX because it consists of multiple INDEPENDENT CLAUSES, and it also contains a DEPENDENT CLAUSE ("swaying her thin masts" depends on the clause before it). The sentence contains IMAGERY ("greasy" and "slimy"), FIGURATIVE LANGUAGE (C) ("Her ensign dropped limp *like* a rag"), and ALLITERATION (E) ("slimy swell swung . . . swaying").

200. (D) The "she" in line 40 refers to the man-of-war ship that is described previously as "shelling the bush" (36). In lines 40–41, the description continues, describing her as "incomprehensible, firing into a continent."

201. (C) The word "Pop" is an example of ONOMATOPOEIA. The first sentence, containing INDEPENDENT and DEPENDENT CLAUSES, is JUXTAPOSED with the second sentence, consisting of only one INDEPENDENT CLAUSE, creating SENTENCE VARIETY—I, II. The series of descriptions ("a small flame would dart and vanish, a little white smoke would disappear, a tiny projectile would give a feeble screech") lacks conjunctions, making it an example of ASYNDETON—II. The projectile's "feeble screech" is an example of PERSONIFICATION—II.

202. (D) What the speaker has been describing is dark and absurd—a ship is "incomprehensible, firing into a continent" with no visible targets (40–41). He goes on to call this proceeding "insanity" (44), making the "lugubrious drollery" (44) a clear reference to the dark absurdity of what he is observing.

203. (B) The speaker is incredulous (surprised disbelief) that "somebody on board" was so certain he was firing at enemies. The EM DASHES and the exclamation point show the speaker's shock, and the previous lines suggest his incredulity because he clearly does not see any enemies—the ship is incomprehensibly firing; the proceeding is insane.

204. (C) In the passage, the speaker describes countless scenes he witnesses while aboard a French steamer, such as the cold indifference with which his shipmates treat the possible drowning of the clerks they are dropping off, settlements that look "centuries old" but still "no bigger than a pinhead," trading places that appear more like "sordid farce[s]" than legitimate enterprises, and of course the "incomprehensible" man-of-war that fires into the jungle with no visible "enemies" in sight. The speaker's TONE when describing these scenes is slightly tragic—he longs for truth and a world of "straightforward facts" because what he has seen is confusing. The settlements, the French outposts, are not functioning the way he may have expected or hoped.

Passage 4. Mary Shelley, *Frankenstein*

205. (D) The TONE of the first sentence is sanctimonious (self-righteous, proud, arrogant). The speaker is *happy* to affirm that his sister's "evil forebodings" were wrong. There is an air of smugness to the sentence.

206. (D) The verb tense of these lines remains in present tense. The speaker says, "my first task is," "I am," "as I walk," "I feel," "fills me," and "Do you understand."

207. (A) The sentence is COMPLEX because it contains one INDEPENDENT CLAUSE ("I am already far north of London") and multiple DEPENDENT CLAUSES.

208. (E) The speaker has left London and is currently in St. Petersburgh, Russia, and is traveling north, to a colder climate (7–11).

209. (C) The speaker repeatedly implies that he expects his destination to be unparalleled, unmatched by any other land: " . . . we may be wafted to a land surpassing in wonders and in beauty every region hitherto discovered on the habitable globe" (17–18). There, "snow and frost are banished" (16) (E) and there is "eternal light" (21) (D).

210. (A) The SIMILE in lines 18–20 compares the "productions and features" of the speaker's destination to the "phenomena of heavenly bodies" in "those undiscovered solitudes." The heavenly bodies are the stars that lie in the undiscovered regions of the heavens above. The simile emphasizes the speaker's expectation that his destination will be unmatched by any other on earth; its features will be as mysterious as the features of the unexplored universe.

211. (D) The repetition of a word at the start of successive sentences or clauses is called ANAPHORA. The word "there" is repeated at the start of two sentences and one clause.

212. (E) The speaker is clearly enticed by the promise of discovering "the wondrous power" (21) and "a land never before imprinted by the foot of man" (25) (A, C). He also hopes "to regulate a thousand celestial observations that require only this voyage to render their seeming eccentricities consistent forever" (22–23) (B). His journey holds, for him, unlimited expectations because he describes his destination as "surpassing in wonders . . . its productions and features [are] without example" (17–19) (D). While it may be inferred that the speaker desires fame and approbation (recognition) for his discoveries, there are no indications that he desires to be notorious (disreputable).

213. (D) The speaker compares his own joy to the joy "a child feels when he embarks on a little boat, with his holiday mates, on an expedition of discovery up his native river" (27–28). Comparing his joy to the joy of a child emphasizes the innocence, ingenuousness (sincerity) of his own enthusiasm.

214. (C) In both sets of lines, the speaker is attempting to convince his sister of something. In lines 3–6 he asserts that her initial judgments were false, and in lines 29–30 he insists that she "cannot contest" that some "inestimable benefit" will come from his expedition.

215. (B) The speaker believes immeasurable gains will result from his journey to this undiscovered land. His discovery of a convenient passage and his ascertainment of "the secret of the magnet" will be immeasurably worthwhile.

216. (C) While Shelley's *Frankenstein* is, in fact, a GOTHIC novel, the given passage is clearly a letter from the narrator to his sister, indicating that its STYLE resembles the style of an EPISTOLARY novel, which is a novel composed mostly of letters. While the speaker does embark on a journey that he seems to deem heroic and adventurous, there are not enough elements to suggest that the passage is a MYTH (B) because there are no references to gods or goddesses or other characteristics of myths. There are also not enough details to indicate that the story is a LEGEND. (C) is the only answer with concrete evidence.

217. (B) The passage contains many examples of SENSORY IMAGERY. We *feel* the cold the speaker feels when he says, "I feel a cold northern breeze play upon my cheeks, which braces my nerves and fills me with delight" (7–9), and we can *see* the sun as the speaker imagines it: "its broad disk just skirting the horizon and diffusing a perpetual splendour" (14–15). The speaker makes use of RHETORICAL QUESTIONS in line 9 and lines 20–21. There are no examples of INVOCATION in the passage.

Passage 5. Mary Shelley, *Frankenstein*

218. (A) The first, second, and fourth sentences all begin with the same phrase, "There was a . . . ," a device known as ANAPHORA.

219. (C) The sentence begins with the subject to which "it" refers: "There was a show of gratitude and worship . . . for it was inspired. . . ."

220. (C) The speaker's mother is described as virtuous in line 8 (A), munificent (generous) in lines 13, 36–39 (B), convalescent (recovering from illness) in line 22 (D), and enervated (weak) in line 19 (E). While the speaker's father is eager to attend to her needs, there are no details to suggest that the mother demands this attention and care; therefore, she is not presented as importunate (annoyingly demanding).

221. (C) While the comparison of the father to a gardener and the mother to a fair exotic might imply that the father is officious (overbearing and fussy) in his protection of the mother, the TONE of the lines does not indicate that the speaker intends to portray the father in such a negative way. The speaker makes the comparison, more likely, to emphasize how his father nurtures his mother the way an attentive gardener would care for a rare flower.

222. (D) The first paragraph gives helpful background for comprehending the details in the second paragraph. The first paragraph explains the relationship between the speaker's parents and characterizes the mother. These details are useful in interpreting the second paragraph, in which we see the mother's specific actions and behavior (she helps the poor). The background from the first paragraph helps us understand the motives and reasons behind her actions.

223. (A) The METAPHOR compares the parents' love to a mine from which they extract unlimited amounts of affection for their son. The speaker implies that, even though they expended so much love and devotion on each other, their capacity to love was so inexhaustible that they still were able to love him without conservation.

224. (E) The speaker mentions that his parents saw him as "their plaything and their idol . . . ," implying that they adored him so much it was as if they worshipped him the way an acolyte (a religious follower, a worshipper at an altar) might worship a religious idol.

225. (B) The sentence is PERIODIC because the main clause is at the end of the sentence, after a series of explanatory DEPENDENT CLAUSES: "With this . . . added to the . . . it may be imagined that while . . . I was so guided by a silken cord that all seemed but one train of enjoyment to me."

226. (C) The cord is a METAPHOR for the parents' guidance of their child. The child holds on to a rope from his parents throughout childhood, and the speaker's cord is silken, implying that his parents' guidance was filled with an "active spirit of tenderness" and his discipline was full of "enjoyment."

227. (A) The children that "spoke of penury in its worst shape" are described as "poor," "half-clothed," "afflicted," and "hungry," all suggesting destitution (poverty).

228. (E) The girl is characterized as visually striking by the words "very fair" and by the contrast made between her and her "dark-eyed, hardy little vagrant" peers—I. She is tow-headed (blonde)—her "hair was the brightest living gold"—but she is not inhuman—II. Though line 52 describes her as heavenly, celestial, and "of a distinct species," the word *inhuman* means ruthless and cruel. She is described as sartorially spartan (very little clothing) in the description "poverty of clothing"—III.

229. (A) The description of the girl contains ALLITERATION ("*s*o expressive of *s*ensibility and *s*weetness") (C), POLYSYNDETON ("thin *and* very fair . . . clear *and* ample . . . her blue eyes cloudless, *and* her lips *and* the moulding of her face") (E), SIMILE ("*as* of a distinct species") (B), and HYPERBOLE ("heaven-sent, and bearing a celestial stamp") (D). There are no ALLUSIONS in these lines.

230. (C) The TONE is not factual; the speaker speculates and recalls his impressions of his parents (B). It is not resentful but rather exceedingly praiseworthy of his parents (D). It is not grave (serious); he mostly recalls sweet, sentimental moments (A). Even his mother's physical weakness is described in the context of how much his father loved and cared for her. It is certainly not sardonic (mocking) (E). The tone, however, can be described as mawkish because every sentence contains HYPERBOLIC descriptions of how wonderful his parents, the "celestial" girl, and their relationships are. The descriptions of their love for each other saturate the passage, creating a mawkish, overly sentimental tone.

231. (A) While the passage does include characterization of the mother, father, speaker, and family (E), the main purpose of the passage as a whole is to characterize the mother. The speaker describes the father only in the context of describing the mother (C). The speaker describes himself only in the context of describing his parents (B). The second paragraph continues with characterization of the mother and does not mention the father or the speaker. Even the girl is described only in the context of her standing out to the mother. The mother is consistently described and characterized throughout the entire passage.

Passage 6. Jonathan Swift, *Gulliver's Travels*

232. (E) The first sentence's SYNTACTICAL STYLE is distinct in its use of multiple APPOSITIVES, which are phrases that further describe a noun nearby. The morning is described further in an appositive to be "about a fortnight after I had obtained my liberty." Reldresal is described in an appositive to be "principal secretary (as they style him) for private affairs." He also "came to my house, attended only by one servant." The sentence contains only one (not multiple) proper nouns ("Reldresal") (C) and only one INDEPENDENT CLAUSE (D).

233. (A) The phrase "(as they style him)" is set off in parentheses, indicating that the speaker may not believe Reldresal to be an authentic "principal secretary"; rather, the community merely *styles* him that way. The CONNOTATION of the word "style" is fabrication and artificiality.

234. (C) In the first paragraph, the speaker mentions that he "obtained [his] liberty" in the past "fortnight," indicating that he has been recently emancipated (B). He mentions that he was willing to give Reldresal his time "on account of his quality and personal merits, as well as of the many good offices he has done [him] . . . ," making him grateful (A). He shows that he is gracious when he "offered to lie down, that he [Reldresal] might the more conveniently reach [the speaker's] ear" (D). Since the speaker has to either lie down so Reldresal can speak into his ear or hold Reldresal in his hand, it is clear that the speaker may be quite large (E).

235. (E) The word "it" in the phrase refers to the speaker's "liberty," suggesting that Reldresal will pretend that the speaker earned his liberty but does not actually believe he did.

236. (A) Line 12 begins with "For, said he, as flourishing . . ." The "he" in this line refers to Reldresal, who is identified in the first paragraph as the principal secretary. After line 12, Reldresal continues to be the speaker of the second paragraph.

237. (D) In lines 15–22, the speaker explains that the empire has "two struggling parties" that are distinguished by the high or low heels of their shoes. In the sentence "It is alleged, indeed, that the high heels are most agreeable to our ancient constitution; but, however this may be, his majesty hath determined to make use only of low heels in the administration of the government . . . ," the clause beginning with "but" suggests that there is some perceived problem with his majesty's partiality toward (preference for) the low heels.

238. (C) In lines 24–25, the speaker says, "We compute the *Tramecksan*, or high heels, to exceed us in number; but the power is wholly on *our side*," implying that he is a member of the opposing party, that of the low heels, also called "*Slamecksan*."

239. (B) The speaker explains, "We apprehend his imperial highness, the heir to the crown, to have some tendency towards the high heels . . . we can plainly discover that one of his heels is higher than the other, which gives him a hobble. . . ." Since it has already been determined that the speaker and his imperial majesty are low heels, it would make sense that they would be apprehensive (nervous, fearful) that the heir to the crown has displayed some preference to the high heels by wearing one high heel and one low heel, resulting in his hobble. The hobble then implies that the heir is defecting (switching, betraying) from one party to the other.

240. (D) "These intestine disquiets" that the speaker has been describing have been the domestic (existing within their home country) problems and strifes (struggles) between opposing factions in the empire.

241. (E) The speaker explains that the empire is skeptical about the truth of the addressee's claims "that there are other kingdoms and states in the world, inhabited by human creatures as large as [himself]" because their "philosophers . . . would rather conjecture that [he] dropped from the moon" (B). The speaker says the empire's doubts also stem from the facts that their "fruits and cattle" (agriculture) are still intact (A) and their "histories [annals (C) and ken (D)] . . . make no mention of any other regions. . . ." The speaker does not cite Lilliput and Blefuscu's superiority as reasons for the empire's doubts.

242. (A) The word "fomented" most closely means goaded (motivated, encouraged) in this context because the speaker goes on to explain that the monarchs of Blefuscu contributed to the war's continuance by providing "refuge" to Lilliput's "exiles."

243. (E) When he describes Blefuscu's "*Blundecral*" as "our *Alcoran*," he suggests that the *Alcoran* is Lilliput's equivalent to Blefuscu's *Blundecral*. Both of these texts are implied to be each nation's sacred holy text because they contain chapters and "fundamental doctrine" of a prophet.

244. (D) The argument between Blefuscu and Lilliput is an argument about SEMANTICS, the study of language's meaning, of linguistic signs and their signifiers, because both nations interpret the words of the "great prophet Lustrog" differently. The words "the convenient end" are interpreted by one nation to be the "big end" and by the other nation to be the "small end." The speaker says, " . . . which is the convenient end, seems, in my humble opinion, to be left to every man's conscience."

245. (E) The style of the passage is similar to a LAMPOON in that the author is clearly satirizing the silly nature of a country's wars and civic disputes, comparing them to quibbles over nonsensical things like arguing over which side of an egg the citizens should crack and what size heel a citizen wears on his shoe. A lampoon is a work of literature or art that sharply satirizes a person, issue, concept, etc.

246. (C) All of the words printed in italics ("*Slamecksan*," "*Tramecksan*," "*drurr*," "*Alcoran*," and "*Blundecral*") refer to objects or names in Lilliput and Blefuscu's language.

247. (E) Reldresal explains that "his imperial majesty, plac[es] great confidence in [the first paragraph's speaker's] valor and strength" (68–69), making him doughty (brave)—III. His strength is suggested to come from his large size—II—which is described in the first paragraph. The first paragraph also explains that the speaker of that paragraph has recently been given his freedom—I—for which he may be so grateful that he would return a favor to his majesty for his acquittal.

248. (A) While the passage as a whole carries an ironic and satirical TONE, Reldresal's tone in lines 11–70 is quite serious. He describes Lilliput's problems in a grave tone to persuade his addressee to assist the nation in its war against Blefuscu.

Passage 7. Oscar Wilde, *The Picture of Dorian Gray*

249. (E) In lines 15–16, the author compares two things, London and the bourdon note, using the word "as," making the sentence an example of a SIMILE—I. There is an example of PASSIVE VOICE—II—in the second paragraph: "Persian saddle-bags on which he was lying" (4–5). The subject of the sentence is placed after the action it performs, making the sentence passive instead of active. The entire first paragraph is a COMPOUND SENTENCE—III—as is the sentence in lines 4–12 ("From the corner . . . motion") because they consist of more than one INDEPENDENT CLAUSE with no dependent clauses necessary.

250. (B) The "birds in flight" (8–9) make Lord Henry recall the Japanese painters who "convey the sense of swiftness and motion" in the "immobile" medium of art (12). The narrator goes on to emphasize the oppressive stillness in the room (15), further communicating the contrast between the movement of the birds and the stillness in the room.

251. (B) The tremulous (trembling) branches can hardly bear the burden of the beauty of "the honey-sweet and honey-coloured blossoms of a laburnum" (6–7), the subject to which "theirs" refers.

252. (A) While there are some details to suggest Lord Henry could be bored (A), he is actually described as having thoughts (10–11) and being relaxed (4–5), which do not imply boredom. The characters appear to be familiar with the art of foreign countries (B) because Basil Hallward's studio contains a "divan of Persian saddle-bags" (4) and Lord Henry describes Japanese painters with some familiarity. Both the characters are presented as bourgeois (C) through their familiarity with luxury items and foreign art. The first two paragraphs describe both the abundance in nature (the "odour of roses," the "heavy scent of lilac," the burdensome beauty of the blossoms and the "unmown grass") alongside the introduction of Lord Henry, who rests on a luxurious and imported divan, relaxing and smoking (4–5), implying the abundance of material wealth in the room (D). There is a lethargic (sluggish) mood (E) to the scene, indicated by the "monotonous insistence" of the circling bees (13–14), the oppressive stillness (15), and the image of Lord Henry "lying, smoking, as was his custom, innumerable cigarettes" (5).

253. (D) The emphasis in this paragraph has been on the silence and stillness, "the sullen murmur" (13). London's "roar" is "dim" (15–16) because of its distance to the stillness and calmness of the current environment, "like the bourdon note of a distant organ."

254. (C) Lord Henry speaks in EPIGRAMS (quips, witticisms), such as in lines 39–40, which are *not* CLICHÉ—II—because they are original and witty. Much of what he says to Basil is counsel, or advice on what he should do with his painting (26–31), that he should send it somewhere so as to be "talked about" and to make others "jealous" (40–42).

255. (C) Basil Hallward's assertion that he won't "'send it anywhere'" (32) is not indicative of insecurity (C). There are no details to suggest that Basil is insecure about his work, as indicated by his "smile of pleasure" (23) when he looks at his painting, which also indicates that he likes his painting (E). That he is well educated (B) is indicated by the mention of his having studied at Oxford (33); he has been excoriated (criticized) in the past (D), indicated by the many "conjectures" about his absence (21) and the friends who would laugh at him for the way he "tossed his head back" (32). He is definitely a notable painter (A) since he is publicly known as an artist and, as Lord Henry suggests, he already has a reputation (37–38).

256. (C) The dialogue in the passage is predominantly comprised of Lord Henry's exhortations (urgings) to Basil Hallward to display his painting. In his speech, Lord Henry expresses his views on artists, the Academy, the Grosvenor, reputation, and old men.

257. (E) While Lord Henry's thoughts on what he sees are clearly described in the second paragraph, Basil's perspective and thoughts on the setting of the room are absent from the passage. Both their pasts (D) are referred to (Basil's recent absence, his time at Oxford, etc., and Lord Henry's "custom" of smoking "innumerable cigarettes"). Their physical descriptions (C) are mentioned (Lord Henry's lying on the divan, his elevated eyebrows, and Basil "placed his fingers on his eyelids"). They both speak (B) in the passage, and their perspectives are enhanced by the use of SIMILE (A) (15–16, 25).

258. (D) While both Lord Henry and Basil share the scene and speak to each other, the focus of the passage is not on their friendship (B). The subject of their dialogue, however, is the painting, the galleries, and the artist's reputation. Lord Henry's views on the subject are evident in the counsel he offers Basil, and Basil's perspective is implied through his refusal to "send [his painting] anywhere" (32).

Chapter 5: American Fiction

Passage 1. Kate Chopin, "The Kiss"

259. (E) Even though the setting appears to be romantic (A, B) because of the fire, darkness, and the word "ardently" (5), a closer look at the IMAGERY of the opening paragraph reveals a surreptitious (sneaky, underhanded) atmosphere, especially with the phrases "uncertain glow" and "deep shadows." The shadows alone evoke darkness and deception, but their depth evokes an even more extreme trickery. These deep shadows added to the "uncertain glow" further cement a surreptitious TONE to the story. We cannot be certain that the glow is even a glow. These phrases conjure up doubt, skepticism, mystery, and perhaps even fraud.

260. (D) Brantain is meek compared to the more up-front and audacious Mr. Harvy, who "pressed an ardent, lingering kiss upon" Nathalie's lips (21–22), confidently responds to her angry questions (36–40), and "with an insolent smile" (73–74) rejects her kiss (78–79). Brantain, on the other hand, is less confident in expressing his desire for Nathalie. In the second paragraph, he is relieved by and thankful for the dark shadows because they allow him to develop the "courage to keep his eyes fastened as ardently as he liked upon the girl" (5–6). While the word "ardent" is used to describe Mr. Harvy's kiss, it merely describes Mr. Brantain's stare, further contrasting their personalities. Braintain is also hesitant in confessing his feelings for Nathalie, unlike the more up-front Mr. Harvy: "She was confidently waiting for him [Brantain] to declare himself . . ." (14). Brantain also unquestionably believes and accepts Nathalie's dubious explanation of her kiss with Mr. Harvy (55–59, 60–61).

261. (D) Up until these lines, we may have still assumed that Nathalie is genuinely attracted to and sexually interested in Brantain because of her occasional "slow glance into the shadow where [he] sat" (9–10) and the fact that "she was confidently waiting for him to declare himself and she meant to accept him" (14–15). However, the next sentence (15–16) reveals that the girl is primarily interested in Brantain for "the entourage which [his] wealth could give her" (16). Her flirtations reveal her to be opportunistic (one who seeks opportunities for advancement without regard for morals or principles).

262. (C) The phrase "'deuced awkward'" is an example of Mr. Harvy's own COLLOQUIAL style of speaking, an example of his slang and vernacular (daily language, lingo).

263. (E) The adjective "delicious" is not usually paired with the noun "frankness," and this pairing makes the reader question the authenticity of Nathalie's frankness. The adjective "delicious" conjures up an image of Nathalie licking her lips, eagerly anticipating approaching Brantain with such a frank manner. The adjective "delicious" depicts Nathalie as more wily (cunning, strategic) than frank. She clearly has some ulterior motive in approaching Brantain; perhaps it has to do with her desire to marry him for his "wealth" (16).

264. (B) While Brantain's face is "radiant," Nathalie's is "triumphant." The word "triumphant" implies that she has achieved something great, that she is happy because she has accomplished a task or goal and not because she is genuinely pleased to make Brantain happy. The word helps to characterize Nathalie as someone who is guileful (full of trickery and deceit) and has ulterior motives beyond love and affection when flirting with men.

265. (E) In contrast to her "delicious frankness" and "triumphant" face when speaking with Brantain, Nathalie's face is now "bright," "tender," and "hungry" in front of Harvy. With Brantain, she uses trickery and deception to convince him that she genuinely cares what he thinks and is genuinely interested in him when she is, in fact, interested only in his "wealth" (16). However, with Mr. Harvy, she abandons such ruses, and her face is described with straightforwardly honest emotion.

266. (A) In the SIMILE in lines 75–76, Nathalie feels as if she is a chess player who has cleverly handled her pieces and sees her triumph is imminent (definite). This same feeling is also revealed when she is described as having a triumphant face in line 66, after it is clear that she has assuaged (eased) Brantain's doubts and restored his interest in her, as she had cleverly planned to do.

267. (D) After Mr. Harvy rejects Nathalie's kiss, she recovers by reminding herself that "she had Brantain and his million left." She does not mind that she cannot have "everything," meaning both Brantain's money (financial needs) and Mr. Harvy's kiss (emotional needs), because she at least has secured her financial stability.

268. (E) In the final paragraph, the narrator adopts Nathalie's voice and thoughts in the narration. There are no indications that Nathalie is speaking these lines. There is no clear distinction between the narrator's voice and the character's, which makes these lines examples of FREE INDIRECT STYLE.

Passage 2. Nathaniel Hawthorne, *The Scarlet Letter*

269. (A) The MOOD is somber (sad, dismal, depressing), as indicated by the "sad-coloured garments" (1), "grey steeple-crowned hats" and oppressive, as indicated by the "heavily timbered" door that is "studded with iron spikes." The fact that the paragraph is describing a prison and a throng (crowd) of people may convey a claustrophobic (B) mood, but these two details also support the broader, more prevalent mood of somberness and oppression.

270. (C) A quick read through the sentence might lead to answer (E), Utopia, because it is mentioned in the clause preceding the word "it." However, "it" is "among [the founders'] earliest practical [first] necessities to allot a portion of the virgin soil as a cemetery" (6–7). Reading the entire sentence will make the subject clear.

271. (E) Isaac Johnson's burial-ground and "round about his grave" (11) became the "nucleus," or center, of all other graves to be gathered there. A grave is a place of interment (burial).

272. (E) The setting is explained through the use of METAPHOR (the cemetery, prison, and rose-bush) (A), ALLUSIONS (Vicinity of Cornhill, Isaac Johnson, King's Chapel, Ann Hutchinson) (B), SENTENCE VARIETY (COMPOUND SENTENCES and COMPLEX SENTENCES) (C), and PERSONIFICATION (the "delicate gems" of the rose-bush offer their beauty to the prisoners) (D). There are no examples of ANAPHORA in the passage; there is no repetition of a word or phrase at the start of multiple clauses or sentences.

273. (A) Line 22 describes the prison as a "portal," which is repeated in line 33, "that inauspicious portal." The phrase's antecedent can also be found by looking in the previous sentence. The "inauspicious portal" refers to "the prison-door" in line 31. It makes sense that the prison door would be the "portal" because a portal is an entrance, a gateway to something. If the portal in reference is the opening to a prison, that would make the portal inauspicious (unfavorable).

274. (B) As explained in the final paragraph, the reader is about to hear a "tale of human frailty and sorrow" (36). The passage prefaces that tale.

275. (B) The narrator's critical attitude toward the setting is evident in his characterization of the new colony as depressing—the clothes are "sad," the prison is "ugly," the vegetation is "unsightly," and the wilderness is "stern" and "old." The narrator is critical of the setting and the new colony for its emphasis on condemning criminals who deserve the "deep heart of Nature" and its "pity" (26). The narrator's DICTION belies (contradicts) objectivity (A) and reverence (D). There is no evidence to suggest the narrator is bewildered (C) or frustrated (E) by the subject.

276. (E) As the final paragraph indicates, the passage precedes a "tale of human frailty and sorrow" (36), so its primary function is to establish a setting (the prison, the throng, the history of the community) and introduce meaningful SYMBOLS, like the rose-bush that will "symbolize some sweet moral blossom" (35). It also establishes the MOOD as lugubrious (mournful, grave, serious, gloomy) through severe descriptions of the people, their clothes, and the structure of the prison (see question 269).

277. (C) The narrator mentions Ann Hutchinson as a theory for why the rose-bush "has been kept alive in history" (27). It either "merely survived" or "sprung up under the footsteps of the sainted Ann Hutchinson" (28–31). But "we shall not take upon us to determine" (31–32) because the narrator is uncertain and is suggesting different theories. While it may appear that the narrator's positive description of Ann Hutchinson as "sainted" suggests he is deploring (criticizing) (A) the colonies' disenfranchisement of citizens, this answer choice requires readers to make too large an assumption that is not fully supported by the text.

278. (E) The TONE of the final paragraph is definitely one of optimism and sanguinity because the rose-bush is presented to serve as a mollifying (healing, soothing) agent to alleviate (lessen) the pain of the tragic tale we are about to read. The speaker says that perhaps one of the flowers that strangely grows by the prison-door may serve as a symbol of a "sweet moral blossom that may . . . relieve the darkening close of a tale of human frailty and sorrow" (35–36). The last paragraph also speculates and anticipates (B) by wondering and conjecturing about the flower's role in soothing the reader by the end of the tale, and it expounds on a METAPHOR (A) by assigning a bigger symbolic meaning to the flower, comparing it to a panacea (cure) of sorts.

Passage 3. Nathaniel Hawthorne, *The Scarlet Letter*

279. (E) All devices are used in lines 1–9 except CHIASMUS, a grammatical figure by which the order of words in one of two of parallel clauses is inverted in the other. The sentence is PERIODIC (A): the main point (it is marvelous that "this woman should still call that place her home") is at the end of the COMPLEX SENTENCE (D), preceded by several DEPENDENT CLAUSES. There is a SIMILE (C) in line 19 ("*like* garments put off long ago . . ."), and ANAPHORA (B) is evident in the repetition of the phrase "it may seem marvelous that."

280. (E) The passage as a whole makes consistent use of the EM DASH—III (1, 3, 5, 8, 17, 19, 22, 23, 32, 33)—which indicates a break in the sentence to offer more information or an afterthought. The consistent use of the em dash and ANAPHORA indicates that the passage also makes use of PARALLELISM—I—in that many of the sentences follow the same style and structure. The sentences in lines 20–21 and in lines 25–28 can be considered LOOSE SENTENCES—II—because the dominant idea is found in the opening clause, with the remaining clause(s) containing supporting details.

281. (D) The afterthoughts set off by EM DASHES suggest other paths the character could have taken instead of staying "within the limits of the Puritan settlement" (2). She could have returned to "her birth-place, or to any other European land" (3) or "the passes of the dark, inscrutable forest" (5–6).

282. (B) The "fatality" is explained in the following sentence to be "[h]er sin, her ignominy" (13–14), her transgression.

283. (E) The second paragraph explores Hester's own reasoning (justifications) for why she "compelled herself to believe . . . she reasoned upon as her motive for continuing a resident of New England" (31–33). She reasons it is for "retribution" (28), for "her earthly punishment" (35), for purging her soul (36), and for becoming more "saint-like" (37). The paragraph does mention a "secret" (22) (A), and it does refer indirectly to her sin (B), but these references are not the focus of the paragraph. They are mentioned only in the context of explaining Hester's reasoning. Her ambivalence (C) is suggested by the sentence "She barely looked the idea in the face, and hastened to bar it in its dungeon" (30–31), but, again, this inner conflict is only one feeling she has on her way to "compel[ing] herself to believe . . . reason[ing] upon as her motive for continuing a resident of New England" (31–33). The focus is definitely not on regret (D) but on justifying how she will go about repenting her sin.

284. (E) Since this person is described as one who will join Hester Prynne "before the bar of final judgment . . . for a futurity of endless retribution" (27–28), we can assume he has been her partner (accomplice) in sin.

285. (D) The narrator is curious about Hester Prynne's life, fears, thoughts, emotions, etc. The narrator actively theorizes about her motives, showing curiosity about the character. He never treats her as a saint (C) because he does not automatically assume her to be moral and great. He acknowledges and is intrigued by her sins and quest for redemption. He is not aloof (distant) (E); he thinks about her "secret," her inner turmoil and deepest emotions.

There are no details that depict the narrator as condescending or pejorative (insulting) (A, B) toward Hester.

286. (D) The second paragraph explains that Hester stays in New England, in the town where she committed her crime, to endure punishment, cleanse her soul, and achieve a "saint-like" purity, and martyrdom" (37). A, C, and E are mentioned in the first paragraph, but they are not reasons why Hester decides to stay. While she may have been conflicted internally (B) about identifying all the deeper reasons for her stay (33), she is certain that she is seeking some kind of absolution by enduring the punishment of remaining in a town that has shunned her for her crime.

287. (E) The passage's content is similar to that of an ARISTOTELIAN TRAGEDY in that the TRAGIC HERO exhibits a fatal flaw and makes error in judgment that brings about her own downfall but has a moment of realization and regret, lives and suffers and repents. Though tragic heroes are of noble birth or great eminence and Hester Prynne is not described in this way, the passage's focus on one character's poor judgment, sin, punishment, and retribution resemble the content of an Aristotelian tragedy more than the other choices. The style of the passage may be called GOTHIC because it does contain gloom, a woman in distress, and intense emotions, but the question asks about the content. Though there are references to humans haunting a place "ghost-like," there is no reference to a supernatural presence or event to warrant choosing (A).

288. (B) While the passage does briefly allude to Hester Prynne as wild (6) (D), fearful (23) (A), ghost-like (11–12) (E), and delusional (33) (C), the passage as a whole communicates her perseverance. She is determined to stay in New England, the place of her crime and punishment, despite the many other options available to her, because "[t]he chain that bound her here was of iron links, and galling to her inmost soul, but could never be broken" (20–21). It is this perseverance that intrigues the speaker; the narration is focused on exploring the deeper reasons behind her perseverance, her adamant decision to live on in this town.

Passage 4. Henry James, *The Turn of the Screw*

289. (E) The speaker conveys her anxiety by explaining that she was caught between a "succession of flights and drops," "right and wrong" (1–2). She is full of doubts, yet also "certain" she "had made a mistake" (4). This "seesaw" (1) of emotion suggests she is full of anxiety over a decision she has made.

290. (A) The convenience refers to the "vehicle from the house" that would meet her (6). It is described as a "commodious fly," or a spacious carriage. *Conveyance* means a mode of transportation.

291. (C) The speaker describes how the "summer sweetness" of the June air was a "friendly welcome," which dispelled her former feelings of anxiety and restored her mental and emotional strength.

292. (A) POLYSYNDETON—I—helps communicate the speaker's excitement as she is so excited that she piles on details to her list with conjunctions ("open windows *and* fresh curtains *and* the pair of maids looking out" (13–14). The word "crunch" is ONOMATOPOEIC—

I—as it sounds like the action it describes. We can hear, through her language, what she hears. While there is an example of ANAPHORA in these lines, there are no IDIOMS—III. While there is IMAGERY, there is no HYPERBOLE—II.

293. (B) The first paragraph implies that the speaker is not upper class herself because she explains that the descriptions of this grand home "had a greatness that made it a different affair from [her] own scant home" (17) and she says that the curtsy given her by the civil person at the door was as decent "as if [she] had been a mistress or a distinguished visitor" (18–19), suggesting that she is neither of those. The speaker cannot be male (C) because she uses the word "mistress" to refer to herself when describing how the civil person treated her. There are no details to suggest that the speaker is precocious (knowledgeable beyond her years) (A), the overseer (D), or the proprietor (E).

294. (C) The "drop" echoes the drops mentioned in line 2 of the passage—the flights and drops that characterized the speaker's emotional state as she set out on her journey. The drops referred to her hesitation, so in the second paragraph she explains that she did not have any more drops, or doubts, until the next day.

295. (C) What "remained" with the speaker in line 29 is the same thing that she says "astonished [her] too." The subject, "this," both astonished and remained with her, which adds to her sense of the "liberality" with which she was treated.

296. (A) "The only thing" (35–36) refers to why the speaker feels as if she would "shrink again" (36) or feel "uneasy" (41). This cause is explained to be Mrs. Grose's "guard against showing" (39) how "glad" (38) she was to see her.

297. (D) The speaker explains that it is the "sense of liberality [generosity, munificence] with which [she] was treated" (29–30) that makes her so excited she cannot sleep. She goes on to list the things that she has been given: "The large, impressive room, one of the best in the house, the great state bed, as I almost felt it, the full, figured draperies, the long glasses . . ." (30–31).

298. (E) The STYLE of the passage resembles the style of a MEMOIR; the speaker recounts events that have happened to her in the past, events that have played an important role in shaping her. She does not describe events objectively; rather, she infuses the descriptions with her emotions and opinions. She also describes the events in terms of the effects they had on her mental and emotional states. (The passage is not excerpted from an actual memoir, however.)

Passage 5. Sinclair Lewis, *Babbitt*

299. (B) Babbitt "kept himself from the bewilderment of thinking" (1–2), suggesting that he performs his job without thought or effort, in a routine, perfunctory manner. He does the same thing "[e]very evening" (2), and since "the days were blank of face and silent" (3), we can assume that he goes through his routine without much enthusiasm.

300. (C) The "days" (3) are described as having a blank face, a human attribute, making the phrase an example of PERSONIFICATION.

301. (A) This sentence is set off in its own paragraph because it contains the essential point that will be reinforced in the next few paragraphs—Babbitt's apathy toward creating his own experience outside of his monotonous routine. He is excited to be free for the evening, but "not quite sure what" (5) to do, which is reinforced later in the passage by his boredom over "having to take so much trouble to be riotous" (11), his vague (20) desire to look for entertainment that would "enable a fellow to forget his troubles" (28–29).

302. (B) The word "emancipated" suggests that the house has been set free. From the previous sentences, we can assume that the house is set free from the routine of work, wife and neighbors, bridge, the movies, and blank and silent days (1–3). In the previous sentence, Babbitt is described as "free to do . . ." (5), indicating that the "emancipation" is from prescribed routines.

303. (C) It is mentioned that the Babbitt household has a "maid" (18), indicating that Mrs. Babbitt has help keeping house. There is no evidence to suggest she is a Bohemian (B). It is implied that she would not approve of Babbitt staying out late (D) (8–9). She is described as altruistic (A) (generous) in line 2. She is currently visiting family in the East (E) (4).

304. (C) The narrator adopts Babbitt's POINT OF VIEW when describing Verona's opinion. By repeating the word "opinion," he is clearly mocking Verona's fourth-hand knowledge of the topic she is discussing.

305. (E) Babbitt only "vaguely" wants something more diverting than comic strips to read (20), which suggests he is not tenacious (B), determined, or passionately eager about making the most of his evening. He appears to be more apathetic (lazy) about finding something to do.

306. (E) Babbitt and Verona clearly do not share the same interests. It is stated that Babbitt "liked none of the books" (25–26) that he finds in Verona's room.

307. (D) This line is not written in quotation marks, nor is it prefaced with an indicator that it is one of Babbitt's thoughts, yet the statement is written from Babbitt's perspective, in Babbitt's voice. The narrator's voice and Babbitt's voice have commingled, making the sentence an example of the technique of FREE INDIRECT STYLE, where the narrator adopts the voice and POINT OF VIEW of character(s) in his/her own narration.

308. (D) The statement "It would be an adventure story, maybe about counterfeiting— detectives sneaking up on the old house at night" (30–31) coincides with Babbitt's "restless" (19) desire for some "diverting" (20)—II. "He kept himself from the bewilderment of thinking" by not looking for stories that make him think—I—which recalls lines 1–2; instead, he wants an author to help him "forget his troubles" (28–29)—III.

Passage 6. Sinclair Lewis, *Babbitt*

309. (D) The first sentence is a LOOSE SENTENCE—I—in that the main idea is given in the first clause and all subsequent words merely elaborate on the idea. It also contains the SIMILE—II—"sturdy *as* cliffs." The presence of CONJUNCTIONS in the phrase "of steel *and* cement *and* limestone" indicate that the sentence also includes POLYSYNDETON—III.

310. (A) The TONE of the first paragraph is definitely wry (ironic, mocking). The speaker describes the towers of Zenith in almost holy words: they "aspire"; they are "austere" and "delicate as silver rods." Yet the last sentence suggests a wry commentary on the holy emphasis the city places on its office buildings—these are not churches, only office buildings.

311. (C) The second paragraph communicates a sense that the new office buildings are ejecting the older architecture from the city center. The buildings of older generations are described as "hulky," "stingy," "sooted," like "mud," compared to the newer architecture that is "clean" and "shining." The last sentence, however, suggests that the new may not necessarily be better than the old, because they merely "seemed" to be for "laughter and tranquility" but are not necessarily so.

312. (D) The thoughts set off by EM DASHES contribute to the passage's wry TONE. There is a distance between what the city and its designers or inhabitants think and what the speaker thinks. The city dwellers call their city "Zenith," implying that they think it is superior to all other cities, the apogee of modern advanced societies. The speaker, however, is skeptical, as indicated by the thoughts set off by em dashes—the city only *seems* to be for laughter and tranquility and giants, but might not actually be.

313. (A) The name "Zenith" reveals more to us about what the city dwellers think of their city (it is the zenith—pinnacle—of all modern cities) than what the speaker (E) does (the speaker did not name the city).

314. (C) The passage is written in THIRD PERSON POINT OF VIEW. The speaker tells the story in third person by narrating what characters do, say, and think. He is not writing from the point of view of one character (A, D) or multiple characters (E).

315. (B) The "twenty lines of polished steel" refer to the New York Flyer, the name of the train being described in this paragraph. The train of polished steel "booms" past, creating the illusion of twenty lines of steel.

316. (E) All the people mentioned in the passage are referred to as groups (clusters) of people, not individuals. There are "people in evening clothes," "the telegraph operators," "the scrubwomen," and the "cues of men." Most of them are employed, but the people in evening clothes are returning from a rehearsal, which is not necessarily a job (B). Most of the workers are not described as happy (C), and the people in evening clothes are not described as fatigued (weary or tired) (A); they also appear to be of a different class than the workers (D).

317. (D) The TONE and descriptions of the setting of Zenith, with its austere and powerful architecture and industry in contrast to the weary working people who inhabit it (see question 316), could be used to question whether this town of advanced modern objects is actually superior to the towns of "older generations" if all the people are tired and powerless in comparison to their man-made physical environment.

318. (D) Based on the passage's TONE, an appropriate title could be "Progress?" since the speaker is skeptical about the town's vision of itself as superior to older towns because of its modern advancements. After the descriptions of the advanced architecture and technology, the descriptions of the people in the town appear noticeably less powerful (some appear weary, tired, and unhappy in their jobs). The passage is questioning whether the progress in industry has really led to progress in the quality of life for the citizens of Zenith.

Passage 7. Upton Sinclair, *The Jungle*

319. (C) In lines 4–5, the speaker explains that the word "this" in line 2 refers to "such cases of petty graft," or incidents involving theft and deception.

320. (C) The speaker says, "After Jurgis had been there awhile he would know that the plants were simply honeycombed with rottenness of that sort—the bosses grafted off the men, and they grafted off each other . . ." (6–8). Graft is definitely abundant, and the word "simply" implies that this is simply what happens on a routine basis; it is so abundant that it is common.

321. (E) The narrator adopts the voice of the character Tamoszius in much of the first and second paragraphs, a device known as FREE INDIRECT STYLE. This narrative device is evident when Sinclair writes, "Warming to the subject, Tamoszius went on to explain the situation. Here was Durham's . . ." (9–10). The remaining lines do not consist of the OMNISCIENT or THIRD-PERSON NARRATIVE voice; rather, they are written in the adopted voice of Tamoszius.

322. (B) Tamoszius uses METAPHORS when he describes the plants as "honeycombed with rottenness" (7) and as a "seething cauldron of jealousies and hatreds" (18). He uses a SIMILE when he describes the superintendents and foremen as "ranged in ranks and grades like an army" (12–13) (A). RHETORICAL QUESTIONS (C) are found in line 21. Tamoszius also cites examples (D) to support his argument that the plants are corrupt places; he cites the examples of the bosses and the superintendents grafting off subordinates (7–9) and he gives a more concrete example when he says, "Here was Durham's, for instance . . ." (10). He speculates (E) when he wonders, "The reason for that? Who could say? It must have been . . ." (21). There are no examples of ANAPHORA in these lines; though he does repeat the word "simply" twice, the repetition does not occur at the start of sentences or clauses.

323. (E) In line 30, Tamoszius explains that the type of man who rises in Packingtown is a "knave," which he later explains is "the man who told tales and spied upon his fellows" (31–32). A charlatan is a fraud, a swindler, a pretender, a knave.

324. (C) Before the phrase "'speed him up'" (33), Tamoszius is explaining what the bosses would do to a "man who minded his own business and did his work." They would "'speed him up' till they had worn him out, and then they would throw him into the gutter" (33–34). Tamoszius appears to be quoting the bosses' command, but the description of speeding up a man to the point of exhaustion implies that the bosses' command is a EUPHEMISM (a substitution of a mild expression for one thought to be harsh) for overworking a man.

325. (A) While the THIRD-PERSON NARRATOR adopts the voice of Tamoszius in the first and second paragraphs, there is a shift in the third paragraph. The third-person narrative voice is apparent in the first sentence of the third paragraph: "Jurgis went home with his head buzzing" (35). However, in the following sentence, the narrative voice moves into FREE INDIRECT STYLE again (see question 321), and this time the narrator adopts the voice of Jurgis: "no, it could not be so" (36). This line is clearly the voice of Jurgis, not the third-person narrator. The free indirect narration from Jurgis's point of view is predominant in this paragraph.

326. (C) In lines 36–40, Jurgis doubts the validity of Tamoszius' claims about the company's graft and corruption. He reasons that Tamoszius is merely "sore" or making excuses because he "did not feel like work" (38–40). This response is typical of someone who is skeptical about believing new information.

327. (B) In the final sentence of the passage, Jurgis realizes "And yet so many things kept coming to [his] notice every day!" (40–41), suggesting that even though he had his doubts about Tamoszius's claims, much of what Tamoszius described is becoming more and more visible at the company. The exclamation indicates his surprise at the legitimacy of what he was told. The passage ending in this sentence suggests that the following paragraph might explain exactly what Jurgis had been observing that corroborated Tamoszius's claims.

328. (E) Tamoszius explains that deception, graft, knavery, telling "tales," and spying are what help a man rise in Packingtown. In other words, men who are opportunistic and seek advancement through no concern for principles or ethics are the ones who will succeed here.

Chapter 6: World Fiction

Passage 1. Miguel de Cervantes, *Don Quixote*

329. (A) The narrator's attitude toward his protagonist is neither sardonic (scornful) (B) nor acrimonious (bitter) (C), since he describes Quixote in sympathetic terms. He refers to him as a "novice knight" (15) and "our new-fledged adventurer" (23), both being expressions that Quixote thought of himself. Because the narrator does show some sympathy for Don Quixote's idealistic spirit, neither can he be said to be entirely dispassionate (unemotional, detached) (E). Although Quixote fails to give "notice of his intention to anyone" (4–5), he has a "grand purpose" (10) that includes "wrongs he intended to right, grievances to address, injustices to repair, abuses to remove, and duties to discharge" (3–4). By implication, the narrator endorses his ambitions but questions his methods and their likelihood of success. The best answer is (A), magnanimous (fair, generous). Even though the narrator pokes fun at his hero's folly, he demonstrates a subtly generous attitude toward his noble enterprise.

330. (E) The ANAPHORA (A) comes at the beginning of the first two clauses of the sentence, which both begin with the word "scarce." The sentence is HYPERBOLIC (B) in its exaggerated descriptions and overwrought feeling. The "*p*ainted *p*lumage" of the birds offers one count of ALLITERATION (C). EUPHONY (D) is the pleasant, musical combination of sounds, to which this sentence clearly aspires with its soothing alliteration, hyperbolic imagery, and parallel structures and sounds. What is lacking in this sentence is ASYNDETON (E), the omission of conjunctions in a list of items.

331. (D) In keeping with the playful layering of voices typical of *Don Quixote* as a whole, this sentence is a quotation within a quotation, where Don Quixote speaks in the anticipated voice of his future "sage" chronicler. Quixote is imitating the lofty, pretentious style of medieval heroic epic. Some might describe this rhetorical style as sophisticated (C), but the best answer is (D), grandiloquent, because the language is courtly and lofty to the point of being bombastic and arrogant, which is not exactly sarcastic (B) or provincial (simple, unrefined) (E).

332. (D) Nowhere in this passage is it indicated that Don Quixote feared his chivalric ambitions were too great (E). Quixote does leave his home "without giving notice of his intention to anyone" (4–5) (A); and he indeed doesn't know exactly where he is going since "he pursued his way, taking that which his horse chose" (21–22) (B). Also, later in the passage, we learn that an integral part of his heroic fantasy is the "grievous wrong" (40) that Princess Dulcinea has done him (C). Nevertheless, the best answer is (D), since the elucidation of the "terrible thought" (11) arrives immediately in the next sentence: that it "occurred to him that he had not been dubbed a knight" (12–13). The legitimacy of his entire adventure depends on his being a knight.

333. (B) All of the following are true: one, Quixote was unable to reason coherently (A), "his craze being stronger than any reasoning" (17); accordingly, two, he had a tenuous grasp on reality (C); three, he had faith in his good fortune (D), since he was willing to take a path "which his horse chose" (22); and four, he was unwilling to go home (E), given the fact that "he made up his mind to have himself dubbed a knight by the first one he came across" (17–18). Yet it is this last detail that confirms that the best answer is (B), his fantasizing was resourceful. In this instance where he encounters an obstacle to the carrying out of his "grand purpose" (10), it is the resourcefulness of his imagination that provides a way of overcoming that obstacle. His fantasy, in effect, offers both problem and solution.

334. (B) In the sentence, Quixote addresses his anticipated chronicler, which is, slyly, a reference to the writer himself (A), Cervantes, since he is, in fact, Quixote's chronicler. Furthermore, the sentence is BURLESQUE (C) in that it treats a ridiculous subject with mock dignity. There are multiple APPOSITIVES (E) (nouns or noun phrases that further describe a noun nearby), such as, "O sage magician . . . my good Rocinante." The sentence contains the lofty language (D) characteristic of the passage ("thou . . . thou art . . . I entreat thee"), and while the sentence is certainly prose, it is not PROSODY (B) (the study of poetic verse or meter).

335. (D) Quixote laments to Dulcinea, the "lady of this captive heart" (40), that she has banished him from the "presence" of her beauty with "inexorable obduracy" (41). While her behavior very well might be construed as cruel (A), the best answer is (D), stubbornness, the definition of obduracy.

336. (C) The key word in this question is "narrator." In this instance, Quixote, as the speaker, believes that his adventures are and will be entirely veracious, or truthful. Since we readers know Quixote to be delusional, we can appreciate the IRONY of his assertion. His claim is framed, in effect, by ironic distance.

337. (E) *Don Quixote* as a whole satirizes heroic ROMANCE (A) or EPIC (B), narratives that center on the exploits of a hero. There is not enough information in the passage to claim it is part of a TRAGEDY (C), which concerns itself with a flawed hero and usually ends in his death, or a COMEDY (D), which, while also satiric, usually ends in a marriage or union. As a FARCE (E), *Don Quixote* relies on stereotypical characters and outrageous situations and consists of a series of episodes that never culminate in a DENOUEMENT, or conclusive unraveling of the plot. The given passage reveals the protagonist to be a parody of the stereotypical knight who is obsessed with his own heroism and image. In the passage, we see him embark on a journey, an episode, that is not given much serious weight.

338. (C) For Quixote, a knight must not travel directly and purposefully (A), but rather he should pursue "his way, taking that which his horse chose, for in this he believed lay the essence of adventure" (21–22). Quixote obviously does not value plain, succinct speech (B), preferring instead the grandiloquent (pretentious, wordy, long-winded) rhetoric of heroic romance. A knight must not avoid romantic entanglement (D), but rather embrace it, as Quixote does in swearing his undying fealty to the Princess Dulcinea. Although Quixote finds creative ways of circumventing the rules he imposes on himself ("he made his mind to have himself dubbed a knight by the first one he came across"), he certainly claims to make every effort to observe his own chivalric code, however seemingly unreasonable its precepts (E). From the passage, it is clear that Quixote sees self-flattery and extreme confidence (superciliousness) (C) as an acceptable and perhaps necessary quality for a knight to possess.

Passage 2. Fyodor Dostoyevsky, *Crime and Punishment*

339. (A) The passage alone (not necessarily the entire novel) is written in THIRD-PERSON LIMITED narrative; the narrator is not the protagonist (which eliminates choices C and D), but he knows what the protagonist is thinking: " . . . he became acutely aware of his fears. 'I want to attempt . . .'" (22–24). The narrator also provides information and details that the protagonist would not say or notice himself: "An expression of the profoundest disgust gleamed for a moment in the young man's refined face" (39–40). We can imagine the narrator standing beside the protagonist, observing and watching, but also aware of the protagonist's inner state. The narrative is not THIRD PERSON ROTATING (E) because the narrator does not offer the same level of insight and perspective for other characters in the passage. The narrative is not THIRD PERSON OMNISCIENT (B) because the narrator seems to know only the protagonist and his environment.

340. (B) The narrator never states directly that the squalor and stench of the city are what cause the protagonist's "irritable condition" (12), but the detailed descriptions of Petersburg's "airlessness," "bustle," "stench," and "drunken men" show how the environment "worked painfully upon the young man's already overwrought nerves" (35–36). The setting, though not directly, does provide some justification—I—for the protagonist's isolation from others (13–14) and his overall state of petulance (irritability). Since the protagonist is "refined" and "exceptionally handsome" (40–41), it is understandable that he might want to isolate himself from his disgusting environment. The final paragraph shows a contrast between this squalid environment and the protagonist's appearance—II. Upon seeing the drunken men amid the stench and heat, "[a]n expression of the profoundest disgust gleamed for a moment in the young man's refined face. He was, by the way, exceptionally handsome, above the average in height, slim, well-built, with beautiful dark eyes and dark brown hair" (39–42). The protagonist is presented as the opposite of his environment. There are no details to make III a viable answer.

341. (D) The paragraph opens with the declaration that the protagonist "had successfully avoided meeting his landlady on the staircase." In this paragraph, the narrator proceeds to describe the protagonist's living situation and how he always felt "a sick, frightened feeling" when passing his landlady. This feeling is clarified by the last sentence of the paragraph: "He was hopelessly in debt to his landlady, and was afraid of meeting her." This sentence could have been placed at the start of the paragraph, but delaying this clarification creates some suspense and curiosity for the reader, which also occurs with the repeated use of the word "it" in the fifth paragraph (see question 345).

342. (C) Both paragraphs contain DEPENDENT CLAUSES (A), the second paragraph does contain SIMPLE SENTENCES ("He was hopelessly in debt to his landlady, and was afraid of meeting her") (B), both paragraphs mention the same characters (the protagonist and the landlady) (D), and the TONE is constant throughout the passage (see question 348) (E). The second paragraph is more focused on establishing setting and context for the protagonist's feelings; it describes his room, introduces the landlady, and briefly mentions his fear. The third paragraph, however, expands on the reasons behind the protagonist's emotional state. It explains his "overstrained irritable condition" (12) by describing how he has isolated himself from others, was "crushed by poverty" (15), and "has lost all desire to" attend to "matters of practical importance" (16–17) (C).

343. (B) Before the protagonist says "that's an axiom," he says, "all is in a man's hand and he lets it all slip from cowardice." The latter statement *is* the AXIOM, the self-evident truth, the wise adage. A man's cowardice (his timidity) (B) causes him to "let it all slip," to squander opportunities because he is afraid of pursuing them.

344. (A) The two sentences are CHIASTIC because the order of words in one of two parallel clauses is inverted in the other. In the first clause "chatter" is the *cause,* and in the second clause "chatter" is the *result,* but the grammar and phrasing are parallel in both clauses. The sentences are not AXIOMATIC (B) or veracious (truthful) (C) because they do not contain self-evident truths. The protagonist is not necessarily exaggerating, so the sentences are not HYPERBOLIC (D). Perhaps he is in denial or deluding himself, but there is no evidence to suggest this, and the statements themselves are not delusional statements (E).

345. (C) In these lines, the protagonist thinks to himself about "his fears" (23). He says he wants "to attempt a thing like that" but is frightened by "these trifles" (24). We are not told what "that" and "these" are, and he goes on to refer to this deed as "there" (31), "that" (31), and "it" (31–32), keeping us in suspense and confusion over what he is actually contemplating that is so fear-inducing. In addition to creating a sense of mystery (A, D, E) the vague language characterizes the protagonist's own fear (B) because he clearly cannot even *say* what it is he is contemplating; he is afraid even of the words. The vague language definitely does not elucidate (clarify) the protagonist's actual desire (C)—we are purposely made unaware of what he actually wants to do.

346. (A) The final paragraph focuses on describing the putrid, squalid conditions of the protagonist's environment. The "heat in the street was terrible," and "that special Petersburg stench . . . worked painfully upon the young man's already overwrought nerves." The "drunken men" in the streets only "completed the revolting misery of the picture." The contrast between beauty and ugliness is apparent in the next sentence: "An expression of the profoundest disgust gleamed for a moment in the young man's refined face." The narrator goes on to describe the man as "exceptionally handsome, above the average in height, slim, well-built, with beautiful dark eyes. . . ." The contrast between the ugly city and the beautiful man makes why the protagonist "walked along not observing what was about him . . .

not caring to observe it" more understandable. The contrast provides some understanding of his chosen isolation and indifference to people and "matters of practical importance" (16).

347. (E) The protagonist is emotionally detached (A) from his environment: "He had become so completely absorbed in himself [proud (B)], and isolated from his fellows that he dreaded meeting . . . anyone at all" (13–14). He also "had given up attending to matters of practical importance; he had lost all desire to do so" (16–17). The protagonist has given up on life; he even ceased to care about the fact that he was "crushed by poverty" (15) (D). He is described as "irritable" (12) and disgusted (40), making him petulant (irritable, ill-tempered) (C). He is not, however, intrepid (fearless) (E); he "was afraid of meeting [his landlady]" (10) and "on coming out into the street, he became acutely aware of his fears" (22–23). When he thinks to himself, he admits that he is "frightened" by his thoughts (24).

348. (A) The narrator observes the protagonist throughout the passage. He is not predominantly curious, intrusive, or speculative (B, C, D) because he seems to know everything the protagonist knows and more (he describes him as beautiful, and perhaps the protagonist himself would not describe himself that way). The narrator is not quite OMNISCIENT, however, because there are no details to suggest that he knows everything about the other characters, as well (see question 339). While the narrator does agree that the city is putrid when he describes it as such in the final paragraph, these descriptions are more indicative of his being observant (A) than sympathetic (E) because he is merely noticing the "heat . . . airlessness . . . and dust" (33–34), where the stench has come from ("pothouses") and why the city appears "revolting" (39) and not necessarily indicating that he feels the protagonist's pain.

Passage 3. Gustave Flaubert, *Madame Bovary*

349. (C) The passage is in FIRST PERSON PLURAL because the speaker describes the events by saying, "We . . .", implying that these observations were those of the entire class.

350. (B) The first three paragraphs lack speculation. The speaker describes things in a factual TONE, as they happened ("We were in class . . . those who had been asleep woke up . . . The head-master made a sign to us to sit down . . . he said . . ."). In the fourth paragraph, however, the speaker includes his speculations and assumptions. He sees the "'new fellow'" and remarks, "He *looked* reliable, but very ill at ease" (11–12). He also reasons that "his short school jacket . . . *must have been* tight . . ." (12–13). (A) is incorrect because even though the fourth paragraph contains subjective impressions, it also contains objective descriptions (the boy was "taller than any of us," and "He wore stout, ill-cleaned, hobnailed boots"). (C) is also incorrect because the fourth paragraph contains a SIMILE ("*like* a village chorister's") as does the first paragraph ("*as* if just surprised at his work").

351. (B) The speaker perhaps describes the boy sartorially (his clothing) to emphasize how awkward he appeared among the other boys in the school, how he does not fit in. We have already been told that he was "not wearing the school uniform" (2) and that "his short school jacket of green cloth with black buttons must have been tight about the armholes, and showed at the opening of the cuffs red wrists accustomed to being bare" (12–14). The jacket appears not to fit properly, and the red wrists imply that the boy is not used to wearing any kind of school uniform, unlike the other boys in the school. The speaker also notices his boots were "ill-cleaned," suggesting further that the boy does not fit in. (E) makes too large an assumption that is not supported by the text. (D) is incorrect because even though the boy may feel apprehensive and uncomfortable in his clothes, the speaker's intention is to convey his own (and the students') impressions of the boy based on his clothing, and what he seems to point out repeatedly is how he does not match everyone else and looks strange.

352. (C) The new boy is described as "attentive as if at a sermon" during the lesson. The teacher "was obliged to tell him to fall into line with the rest" because he is so immersed in learning that he does not even realize the bell has rung. Though the teacher has to tell him to follow what the others are doing, (A) and (B) misunderstand the teacher's intention; the boy is not being reprimanded for not following the others.

353. (B) The phrase "'the thing'" is in quotation marks because it is what the students call the action to which "the thing" refers (throwing their hats). It is their own VERNACULAR, a COLLOQUIAL phrase to describe an action they take regularly.

354. (B) The speaker notices the cap is ugly, "one of those poor things" but still "full of expression." The fact that it is full of expression shows that the cap carries meaningful significance as a SYMBOL. It is poor but full of expression, just as the boy appears to be poor because of his "ill-cleaned" boots and "short school jacket" that does not quite fit. However, like the cap, the boy is also "full of expression"; he is "attentive as if at a sermon" and he "looked reliable, but very ill at ease." The speaker goes on to describe the cap's "composite order," every type of material, color, and texture that made up the cap. Since this detailed description of the cap follows other speculations and conjectures about the boy, we can logically assume that the cap is somehow equated to the boy. After all, the paragraph ends with a statement that easily suggests the cap's symbolism for the boy: like the boy, "the cap was new; its peak shone." The previous paragraphs have detailed exactly how the boy himself sticks out from the other boys, how his "peak shone."

355. (A) The penultimate sentence contains three INDEPENDENT CLAUSES, multiple DEPENDENT CLAUSES, and it runs for nearly six lines. The last sentence, however, is short, direct, lacking any DEPENDENT CLAUSES or APPOSITIVES. The two sentences JUXTAPOSED create SENTENCE VARIETY.

356. (A) The TONE of the passage is attentive. The speaker is vigilant in his observations and descriptions of the new boy. He notices minute details of his clothes, body ("red wrists"), demeanor, behavior, and emotional state. While the speaker does sound critical (B) of the new boy in parts of the passage, the question asks about the passage's overall tone, and the speaker is not harshly judgmental of the boy in all his descriptions, nor does he intend to describe him to criticize him. The speaker is also not detached (D); rather he is quite involved in his impressions of the boy; he declares, somewhat passionately, that the boy's cap has "dumb ugliness" with "depths of expression, like an imbecile's face." Someone who is detached from a subject would not describe it with such specific and subjective detail.

357. (C) The passage as a whole is devoted entirely to characterizing the "new fellow." Each paragraph contributes to this characterization primarily through the speaker's (who speaks for his classmates) observations.

358. (D) The new boy differs from the speaker in his attire/clothing (2, 12–16, 24–33), his height (10), his deportment/manner/behavior (17–25), and his interests (17–20). Their environment is the same: the classroom and school.

Passage 4. Hermann Hesse, *Siddhartha*

359. (E) The first sentence contains REPETITION, specifically ANAPHORA, because the phrase "In the shade" is repeated three times at the start of different clauses—II. The sentence also contains a METAPHOR when Siddhartha is compared indirectly to a "falcon"—III. The sentence can also be described as PERIODIC because the main clause ("is where Siddhartha grew up . . .") comes after a series of introductory, descriptive clauses ("In the shade . . . in the sunshine . . . in the shade . . . in the shade . . .")—I.

360. (D) An ablution is a cleansing with water or other liquid as a religious ritual. While (C) is correct, (D) is a better answer because it more specifically describes ablutions. We can understand the meaning of the word by looking at the context; Siddhartha performs the sacred ablutions when he is "by the banks of the river . . . bathing."

361. (A) The question asks for the dominant technique, and there are more examples of ANAPHORA than any other technique listed in the answer choices. The phrase "in the shade" is repeated at the start of three clauses, the phrase "the sacred" is repeated twice, and the phrase "to speak" is repeated at the start of two clauses. There are only two sentences containing ASYNDETON (6–8, 9–10) (C) and one sentence containing PERSONIFICATION ("shade poured") (B). While the references to "Om" and "Atman" could be classified as ALLUSIONS, there are still only two of them (D).

362. (D) The word "Om" is mentioned to be something that one would "speak . . . silently" into oneself "while inhaling" and "out of" oneself "while exhaling." It requires "all the concentration" of the soul and "clear-thinking," indicating that it is a recitation that requires thought, effort, concentration—it is meditative (10–14).

363. (A) Siddhartha's parents are impressed by his sagacity/wisdom, "quick to learn, thirsty for knowledge" and likely to "become a great wise man" (B, C); his ecclesiastical (religious) talents, likely to become "a priest" (D); and his litheness, "slender legs" (E). They are not impressed by his corpulence (fatness) (A); on the contrary, he is slim and lithe.

364. (E) Siddhartha is regal ("a prince among the Brahmans," "with the eye of a king") (A), distinct ("he would not become a common Brahman") (B), luminous ("luminous forehead") (C), and coveted (desired) by "the Brahmans' young daughters" (D). He is not described as proud; on the contrary, Govinda says he will *not* become like the other "vain" Brahmans (35) (E).

365. (D) Govinda admires Siddhartha's nonconformity; he was "not a decent, stupid sheep in the herd of many" (31–32) (A). He admires his tenacity, "his ardent will" (28–29) (B). He admires his potential, "his high calling" (29) and how he "would become a God" (35) (C). He also "loved his walk" (26), or his amble (E). Govinda likes that Siddhartha is *not* like the other Brahmans who are like "a greedy merchant with magic spells [incantations]" (30) (D).

366. (E) According to Govinda, many Brahmans are supercilious (proud, arrogant) and "vain" (31)—I. They are also venal (open to bribes), being "greedy" and "deceitful" (30, 31)—II—and banal (common, unoriginal) in that they are "stupid sheep in the herd of many" (32)—III.

367. (E) The entire passage is devoted to praising Siddhartha's many venerable qualities. Every person mentioned in the passage is mentioned only through their admiration for Siddhartha. The TONE is thus lofty and exalted. Though the descriptions of the shade and the calming, meditative rituals may make the passage seem idyllic (A), the tone refers to the author's attitude toward the subject; the subject is Siddhartha, not the peaceful setting, and the attitude toward him is exalted (high-minded).

368. (B) Siddhartha is described to us through what others say and think about him. We learn what his father, his mother, Govinda, and "the Brahmans' young daughters" (22) all think of him. While (C) is somewhat correct, we do not actually meet Siddhartha in this passage, so he is not introduced. Even if we agree that he is figuratively introduced, (B) is still a more specific and accurate answer than (C).

Passage 5. James Joyce, "The Dead"

369. (A) The phrase "literally run off her feet" (1) is not the narrator's phrase; it belongs to Lily, the caretaker's daughter. We can imagine Lily misusing the word "literally," but not the narrator. Since the narrator goes back and forth between his own formal language and Lily's more informal language without any quotation marks or other authorial flagging (like "he said" or "she thought"), the phrase is indicative of FREE INDIRECT STYLE. The narrator adopts the unique voice of the character in the narration. The misuse of "literally," then, is not an example of the author's COLLOQUIAL language (E), nor is it a MALAPROPISM (D), because one word is not being used mistakenly to mean a similar-sounding word.

370. (A) Through FREE INDIRECT STYLE, the speaker introduces us to all of the characters except for Mary Jane. We see things from Lily's POINT OF VIEW ("They were fussy, that was all") and the two aunts' views ("they were dreadfully afraid that Freddy Malins might turn up screwed. They would not wish for worlds that . . ."), but the speaker never narrates from Mary Jane's point of view, and the question asks about "all" the characters.

371. (D) The second sentence of the passage contains multiple CLAUSES and CONJUNCTIONS without any commas or semicolons. When it is read, we feel the frenzy and hurried state Lily must be in as she is "run off her feet" preparing for the party.

372. (C) Both these sentences are CUMULATIVE SENTENCES, also known as LOOSE SENTENCES, because in both sentences the main clause is at the start of the sentence and is followed by explanatory, supporting clauses. For example, one sentence begins with the main clause "Everybody who knew them came to it," and it is followed by additional supporting details describing who these people are.

373. (D) The MOOD in the house is nervous (jumpy, anxious, tense), as indicated by Lily feeling "run off her feet" (1), the two aunts feeling "dreadfully afraid that Freddy Malins might turn up screwed" (34) and "fussy" (32), and their peering over the banister "every two minutes" (38).

374. (A) After it is explained how the two aunts came to live in this house, the speaker says, "That was a good thirty years ago if it was a day," meaning that, for the two aunts, moving to this house feels like it was only yesterday, not thirty years ago.

375. (D) Mary Jane is referred to as the "main prop of the household" right before it is mentioned that she was qualified to teach music and that her students were wealthy (19–23). The next sentence explains that the two aunts also contribute to the household as much as they can, making (A) and (B) incorrect. (C) and (E) are too rash and assuming. There are no other details to suggest that the aunts are merely using Mary Jane or that they actually see her as a prop, an object. Since they themselves contribute to the household in their own ways, it would not make sense for them to view Mary Jane as beneath them for doing the same.

376. (D) The three women are not abstemious (sparing or moderate in eating and drinking), as indicated by the fact that "they believed in eating well; the best of everything: diamond-bone sirloins, three-shilling tea and the best bottled stout" (28). The fact that they enjoy fine foods makes them epicures (gourmands, connoisseurs of food) (A). They are also finicky (E), according to Lily: "she got on well with her three mistresses. They were fussy, that was all" (29–30).

377. (B) All the phrases are examples of the characters' VERNACULAR and FREE INDIRECT STYLE. They are examples of free indirect style in that the characters' COLLOQUIAL phrases are not flagged by the author (with phrases like "he said" and "she thought"); rather, they are written into the narration. The phrases are not written in THIRD-PERSON LIMITED point of view because the speaker adopts the vernacular/points of view of multiple characters, not just one.

378. (C) The first paragraph does set the scene; it introduces the event that is taking place by describing what the housemaid and hosts are doing. The second paragraph, however, provides background information on who these characters are, how they know each other, and what the event is. (D) is incorrect because the second paragraph does contain simple sentences ("They were fussy, that was all"). (E) is incorrect because the first paragraph mentions Lily and the two aunts, all of whom are also mentioned in the second paragraph. (A) is incorrect because the first paragraph does contain Lily's perspective. She (and the speaker) tells us that she is "run off her feet" because she is scampering around greeting guests. No problem is set up and solved in the two paragraphs (B).

Passage 6. Franz Kafka, "Metamorphosis"

379. (A) Each sentence in the first paragraph contains one or more DEPENDENT CLAUSES. For example, the clause "when Gregor Samsa woke from troubled dreams" cannot exist on its own. It depends on the following clause, "he found himself transformed in his bed into a horrible vermin."

380. (C) While the descriptions of Gregor's insectlike appearance would confound (confuse) a reader (B), the main purpose of these descriptions is to pique the reader's interest by setting up a problem (C). The problem is Gregor's transformation into an insect, which will be described in more detail in subsequent paragraphs. By emphasizing the specific details of Gregor's bewildering transformation, the opening paragraph motivates readers to read on and learn more about his condition and how he might deal with this perplexing problem.

381. (B) Through descriptions of the objects in his room ("a collection of textile samples" and "a picture . . . in a nice gilded frame"), we understand a little more about Gregor as a person. The textile samples reveal his line of work, and the framed picture of a woman dressed in fur evokes masochism (for readers familiar with Leopold von Sacher- Masoch's story "Venus in Furs"), or less specifically, it reveals Gregor's desires. While the picture of the woman can be interpreted as a METAPHOR, (A) is incorrect because the first paragraph arguably contains a metaphor as well (Gregor's insect body), which is a similarity between both paragraphs and not a difference.

382. (D) The third paragraph makes effective use of SENSORY IMAGES to help the reader see what Gregor sees ("the dull weather," "shut his eyes"), hear what he hears ("drops of rain could be heard hitting the pane"), and feel what he feels ("a mild, dull pain").

383. (C) It is surprising to us that even though Gregor has awoken to find himself transformed into an insect, his thoughts are focused on his hatred of his job. We can assume that Gregor would be having the same thoughts on any morning since they appear to be disconnected from the bigger problem at hand. This makes us see that Gregor's unhappiness with his daily routine and responsibilities is so great that even an insurmountable and grotesque problem like being turned into an insect does not outweigh his problem of just having to go to work for another day. (B) is incorrect because even though these thoughts can also be described as symbolic, they do not *introduce* a new SYMBOL; rather, they further develop a symbol already introduced in previous paragraphs.

384. (D) After Gregor says that getting up early "'makes you stupid,'" he goes on to explain that "'You've got to get enough sleep,'" implying that "stupid" in this context means foggy, in a daze from lack of sleep.

385. (E) Gregor's thoughts in lines 35–48 reveal how he is treated like an insect in his regular human life. He describes his boss as unrelenting and demanding, demeaning "his subordinates from up there." Unlike the "other traveling salesmen [who] live a life of luxury," Gregor has to scurry around like a weak and powerless insect. The METAPHOR of his physical transformation into an insect (introduced in the first paragraph) is further developed here by explaining how Gregor's emotional and working life is similar to that of an insect. While the lines may elicit some empathy from readers (B), their symbolic resonance is their primary purpose.

386. (A) The narrator's TONE is clear and straightforward. It does not express dismay at Gregor's shocking transformation; on the contrary, the tone is more objective and matter-of-fact, as if Gregor has awoken this way every morning. The passage begins with a calm, objective description of Gregor's morning. The following sentence does not ask questions or reveal Gregor's own bewilderment; it merely goes on to offer a factual rendering of what Gregor does and how he looks.

387. (A) In the last sentence, Gregor declares that he has "got to get up [because his] train leaves at five." It is astounding to us that, despite his physical transformation into an insect, Gregor is still determined to go to his horrible job. His decision suggests that being an insect physically is not so shocking or noticeably terrible to Gregor because he is already like an insect emotionally because of his work situation. Gregor's indifference to his physical transformation emphasizes how habituated he has become to being treated like an insect in his life. We are not angry (D) at, impressed by (B), or distanced from (E) Gregor because of his decision. Also, we are not dumbfounded (C) by his obliviousness because we know that

Gregor is aware he has turned into an insect; we are amazed, surprised, and curious about his indifference to this situation and his preoccupation with his work.

388. (A) In contrast to the narrator's objective and straightforward TONE (see question 386), the tone of Gregor's thoughts is marked by frustration and annoyance toward his job. Exclamation points indicate his anger at choosing such "'a strenuous career'" (23). He thinks, "'It can all go to Hell!'" (28).

Chapter 7: Drama

Passage 1. Euripides, *Medea*

389. (D) In the first paragraph, Medea explains that she has come forth "from the house" out of "fear lest [the ladies will] be blaming her" (1–2), meaning if she were to stay in her house, "showing pride," she would gain an "ill name and a reputation for indifference" (3–4). She leaves and speaks to the "Corinthian ladies" so that they will not "blame" or judge her. She is trying to mitigate (lessen) their judgment of her. Though she does say that "there is no just discernment in the eyes of men" (6), this is merely a digression from her main point in this paragraph; labeling the people as unjust is not her purpose in leaving her house (B).

390. (C) Medea says that there is "no just discernment in the eyes of men" because they "loathe [a person] at first sight, though never wronged by him" (8), making I incorrect. People will form unrelenting judgments of others even if they are "stranger[s]" (9). Regarding II, Medea says that she does not wish to commend (praise) a citizen who "resents the city's will" (11) and out of "stubbornness of heart" refuses to hate those whom the city hates.

391. (B) In the first paragraph, Medea introduces the topic of her speech. She is here to persuade the Corinthian women not to blame her. She explains why she needs to leave her house to lessen their hatred for her. In the second paragraph, she develops this topic by explaining how she was wronged, perhaps to help them understand her situation and the reasons for her crime or sin. She says, "on me hath fallen this unforeseen disaster, and sapped my life; ruined I am . . ." (12–13). Both paragraphs are addressed to the "Corinthian ladies" (A). No questions are posed in the first paragraph (C). Both paragraphs contain specifics (D); the first gives examples of the men's unjust discernment, and the second gives examples of why "women are the most hapless creatures" (16). While the first paragraph does contain some mild excoriation (criticism) of the unjust discernment of men, it also contains understanding of such judgment (9–10) as well as explanations of why she has come forth from her house. It is not primarily an excoriation, nor is the second paragraph necessarily a justification (E); Medea only explains the hardships women have to endure.

392. (A) Medea says that since her life is "sapped" and "ruined" by an "unforeseen disaster," she must "resign the boon of existence" (12–13). The context tells us that a "boon" is something positive because she has to "resign" it only because of her unfortunate situation. This eliminates (E) and (B) as possible answers. Though the word "resign" is often used in modern vernacular in the context of resigning from a job, (D) is incorrect because the context of the passage does not indicate that "existence" is a "job" from which she must resign.

393. **(E)** The word "yoke" means burden, oppression. In this paragraph, Medea complains about the sad plight of women. She says that if women do not resent the yoke/impositions/burdens of marriage to a man, they will be happy.

394. **(C)** In the second paragraph, Medea cites examples of women's unfortunate lot in life. She says they have to "buy a husband at a great price" (17) (B), and if they make a bad choice in spouse, they cannot be unfettered (E) from a bad marriage because "divorce is not honourable to women" (20), and while the husbands have the option to leave the house and seek the company of friends, women "must needs regard his single self" (28–29), which means they do not have that same option (A). A woman, according to Medea, also must "have a diviner's eye" (22–23) to be able to determine how best to please her husband, though she has not been taught how to do this. All these examples imply that women's submission to men causes their haplessness (D), but nowhere does she mention their obligation to bear children (C).

395. **(C)** Medea says, "But enough!" after she has gone on complaining about the plight of women for nearly the whole passage. She then says, "this language suits not thee as it does me," meaning she should stop herself from detailing the obstacles women may experience because they apply directly to her but not necessarily to her audience of Corinthian ladies. Therefore, she stops her griping (complaining) (C).

396. **(D)** In lines 33–38, Medea says that she should stop griping about the lot of women because it applies only to her situation and not to the women she is addressing. She goes on, "thou hast a city here, a father's house . . . but I am destitute, without a city . . . a captive. . . ." Medea distinguishes between herself and them by assuming they all have what she does not. Though she does mention she is without a family or husband (A, B) she is assuming they still have these things, making (D) the better answer choice. She does catalog (list) all her misfortunes, but this alone does not distinguish her from them; again, it is her assumption that they do not have the same misfortunes that allows her to make this distinction.

397. **(E)** Medea acknowledges that though women are "timorous" and "coward[s] at the mere sight of steel," she abandons this timorous nature and becomes courageous (full of temerity) when her honor is wronged.

398. **(A)** Medea is not remorseful (C) or penitent (E) for whatever crime/sin she has committed. In the passage, her main purpose is to explain herself to the Corinthian ladies to gain their understanding so that she may convince them to grant her their "silence" (39) about the vengeance she is seeking against her husband, his new wife and father-in-law. She is by no means objective (D) in this speech; on the contrary, she quite subjectively expresses her opinions of what life is like for women. While she may seem ruthless (B) at certain points, such as when she expresses her wish to "avenge" herself (40) and when she alludes to her heart being "filled with deadlier thoughts" (44), these are just examples of how resolute she is about the way she sees her situation. Throughout the entire passage, Medea conveys a confident, assertive attitude and TONE about how she has been wronged and what she has decided to do about it.

Passage 2. Euripides, *Medea*

399. (D) After Medea says, "For dost thou think I ever would have fawned upon *this man* . . . ," and every "he" and "him" until line 9 refers to the same man.

400. (B) Medea opens these lines with a question ("Whether shall I . . ."), followed by logical reasoning in which she considers the consequences and then decides to stick to using a method she is best skilled in ("to take them off by poison"). She then comes to a conclusion ("Let it be so"), but then considers more alternatives ("Waiting then yet a little time . . . But if . . ."). Though (E) is a reasonable answer because Medea does use rhetorical questioning, weighs consequences, and then becomes temporarily undecided, this answer is not as complete as (B) because Medea does eventually come to a firm decision. She even swears on Hecate that she will not allow her victims to live on and torture her with "impunity" (28–29).

401. (A) Medea says this line when she is referring to her plan to murder her victims ("the father, the bride, and my husband"). She vows that she will summon the courage and risk her life to "kill them" (25) and not allow "any one of them wring [her] heart with grief with impunity" (29).

402. (D) "Impunity" means freedom, liberty, license to do something. Medea does not want her victims to live so that they may "wring [her] heart with grief with impunity," meaning she does not want them to have free license to torture her, which she thinks they will have if they remain alive.

403. (C) A person who refers to himself or herself by name is using THIRD PERSON. Medea tells herself, "But come, spare none of these sciences in which thou art skilled, Medea" (31–32).

404. (E) In these lines, Medea is summoning up her courage and determination to go through with her plan. She refers to herself in THIRD PERSON, giving herself a pep talk, motivating herself to act. She tells herself, "Spare none . . . Proceed . . . now is the time . . . thou art skilled . . ." (31–33).

405. (E) Throughout the passage, Medea has a proud—I—TONE. She belittles the man who "at such a height of folly" (7) allows her to stay in the city of her future victims instead of banishing her. She also tells herself twice, "thou art skilled" (32, 37). She has a tenacious (determined)—II—tone in that she is passionate about executing this plan—she carefully thinks it through in its entirety, using rational—III—reasoning, meaning she considers the consequences ("If I should be caught") and alternatives ("which shall I") and comes to (what appears to her as) a logical solution to her problem ("Best then is to"). Her tenacity is clear when she swears by Hecate that she will go through with this, even risking her life to do so (25–28).

Passage 3. William Shakespeare, *Hamlet*

406. (A) All three choices describe things the Queen does mention, directly or indirectly, to Hamlet, but choice I *best* summarizes the Queen's lines, which is what the question asks for. She tells him to "look like a friend on Denmark" (2), which can be interpreted to mean that he must be cheery for the people. She is a Queen, and the other speaker is a King, and we know that Hamlet is also an heir to the throne (43), so smiling on Denmark does mean looking cheery for his people—II. However, choice II does not *summarize* the Queen's lines; she says more than simply this. Choice III conveys a slight misunderstanding of the Queen's lines; she is not saying that Hamlet's grief is entirely unwarranted, but rather that the continuance of his grieving is needless.

407. (C) Hamlet is shocked that the Queen would use the word "seems" because it implies that Hamlet only "seems" or merely appears to be grieving when he actually is grieving. After line 10, he goes on to explain how one's clothes, tears, heavy breathing, etc., might all make it seem that one is in mourning, but he "know[s] not seems." He finds her use of the word "seems" insulting and inaccurate, and he clearly takes offense.

408. (E) When a word or phrase is repeated at the start of multiple sentences or clauses, the device being used is ANAPHORA. The repetition of the same word here does not result in redundancy (A) because the repetition is not gratuitous; it has an intended effect. We can imagine and hear Hamlet emphasizing the word as he repeats it so as to make his point clearer to the Queen.

409. (A) The clause is PERIODIC in that the main point is given at the end, after a series of other clauses that provide supporting/background/explanatory details. Though he does repeat the word "nor" four times and almost endlessly adds to his list, Hamlet's TONE here would not be monotonous (E). The opening exclamation point and the ANAPHORA (see question 408) all indicate that he is quite passionate about and interested in the point he is trying to make. The clause is also not an example of ASYNDETON; the word "nor" is a CONJUNCTION, and he repeats it four times, making it an example of POLYSYNDETON.

410. (B) In these lines, Hamlet is distinguishing between those who only "seem," or appear, to mourn and those (he) who actually and truly mourn. In line 19, he says, "But I" to emphasize that he does not merely do what he just described in the previous lines: wear "customary suits of solemn black," cry and breathe heavily to show his grief, for these are mere "actions that a man might play" to give the impression that he is in mourning. Hamlet, on the other hand, is proud to assert that he has "within which passeth show," that he is superior to these inauthentic mourners. *Sanctimonious* means smug, holier than thou.

411. (D) "These" in line 20 refers to all the "actions that a man might play" (18) to show his grief, everything Hamlet has just listed in lines 11–15, which can be summarized as "all forms, moods, shows of grief" (16).

412. (A) In line 20, Hamlet says "suits of woe," and the word "suits" carries two meanings here, both of which are intended, making it a DOUBLE ENTENDRE. Suits, as a plural noun, are clothes that one wears, and he has been describing the "customary suits of solemn black" and other outward appearances a person might wear to show grief on the outside. These "suits of woe" also "suit," as a verb (to make appropriate, adapt, or accommodate), the person "wearing" them because he is wearing them for a purpose, to achieve a goal, such as to convince others he is grieving. (D) is a close answer, but when a word's dual meanings are used for comic effect, it is called a PUN and not double entendre.

413. (E) The King's main point is that Hamlet, in grieving so long for his dead father, is being quite unreasonable and illogical. According to the King, Hamlet's excessive grieving is "unmanly" (28) (B), even sinful ("'tis a fault to heaven") (C). His heart is "unfortified" and his "mind impatient" (30), which means Hamlet lacks fortitude (mental and emotional strength to deal with the hardship of losing a father) (B). He sees Hamlet's "understanding [as] simple and unschool'd" (31) (D).

414. (C) The King declares his love for Hamlet in a roundabout way, without actually saying he loves him in a direct and up-front manner. The sentence consists of four clauses, and the "love" clause is buried at the end of the sentence, in an abstract comparison to an actual "dearest father" and his love for his son. He cleverly and suspiciously avoids actually using the word *love* to refer to his own feelings toward Hamlet. The syntax of the sentence allows the King to be very indirect.

415. (A) The King does not at all appear to be Hamlet's confidant. While the King does speak to Hamlet for 30 lines about a personal matter, there are no lines in the passage that show Hamlet confiding in the King—II. The King is not Hamlet's successor; rather, the King mentions that Hamlet is "the most immediate to our throne" (43), the heir to the current King—III. If Hamlet is the heir to the throne, that makes him the prince, and his dead father whom he is mourning must have been the former King; we can infer that the current King in the passage is the old King's replacement by marriage since Hamlet is still the heir. The King is Hamlet's new father—I.

Passage 4. William Shakespeare, *Macbeth*

416. (C) The words "thee" and "thou" in these sentences are examples of the literary device called APOSTROPHE in that Macbeth is addressing inanimate things that cannot possibly answer him, like a dagger and night. This is not an actual dialogue in that they do not respond (B). Though his sighting of a dagger is plausibly a hallucination (E), he is not hallucinating the night when he addresses it.

417. (E) The sentence is an example of ANTITHESIS; there is a juxtaposition of opposite ideas in a similar grammatical structure. It cannot be part of an actual dialogue because the addressee cannot respond (it is a dagger) (A). Even though Macbeth's conversation with the dagger, or his imagining of it, or even the dagger itself could be seen as a METAPHOR (B), the metaphor is not apparent in this line alone, which the question directs our attention to. It is not an OXYMORON, which is two opposite words side by side, since it is an entire phrase (D).

418. (B) In the phrase "Thou marshal'st me," Macbeth is speaking to a dagger, which he refers to as "thou." The dagger is performing the action in the sentence (marshaling), making it the subject of the sentence. Macbeth is the one receiving the action, making him the object of the sentence.

419. (E) After Macbeth questions whether the dagger he sees is real ("Art thou not, fatal vision, sensible/ To feeling as to sight? Or art thou but/ A dagger of the mind, a false creation,/ Proceeding from the heat-oppressed brain?"), he says that either his eyes are being made the "fool" of the other senses (meaning his eyes look foolish because they are not seeing properly) or his eyes alone are worth "all the rest," all the other senses put together. In other words, either his eyes are seeing inaccurately and failing him, or they are seeing accurately and his other senses are failing him.

420. (E) Macbeth's references to Hecate, a Greek goddess, and Tarquin, a character in Shakespeare's narrative poem *The Rape of Lucrece* and a historical Roman figure, are known as ALLUSIONS.

421. (E) In this long sentence, we must carefully trace back the original subject of the verb "move." In the clause beginning in line 22, Macbeth says that withered Murther (PERSONI-FIED here as a man), which is alarmed by his sentinel (guard), who is the wolf whose howl serves as Murther's warning, with a stealthy (sneaky) pace, with the movements Tarquin used when he raped Lucrece, moves like a ghost. It is Murther who is the subject of these clauses, the one who moves.

422. (A) When Macbeth describes the atmosphere of the night, he describes nature as "dead" and "wicked dreams" abusing our sleep. Witchcraft is celebrated, and murder is PER-SONIFIED as a man here, moving like a ghost, the way Tarquin moved toward his "design," Lucrece, his rape victim. He used "ravishing strides" and a "stealthy pace." These descriptions of Tarquin allow us to actually see him moving toward his innocent victim in all his cruelty and ruthlessness. Since "Murther" is the one moving this way (like Tarquin), Macbeth is characterizing murder as heinous. The actual ALLUSION to Tarquin does not yet imply Macbeth himself is cruel—II—because we have not yet seen him commit murder, though he will. Here, the allusion merely comments on the cruelty of murder ("Murther").

423. (E) Most of Shakespeare's plays (especially the soliloquies of royals, like this passage) are written in BLANK VERSE, which is unrhymed IAMBIC PENTAMETER. An easy way to determine this is to notice that each line begins with a capital letter regardless of whether the word is a proper noun or the start of a sentence. Also, when we read each line, we notice a regular alternating pattern of stressed and unstressed syllables; this pattern mimics the rhythm of regular speech, which is what iambic pentameter does.

424. (B) While the last two lines rhyming in their end words would generally be considered a COUPLET (C), when those lines are also written in IAMBIC PENTAMETER (see question 423) the couplet is called a HEROIC COUPLET. In Shakespeare's plays, characters often speak a heroic couplet before ending a scene.

425. (A) Though it is hard to know when the passage is taken out of context of the larger scene, we can logically infer that lines 3–35 constitute Macbeth's SOLILOQUY. Some clues are that the servant exits in line 2, suggesting that Macbeth is alone. Throughout the lines, he never addresses another person (though he does address inanimate objects and concepts that cannot answer him), suggesting he is talking to himself. When a character recites lines when he is alone and only he and the audience can hear him, this speech is called a *soliloquy*. In an ASIDE (B) the character says lines that only he and the audience can hear, but he is not alone. In Shakespeare's plays, asides are labeled in the script.

Passage 5. Sophocles, *Oedipus the King*

426. (D) The passage begins with Oedipus asking three questions. He asks why his "children," the citizens of his land, carry "suppliant branches" in prayer and entreaty (1–4). He also inquires whether the priest stands there in "dread or sure hope" (12). He then asks if the priest knows that he is there for them "'gainst all" (13). As these are all actual questions directed to another person who is about to answer in the following lines, they are not RHETORICAL QUESTIONS (B).

427. (A) The word "us" refers to the King, Oedipus. It is common for monarchs to refer to themselves as "we" and "us," the "royal we" form. Shakespeare's plays provide abundant examples of this.

428. (C) The PERSONIFICATION in these lines characterizes the city and its people as desperately in need of assistance. The city "breathes/ Heavy with incense, heavy with dim prayer/ And shrieks to affright the Slayer." A city cannot actually breathe, pray, and shriek; these actions all personify the city as pleading for help. While the technique of personification does imply that the object is alive (D), that is not the sole purpose of the device. It presents things as alive for a reason, and in these lines the city is given human qualities to emphasize its desperation.

429. (A) The words "prayer" and "care" are examples of SLANT RHYME because they almost rhyme, like the words port and heart. They are not EXACT RHYMES like the words that end the first four lines of the passage: "tree" and "knee," "wreathes" and "breathes."

430. (A) Oedipus first says that he notices how the city "breathes," is heavy with "dim prayer," and "shrieks"; then he says "this moves me." The word "this" refers to the city's heavy breathing, dim prayers, and shrieks; in other words, what concerns him is the city's plight.

431. (D) The first two lines end in rhyming words (tree, knee), which would be marked as "*aa.*" The next two lines end in rhyming words (wreathes, breathes), which would be marked as "*bb.*" The next lines continue in this pattern to form the RHYME SCHEME.

432. (E) The priest explains that "A burning and a loathly god hath lit/ Sudden, and sweeps our land, this Plague of power" (30–31). Another word for a plague is a scourge. It is ruthless in having sent the land's people to "Hell's house" (33).

433. (A) The METAPHOR compares the ship to the city and its woes. Like the city, the ship is "weak and sore" (24). The ship is "shaken with storms" (25), and the city is shaken by the "Plague of power" (31). The ship cannot keep "her head above the waves whose trough is death" (26), like the citizens of the city who are dying in droves.

434. (C) Oedipus makes sure to mention that he is so moved by the citizens' plight that he has "scorned withal/ Message or writing" once he knew that he was called by his people—II. He calls himself "world-honoured Oedipus," clearly characterizing himself as venerable, deserving of great honor and respect—I. In lines 12–14, he emphasizes that he is there for the citizens above all else; his "will is [theirs]." He reiterates how moved he is by their hardships by saying only "stern" hearts would not feel for "so dire a need," indicating that he is not preoccupied but is here to assist the people—III.

435. (D) The priest says to Oedipus that "we kneel before thine hearth,/ Children and old men, praying." The "we" refers to children and old men. *Senescent* means old and aging, making (D) the right answer.

436. (C) The priest says, "O King, not God indeed nor peer to God/ We deem thee" (34–35). This line reveals that the people do see Oedipus as their monarch (A) but do not see him as God's peer (C). He is their liberator (B) in that he "made [them] free" (41) and their intellectual equal (D) in that he came to their city "naught knowing more than [them],/ Nor taught of any man" (42–43). He is clearly capable (E) because he "so swift[ly] . . . swept away/ The Sphinx's song" (39–40).

437. (A) The priest's TONE is grave as he explains to Oedipus the gravity (importance, severity) of the situation the citizens are in—they are suffering from a "Plague of power" (31). Oedipus's TONE, on the other hand, is mostly compassionate. He urges the priest to tell him what causes them to approach him with "suppliant branches" (4), and he insists that their hardship "moves [him]" (7), that his "will/ Is [theirs] for aid 'gainst all" (12–13). (E) is an understandable answer choice, but the priest's tone is not entirely laudatory (full of praise). While the priest does praise Oedipus for freeing the people in the past, and for being full of "God's breath" (43), the main purpose of his speech is to convey the seriousness of the city's turmoil, which his tone reflects. Also, while Oedipus is unaware of the specifics of the city's dire needs, calling his tone naive is too extreme. His lines do not stress his ignorance of the issue.

438. (A) Cadmus is the name of the founder of the city of Thebes, the setting of the passage. In the opening line of the passage, Oedipus addresses his city's citizens as his "children, fruit of Cadmus' ancient tree." Here, he uses a METAPHOR to compare the people of the land to fruit that has been born from a tree, implying that the citizens have been born from Cadmus; Cadmus is the father of the people the way a tree fathers its fruit. The second reference to Cadmus is also a METAPHOR. The priest now compares the city and the citizens to "Cadmus' house" and family. As the plague festers, "Cadmus' house grows empty, hour by hour/ And Hell's house rich with steam of tears and blood" (32–33). The dead citizens leave their land ("Cadmus' house") and enter Hell. The vivid IMAGERY contained in these metaphors also helps us imagine the depths of the people's despair. We can see and smell the "steam of tears and blood." In line 39, the city's name is revealed to be Thebes, making (A) correct.

Chapter 8: Expository Prose

Passage 1. Charles Darwin, *On the Origin of Species*

439. (A) In the first sentence of this passage, Darwin summarizes the points he has made previously ("I have now recapitulated [summarized] the main facts . . .") so that he may now address some of the anticipated objections to those points and provide COUNTERARGUMENTS.

440. (A) In the second paragraph of the passage, Darwin states that "most eminent living naturalists and geologists" have rejected the notion of the "mutability of species." Throughout the passage, he offers COUNTERARGUMENTS to the position of these naturalists and geologists, namely, that species are immutable (unchanging).

441. (D) Darwin does not agree with (B) or defer to (E) the opinions of "eminent living" geologists, but he certainly understands them. By taking the time to address their opinions, he demonstrates that he neither discounts (A) nor disrespects (C) those opinions.

442. (A) "Mutability" means changeability, variability. Darwin asks why many have rejected the idea of the "mutability of species" and then responds by saying that "It cannot be asserted that organic beings in a state of nature are subject to no variation" (13–14).

443. (D) The first sentence begins with "It cannot" and repeats "it cannot" after the semi-colon. The sentence that follows also begins with "It cannot." The repetition of the same word or phrase at the beginning of clauses or sentences is called ANAPHORA.

444. (E) The TONE of the passage is EXPOSITORY. It sets out to explain in a calm, straight-forward manner the theory of natural selection and to provide COUNTERARGUMENTS to objections.

445. (B) The sentence refers to "the history of the world" and, implicitly, the relatively recent origins of the world. Cosmogony is the study of the origin or creation of the world.

446. (C) Natural selection is certainly a theory. According to most philosophers of science, all theories must be both coherent and falsifiable; that is, evidence that contradicts a given theory can prove the theory wrong. As a deist, Darwin sees no contradiction between his theory and his religion. The one thing natural selection is not is ephemeral (short-lived). Mutation that results in the differentiation of species requires a long period of time to occur.

447. (E) According to the theory of natural selection, changes in species accumulate over many generations—II. And because humans live for only a relatively short period of time, it is difficult for us to perceive change over long periods of time—III. Darwin insists that with respect to evolution *most*, if not all (not a few), variations are slight—I.

448. (D) Darwin assumes that his audience is receptive but skeptical. As a consequence, he takes pains to address what he anticipates will be the key objections to his theory.

449. (C) In defense of his theory of natural selection, Darwin quotes "a celebrated author and divine" who expresses a position consistent with deism. Deism posits a divine creator who makes the universe and then, without intervening, allows the universe to change and develop according to a set of natural laws. Through deism, Darwin can reconcile natural selection with belief in a creator.

Passage 2. Nathaniel Hawthorne, "The Custom House" (preface to *The Scarlet Letter*)

450. (D) The "figure" of the ancestor has been "invested by family tradition with a dim and dusky grandeur" (1–2), meaning his eminent reputation is foggy. The truth of his "grandeur," of his reputation and identity, is not entirely clear. This is reinforced later in the passage when the speaker describes his ancestor's "cruelty" (18–20).

451. (C) There is no evidence to suggest that the speaker's ancestor is a philistine (one who does not appreciate the arts). Even though the second paragraph suggests that the ancestor would disapprove of the speaker's profession as a writer of literature, this does not necessarily mean he is a philistine. The second part of this answer choice is correct; the ancestor is described as a "ruler in the church" (10).

452. (E) The progenitor's appearance and behavior are described as stately ("grave, bearded, sable-cloaked and steeple-crowned . . . trode the unworn street"), so the phrase "stately port" describes his overall appearance and the way he conducts himself, his demeanor.

453. (B) The phrase "He was a soldier, legislator, judge . . ." contains a list of nouns without any CONJUNCTIONS. It is an example of ASYNDETON.

454. (A) The two sentences are LOOSE SENTENCES; the main clause of each sentence ("He was likewise a better persecutor" and "His son, too, inherited the persecuting spirit") is at the beginning of the sentence and followed by supporting details—I. The first sentence is not a SIMPLE SENTENCE—II—because it contains more than one INDEPENDENT CLAUSE. Neither of the two sentences is a BALANCED SENTENCE—III.

455. (C) The Quakers deem the speaker's ancestor as a "hard" and severe persecutor (12–13) who harshly judged a "woman of their sect" (13). In their "histories," the Quakers will remember the bad deeds of the speaker's ancestor as opposed to "his better deeds" (14). The Quakers are most like a student who deems a judgment or punishment from a disciplinarian as unfair.

456. (B) "Either of these" refers to the main subjects of the previous paragraph, the speaker's "grave, bearded, sable-cloaked and steeple-crowned progenitor" (6) and "His son" (14), his offspring.

457. (B) The words "idler" and "compliments" are meant to be read sarcastically, or ironically. The speaker does not really think of himself as a mere idler (someone who wastes time on meaningless activities), and he also does not genuinely believe the comments from his ancestors to be "compliments" when they are clearly insults.

458. (A) The dialogue is the speaker's imitation of what his own ancestors might say about him and his profession. The exclamation points and comparison to a fiddler suggest he is exaggerating (for effect) his ancestors' disapproval of his accomplishments.

459. (B) Both of the paragraphs elaborate on specific details of the speaker's ancestors. There is no emphasis throughout the passage on the speaker's innocence (E) or his superiority to his family (C). While the speaker does see his ancestors as sinful and in need of repentance, the passage as a whole does not emphasize the speaker's supremacy. There is not enough evidence to suggest the passage precedes an autobiographical BILDUNGSROMAN narrative (D). The passage does mention some bad traits of the Puritans (11), but the passage does not go so far as to lambaste (criticize) all Puritanical ideals (A).

Passage 3. Thomas Hobbes, *Leviathan*

460. (C) The sentence uses many CONJUNCTIONS ("and," "because," and "nor") and as such it employs POLYSYNDETON—II. The last phrase is incomplete in that it elides the verb "is" with a comma—an example of ELLIPSIS—I. The word or phrase that begins the sentence does not appear at its end; therefore, it does not use EPANALEPSIS—III.

461. (A) Both first sentences begin with "It may," which expresses possibility and thus anticipation. In the second paragraph, Hobbes anticipates the objection to his assertion that in a state of nature "every man is Enemy to every man" (1–2). Given the boldness of this assertion, his hypothetical reader may require more tangible evidence than simply the inference he provides through his notion that human passion, such as it is, necessarily leads to conflict. In the third paragraph, Hobbes anticipates the COUNTERARGUMENT that such a state of nature akin to a state of war has never existed. He then provides two examples—natives in America and civil war—to back his original argument. The sentences do not have an ironic (E) or skeptical (B) TONE. His attention to counterarguments does not cast doubt on his own argument (D) but rather strengthens it. Nowhere does he suggest that these counterarguments are in any way authoritative (C).

462. (C) Hobbes asserts that desires, even, by implication, harmful ones, and actions motivated by those desires, are not sins if the perpetrator does not "know a Law that forbids them" (23–24). No laws can be made, he claims, except by someone with the authority to make those laws. Accordingly, the best answer here is (C), installment of a legitimate sovereign, since it is the legitimate sovereign who has the authority to make and enforce laws that check man's naturally selfish desires. A state of anarchy (B) is a situation of lawlessness, as is civil war (D); therefore, they are both akin to a state of nature, where conflict presides. Hobbes is not concerned with the church (E) directly in this passage but with secular political authority.

463. (D) It is a common rhetorical strategy in EXPOSITORY prose for the writer to address potential objections to his or her argument. In effect, the passage is imagined as part of a larger conversation or debate. While Hobbes certainly had contemporaneous rivals, that he addresses "some man" suggests an imagined adversary rather than a known one (A). Furthermore, although the entire passage is addressed to an implied audience (C), this particular sentence singles out a participant in the larger debate who is less sympathetic to Hobbes's claims than an implied audience generally would be.

464. (A) The main purpose of the book *Leviathan* as a whole is to argue for the legitimacy and value of absolute monarchy (B). An important preparatory element of this argument is to elaborate the natural state of man, which Hobbes describes in this passage as a state of perpetual and debilitating war. That Hobbes does disparage Native Americans as "savage" (28) (C) and does equate total "Liberty" (42) with this state of war (E) is secondary to his main point in this passage, that the natural state of man is war.

465. (B) In the last paragraph of the passage, Hobbes points out that kings, "because of their Independency" (37), are in perpetual conflict with each other. On the other hand, since kings impose laws on their subjects, these subjects' relative lack of liberty allows them to be industrious and thus free from the misery of the natural state of man. Individual liberty, in effect, is akin to a state of war, which Hobbes elaborates in the first paragraph as a state of fear (A), ignorance (C), immobility (D), and misery (E). In such a state, no one is motivated to be industrious (hardworking, productive) "because the fruit thereof is uncertain" (5–6).

466. (A) One of Hobbes's most counterintuitive points in this passage is that independence (A) is generally undesirable as it results in reversion to a state of war, man's natural state. Kings watch over their subjects, protect (C) them from invaders and, significantly, from each other, through the enforcement of laws (B). This dependence allows the subjects of a kingdom, in turn, to be both neighborly (D) and productive (E), since they all enjoy the protection of the king.

467. (D) While Hobbes does contend that Native Americans have a relatively small government that is essentially that of "small Families" (29), he says that government is not particularly effective, since life under it is "brutish" (31) (A), an allusion to the wholly natural state (B) of man where life is "solitary, poore, nasty, brutish, and short" (10). Accordingly, for Hobbes, there is nothing noble (C) about such a "savage people" (28). The problem for Hobbes is that the Native Americans, among others, do not enjoy the authority of an absolute sovereign (D), and thus they miss out on all the benefits of law-abiding subjectivity.

468. (E) Hobbes does not seem particularly idealistic (D) about humanity, since he suggests that, left to its own devices, a state of war inevitably results. For Hobbes, people are not naturally good, but must be induced by sovereignty to be so. On the other hand, it would be unfair to say that he is cynical (B) about or contemptuous (C) of humanity, since he does offer a way out of the naturally miserable state of man. While Hobbes writes with some aplomb (assurance, confidence) (A) about humanity, "aplomb" is self-referential—it describes his attitude about his own thinking and writing and the question asks about his attitude toward humanity. The best answer here is (E), REALISM. Hobbes seems to make a concerted effort to consider the best and worst of humanity and to provide a realistic political solution to the problems of the world, as he understands them.

469. (B) To address the COUNTERARGUMENT that a hypothetical "some man" (11) may make, Hobbes provides examples that are "confirmed by Experience" (14) to defend his point that the natural state of man is to "dissociate" (12) into a state of war. An EMPIRICAL METHOD aims to give evidence based on experience in support of an argument. Apodictic (A), a priori (C), and DEDUCTIVE arguments (D), generally speaking, work by proving PROPOSITIONS through reasoning, irrespective of experiential evidence. An ad absurdum (E) approach attempts to refute an argument by reducing it to an absurdity.

Passage 4. Friedrich Nietzsche, *Beyond Good and Evil*

470. (D) While Nietzsche does take pains to describe the "moral hypocrisy of the commanding class" (20) (B) and implicitly makes a case against democracy (the rule of the people) (E) when he writes that "nowadays" in Europe there is "attempt after attempt" to "replace commanders by the summing together of clever gregarious [outgoing, sociable] men" (31–32), the best answer here is (D), criticize group behavior. The entire passage is dedicated to criticizing the "herd-instinct" (14), and the previous two points fall under its purview.

471. (B) Nietzsche asserts that because "obedience has been most practiced and fostered among mankind" (4–5), "Thou shalt . . . do" and "refrain" reduce simply to "Thou shalt" (8), which he describes as a "need" that, with an "omnivorous appetite," fills "its form with a content" (9). Although many commandments are indeed unconditional (E), the point he is making is that specific rules of conduct are inconsequential (B). Rather, it is the compulsion to obey that is all important. This is a dynamic more in keeping with the notion that means are everything.

472. (B) The simile uses the word "as" to compare a desire to satisfy to a desire to devour. Nietzsche writes, "This need tries to satisfy itself and to fill its form with a content . . . it at once seizes as an omnivorous appetite with little selection . . ." (8–11).

473. (A) (B) through (E) are certainly all conventional criticisms of leaders' hypocrisy. But Nietzsche's point is an unconventional one: that rulers are hypocritical when they call themselves "servants of their people" or "instruments of the public weal" (25). According to him, leaders ought to command confidently without such backhanded justifications.

474. (D) Nietzsche at times does write with IRONY (A), such as when he calls democratic representatives "clever gregarious men" (32). But the best answer is (D), polemical (argumentative, controversial), because Nietzsche unapologetically offers up counterintuitive arguments against conventional liberal notions of leadership, partially in an effort to be controversial. Providing evidence and addressing objections are only secondary concerns; therefore, the TONE is not EXPOSITORY (E). Nor is it apodictic (C), a form of reasoning that works methodically to clearly and incontrovertibly demonstrate absolute truths.

475. (B) In this passage, Nietzsche offers up Napoleon as a perfect example of a commander who rules resolutely without hypocritical justification, the kind of leader that represents for "clever gregarious men" (32) a "deliverance from a weight becoming unendurable" (33–34), that is, the burden of leadership. According to Nietzsche, rulers like Napoleon, as "its worthiest individuals," can give an "entire century" a "higher happiness" (37–38).

476. (D) The first sentence of the passage is a COMPLEX SENTENCE, but not a COMPOUND SENTENCE or a LOOSE SENTENCE. It has only one INDEPENDENT CLAUSE: "one may reasonably suppose that, generally speaking, the need thereof is now innate in every one" (5–6). The main clause must come at the start of the sentence for it to be loose. To be compound, it must have more than one independent clause.

477. (E) Nietzsche certainly finds herds reprehensible (worthy of blame) (A) inasmuch as he takes pains to criticize them and the "herd-instinct" (14) in this passage. By implication he finds human herds obdurate (stubborn) (B), self-perpetuating (D), and autocratic (despotic) (C). What they are not is transitory, or short-lived. He asserts that "as long as mankind has existed, there have also been human herds" (1–2).

478. (E) Nietzsche seems to have nothing but contempt for democratic institutions ("representative constitutions"), which he describes as collections of "clever gregarious men" (32), where leaders, by justifying their rule as "executors of older and higher orders" (22), exercise a form of "moral hypocrisy" (20) and yet are quick to relinquish command as soon as an "absolute ruler" such as Napoleon appears on the scene (34). Given Nietzsche's polemical TONE (see question 474), one that relentlessly and ironically attacks conventional wisdom, his attitude toward democracy here can best be described as sarcastic.

479. (A) The "herd-instinct" does indeed often manifest as "representative constitutions" (32) (B). And since it values obedience above all else, it does tend to encourage a cohesive public opinion in groups (E). Yet Nietzsche clearly is more concerned that the "herd-instinct" (14) may result, eventually, in a dearth (total absence) of strong leadership (A) when he writes that if "one imagines this instinct increasing to its greatest extent, commanders and independent individuals will finally be lacking altogether" (15–17). He does not see

Napoleon as a tyrant (C) at all, more as a worthy individual (37–38). In the passage, he has nothing explicit to say about class conflict (D).

480. (C) Nietzsche makes it clear that contemporaneous European leaders do all of the following: they celebrate self-effacing values (A) such as "kindness" and "deference" (27–28); they embrace public opinion (B) inasmuch as they claim to be "servants of their people" (25); they encourage collegiality (D) with values such as "public spirit," "modesty," and "sympathy" (27–28); and they would seem to respect consensus (E) in that they are members of "representative" governments (32). Counterintuitively, Nietzsche suggests that what they do not do is vilify (or denounce) absolute rulers (C) such as Napoleon. Rather, they embrace them as a relief from the burden of having to rule.

Passage 5. Oscar Wilde, Preface to *The Picture of Dorian Gray*

481. (D) Wilde's ideas mirror the philosophy of AESTHETICISM and its principles of "art for art's sake." Art should not be didactic (instructive, moral) and "those who go beneath the surface do so at their peril" (22–23) because "no artist desires to prove anything" (16).

482. (D) The sentence means that art's goal is to merely reveal art, *not* to reveal the artist and his beliefs, intentions, etc. In other words, the artist's purpose is irrelevant when we view art.

483. (D) The "fault" refers to "Those who find ugly meanings in beautiful things . . ." (4–5), or people who read base meaning or significance into the art instead of appreciating it solely for its beauty. (E) is partially correct because the fault also refers to people finding ugly meanings in art without being charming, but (E) says only "people" lacking charm—it is too vague.

484. (A) The cultivated, according to Wilde, are the optimists, "Those who find beautiful meanings in beautiful things" (7) (A), as opposed to those who interpret ugly meanings in beautiful things (4–5)—the cynics (B) or skeptics (C)—and those to whom beautiful things mean more than beauty (8–9).

485. (A) The passage is a series of EPIGRAMS, or concise, witty statements, that express the major points of Wilde's aesthetic philosophy. The epigrams laud beauty and reject the notion that art serves a moral purpose. Wilde also uses PARALLEL STRUCTURE, as shown in lines 19–20.

486. (B) Wilde uses the ALLUSION to Caliban to explain that people of the nineteenth century PARADOXICALLY (inconsistently) dislike both realism and romanticism: they do not want to be shown their own flaws or savagery but then are upset that they are not being shown their flaws.

487. (E) Wilde writes, "Those who read the symbol do so at their peril" (23), indicating that people should not look for a bigger meaning or message—I, II—in a work of art because "no artist desires to prove anything" (16).

488. (E) The TONE is serious in that Wilde earnestly explains his aesthetic philosophy. He is not vituperative (angry) (D), vindictive (vengeful) (A), sarcastic (mocking) (C), or maudlin (overly sentimental) (B) toward the subject.

489. (E) Wilde mentions that art is not theoretical, didactic, ethical, or purposeful, "All art is quite useless" (29). However, he does suggest that art is a mirror, "It is the spectator, and not life, that art really mirrors" (23–24).

490. (B) The final line summarizes the THEME of the whole passage—that art is for art's sake. One should not seek social commentary, moralizing, instruction, or great significance other than pure beauty in art. Art is thus without a specific "use."

Passage 6. Zhuangzi

491. (C) The sentence has only one INDEPENDENT CLAUSE, "the sounds were all in regular cadence," and several DEPENDENT CLAUSES; therefore, it is COMPLEX and not COMPOUND. It is also periodic in that a PERIODIC SENTENCE is one in which the main clause comes at the end of the sentence, usually after a series of parallel constructions.

492. (D) Through the proxy of the cook, the writer clearly expresses a certain respect and enthusiasm for the task of butchering the ox. This is reinforced by the ruler Wen Hui's enthusiastic reaction to the cook's speech. *Avidity* means enthusiasm or dedication.

493. (B) While the cook's method of butchering the ox does make his work easier (E), appear somewhat mechanical or automatic in its execution (A), and require only the use of a good knife (D), in his speech he clearly emphasizes that "the method of the Dao" (8) is a form of meditative action where his "senses [are] discarded" and his "spirit acts as it wills" (11–12). There is something beyond conscious decision making (B) in this description of his mental state. That the ruler approves of his method is an important yet secondary concern for the cook (C).

494. (B) The TONE of the passage is utterly sincere (A) and lacking in irony (C). While the ruler Wen Hui's responses may be described as ecstatic (E), the cook's tone, which dominates the passage, is decidedly more levelheaded. There is a certain attention to detail in the passage, but it is not punctilious (D) in that details are given not for their own sake but in service of the overall THEME. The writer shows a clear sympathy for the cook's efforts and, through the dialogue between servant and master, implies a feeling of mutual accord or congeniality (B).

495. (D) There is no hint in the passage that the knife has magical properties of any kind (A), in spite of the seemingly miraculous results. The cook implies that he has not sharpened the knife for nineteen years when he says that it "is as sharp as if it had newly come from the whetstone" (18–19) (B). Clearly, by butchering the ox into pieces, he does not leave the carcass intact (C). Sometimes in his work he moves slowly, in particular when he comes "to a complicated joint" (22), but not always (E), as sometimes the knife moves "easily" along (21). The important point that the cook makes is that through his meditative approach, he is able to feel his way through the butchering in a way that avoids the kinds of abrupt collisions between knife and bone, ligament, and tendon that would quickly blunt the knife (D).

496. (C) The cook does not react to Wen Hui's visit in a way that would suggest that the ruler is being intrusive (A) or sarcastic (D). Wen Hui's responses, likewise, are more than merely tolerant (B), but rather enthusiastic toward what the cook is doing. Permissive (E) generally implies someone in authority allowing a subordinate to get away with bad behavior. The best answer here is (C), enlightened, in that the writer's portrayal of Wen Hui goes against the stereotype of a ruler being arrogant and aloof toward his subjects. The ruler is bright and secure enough to be willing and able to learn life lessons from the cook in the humble act of butchering an ox.

497. (E) Nowhere does the passage indicate which particular hand the cook uses to wield the knife; therefore, we cannot ascertain whether he is ambidextrous (A), or able to use both his right and left hand. The cook is certainly dexterous with the knife, though, so clearly not maladroit (awkward) (C). His "method of the Dao" (8) would seem to be anything but fractious (irritable) (D) or overwrought (B), or highly agitated. The one quality here that the cook's method does exhibit is meticulousness (E) in that he is both careful and precise.

498. (B) While the cook treats the ox carcass with respect, and therefore is not irreverent (disrespectful) (A), he is not necessarily courteous toward it either (E), since courtesy is usually behavior shared between people, not between people and things. Nowhere does the passage indicate that the cook is being religious (C) in the conventional sense of performing a ritual for the benefit of a deity. Nor does the passage suggest that the cook is animistic (D) by attributing a living soul to the inanimate ox carcass. The best answer then is (B), venerating, which suggests that he regards the ox carcass with respect and reverence in that its dismemberment is an occasion to practice a kind of communion with it through meditative action.

499. (C) There would appear to be nothing hypnotic (A) or unconscious (B) about the cook's method in that he is fully aware while he works; for example, at times, he proceeds "attentively and with caution" (23). This approach would seem to be something more than instinct (E), in that instinct is generally understood to be basic innate behavior that is crude and reactive. As his "servant" (8), the cook does indeed defer to the ruler's wishes (D) but, in describing "the method of the Dao" (8), the cook is not talking about the spirit of service, but more likely a spirit of communion with right action in the context of his mind, body, and the situation at hand. As such, that he says that his "senses are discarded" is paradoxical. They are discarded so that he may achieve a certain heightened sensitivity (C) to the knife's movements within the ox carcass.

500. (C) The cook's account of how he butchers an ox is loosely ALLEGORICAL (A) in that it suggests a mode of being—"the method of the Dao" (8)—that can be extended beyond that specific act. The ruler Wen Hui confirms this when he says that he has learned from the cook's words "the nourishment of [our] life" (29). The cook says that with a slight movement of his knife a part of the ox carcass "drops *like* [a clod of] earth to the ground" (25), which is a SIMILE (B). To claim that he has butchered "several thousand oxen" over the course of "nineteen years" (17–18) certainly would seem to be an exaggeration—or HYPERBOLE—for dramatic effect (D). In his responses, Wen Hui makes several exclamations (E), for example, "Admirable!" and "Excellent!" What is missing from the passage is CHIASMUS (C), a grammatical figure by which the order of words in one of two of parallel clauses is inverted in the other.